THE 2011 GUIDE TO

PLANO

NORTH DALLAS AREA

REAL ESTATE

THE 2011 GUIDE TO

PLANO

NORTH DALLAS AREA
REAL ESTATE

Including Plano, Frisco, Allen, McKinney, Richardson, Addison, Carrollton,
Coppell, Irving, Lewisville, Garland, Flower Mound and More…

JAMES SHARP

WEXFORD HOUSE BOOKS

THE 2011 GUIDE TO
PLANO
NORTH DALLAS AREA
REAL ESTATE

Including Plano, Frisco, Allen, McKinney, Richardson,
Addison, Carrollton, Coppell, Irving, Lewisville, Garland,
Flower Mound and More...

JAMES SHARP

Published by:
Wexford House Books

ISBN
978-0-982-64332-7

ABOUT THE AUTHOR

Born and raised in Flint, Michigan, James Sharp has experienced the moving process, having lived in Michigan, Arizona, California and Texas. He currently resides in Plano with his three little boys, Noah, Tucker and Carter.

James is a full-time licensed REALTOR® with Ebby Halliday Realtors, the top independent brokerage in the Dallas/Fort Worth Area and in the state of Texas.

Clients and friends know James has a burning desire to impact and improve the lives of those he works with. He finds personal satisfaction meeting their real estate needs, whether it is through buying, selling or leasing a home. His key to success is treating clients in the way that he would like to be treated and he is intentional about building his business by way of referrals. He currently is coached by Buffini and Company, the world's largest coaching company.

ACKNOWLEDGMENTS

It is so hard to thank everyone that has impacted and influenced me to put together a project like this book. With that I am going to make an attempt to thank the key people who have made this book possible.

My family has been a big inspiration and without their support this wouldn't have been possible. My Ebby Halliday family, who has supported me from the very beginning in giving me a chance to pursue my dream of real estate and who, to this day, still support and encourage me!

Thank you to my entire support staff at Wexford House Books, including Kimberly Martin for formatting, Bill Ferris for his excellent interior graphic design, George Foster for an amazing cover design, Jennifer Ferris for her project management and keen editing and most of all, Mike Regan for having the vision, drive and guidance to help me pull this together.

Of course, I must thank my clients -- both past and present -- for giving me the opportunity to work with them and whom, without their support, this book wouldn't be possible either.

Brian Buffini and his amazing staff at Buffini and Company -- without Brian's push to pursue my dreams and write down my goals in life, this book wouldn't be here today.

To my friends in Clubnet, who may be all over the country but are close to my heart with daily words of encouragement to pursue what matters most.

My BNI family of business partners who have stood by me with their support to see this book come to fruition.

Lastly to my late Grandmother Lucille who always told me, "You can do it James, I believe in you and I know you are going to do great things in life!"

CONTENTS

INTRODUCTION

CHAPTER 1

WHY MOVE TO THE PLANO AREA?

Plano is a city of prosperity and affluence in the heart of Texas, just north of Dallas. Winner of the 1994 "All-American City" designation from the National Civic League, (a non-profit, non-partisan, membership organization dedicated to community building and political reform) the Plano metropolitan area includes such smaller cities and towns as Frisco, Allen, McKinney, Richardson, Addison, Carrollton, Coppell, Irving, Lewisville, Garland and Flower Mound, but the city stands on its own as one of the largest, most beautiful places to live in the country. If you want to experience the relaxed atmosphere Texas can bring mixed with the industrious, entrepreneurial spirit of the big city, Plano is the perfect place to move.

According to a 2008 census report, the city has a population of more than 267,000, meaning Plano is the 70th largest city in the country.

"BEST CITY" DESIGNATIONS

If you're looking for an area of the country that is looking forward and not backward, Plano is it.

INTRODUCTION

Surprising to many, Plano is actually the wealthiest, most affluent city in the country -- more so than New Haven, Montpellier, Seattle or even New York. In 2006, **CNN Money Magazine reported that Plano is the wealthiest city in America.** CNN Money Magazine cited the city's incredibly low 6.4% poverty rate, earning potentials for men and women, average income in certain industries as compared to other areas of the country as well as several other factors.

CNN Money Magazine also said that Plano is the 11th best place to live, taking into account variables that range from how open the job market is to how diverse the arts and entertainment is in the city. Plano was also the most populous city on the list of 100 cities the magazine deemed "best place to live" meaning that Plano knows how to keep a growing metropolitan population happy and healthy.

American publishing and media company Forbes also **said Plano is the top suburb of Dallas,** saying that Plano has been one of the quickest-growing Dallas suburbs, both in income level and population. According to Forbes, the mean income for Plano in 2008 was $77,038.

The Best City...

- Wealthiest City in America – *CNN Money Magazine*, August 2007
- Wealthiest City with Population Over 250,000 – *Census Bureau*, 2008
- #11 Best City To Live – *CNN Money Magazine*, 2006
- #1 Suburb of Dallas – *Forbes.com*, March 2008
- Top-10 Place To Grow Up – *U.S. News & World Report Magazine*, 2009
- #1 in Educational Attainment – *America's Most Literate Cities*, 2008
- #17 Most Inventive City – *Wall Street Journal*, 2007
- #26 Best Place to Raise a Family – *Best Life Magazine*, 2008

ECONOMY

If there's one thing Plano, Texas can hang its hat on, it's the city's local economy.

Nationally renowned media outlets such as Forbes and CNN Money Magazine testify to the financial strength of Plano. In fact, according to a 2008 report by Salary.com **Plano is the top city in America to build personal wealth.** Salary.com is a provider of human resources software that helps businesses and individuals manage pay and performance.

But the most telling testimony is when CNN Money Magazine reported that **Plano has the highest average income of any city: $77,038.**

A city that wasn't strong economically wouldn't have a poverty rate of 6.4%, **the lowest poverty rate of any city in the country.** If you're looking for a city that knows how to build a robust economy, maintain it and plan accordingly for the future, Plano is going to be your best bet.

An Economic Stronghold...

- #1 City in America to Build Personal Wealth – *Salary.com*, 2008
- #1 Most Poverty-Proof City in America – *CNN Money Magazine*, August 2007
- Wealthiest City in America – *CNN Money Magazine*, August 2007

GROWTH AND EXPANSION

But average salaries and low poverty rates are not the only indications of a healthy economy. One way to gauge just how healthy an area is currently is to look at how viable it is for businesses to relocate there or for what kind of success rate small businesses have.

In 2007, the **Texas City Management Association named Plano's City Council the Texas City Council of the Year** for outstanding leadership in the economic and governmental development field.

Also, **Plano earned the AAA distinction, the highest bond rating possible,** from Moody's Investor Service, Standard & Poor's and Fitch IBCA.

With such a solid foundation of leadership, large businesses are moving to Plano every day. **There are currently dozens of multi-national corporations that make their headquarters in or near Plano, including Pizza Hut, Dr Pepper Snapple Group, Dell, HP, Texas Instruments, Rug Doctor, Mary Kay, Cinemark Theatres, Ericsson, Frito-Lay, JC Penney, Rent-A-Center and Siemens.**

EMPLOYMENT

Nationwide, unemployment has not been this high in decades and the recession is affecting every nook and cranny of the U.S., including Plano. But those desiring to move to this great Texas city will take comfort that unemployment has not sunk its teeth as far into this area of the country as it has in many others.

According to **SimplyHired.com, the unemployment rate in Plano as of February 2010 was only 5.9%, a full percentage point lower than the national average of 6.9%.** SimplyHired.com is a job searching website.

In an April 2009 report, the financial media outlet Forbes.com said the **Plano-Dallas-Irving metropolitan is the fifth-best big city to find a job.**

But the praise from Forbes.com doesn't stop there. The financial website said just a few months later in a July 2009 report that **Plano is the 25th best city to relocate to if you're seeking employment,** taking into account the cost of moving, cost of living, average starting salaries, average home sales and how many jobs are actually available. In terms of the workforce, Forbes called Plano a "Reloville" saying that the city has **twice the incomes, twice the home values and home sizes and twice the college degrees when compared with the rest of the U.S.** According to Forbes, that means that Plano is an environment where success is not only rewarded, but expected -- meaning a healthier local economy and a brighter future for the north Texas city.

The entrepreneurial spirit that contributes to such a robust economy and workforce is not lost on national publications. According to a 2008 study by the Ewing Marion Kauffman Foundation, Texas tied for thirteenth-most entrepreneurial, with 0.37 percent of adults starting businesses. That translates to 370 out of every 100,000 residents. Of the largest metro areas, the Dallas-Fort Worth-Plano area ranked sixth in the country for entrepreneurial activity.

The Job Market...

- #1 Most Affluent City in America – *USAToday.com*, August 2008
- #5 Best Big City to Find a Job (Plano-Dallas-Irving) – *Forbes.com*, April 2009
- #6 Most Entrepreneurial City in America, Ewing Marion Kauffman Foundation, January 2008
- #25 Best City to Relocate to Find a Job – *Forbes.com*, July 2009
- Distinction as a Top-25 "Reloville" – *Forbes.com*, July 2009
- #1 State For Business (Texas) – *Directorship Magazine*, June 2009
- #1 State For Business (Texas) – *Chief Executive Magazine*, January 2009

REAL ESTATE

With Plano being a place where poverty is at a minimum, personal wealth is easily built, and so many businesses are either expanding into or relocating to the area, the real estate market must be depreciating in value, right?

Wrong.

The continued increase in home values is just one indicator of how well the Plano, Texas housing market is faring during this recent economic recession. **Trulia.com reported that houses in the Plano area** are appreciating in value, nearly doubling in value in the last ten years. In January 2000, the average property sold for $88,000. Trulia.com, a website focused on the real estate market, also stated that the average price for a property in Plano, as of January 2010, now sells for nearly $150,000.

The Brookings Institute also ranked the Dallas-Fort Worth metropolitan as the third-strongest market for home prices in the nation. Plano is a part of the Dallas-Fort Worth metropolitan.

Housing Health...

- #3 Strongest Home Price (Dallas-Fort Worth Metro) – *Brookings Institute*, 2009
- #4 Strongest Housing Market (Dallas-Fort Worth Metro) – *Brookings Institute,* 2009

SAFETY

With Plano nearly doubling its population in just the last twenty years, it's evident that people like moving to Plano. But with so many new people moving here from all over the country, safety could be a concern. City officials share the concerns of potential residents and that's why they make an effort to keep Plano as safe as possible.

In a 2009 report, **CQ Press ranked Plano as the safest city in North Texas with a population over 100,000, the 6th safest city in the state of Texas, and the 63rd safest city in the nation.** CQ Press is a Washington, D.C. based publisher of books, directories, periodicals, and electronic products about American government and politics.

Men's Health Magazine also ranked Plano as the 8th-safest city in the nation.

Safety First...

- Safest City in North Texas with Population Over 100,000 – *CQ Press*, 2009
- #6 Safest City in Texas – *CQ Press*, 2009
- #63 Safest City in America – *CQ Press*, 2009
- #8 Safest Food Supply in America – *Men's Health Magazine*, 2009

EDUCATION

The city of Plano knows that in order to have a workforce that is second-to-none, education must be top notch. That's why it's a good thing that the north Texas city puts so much time, energy and resources into its public education. And the residents truly reap what they sow.

Residents of the great city of Plano have a lot to hang their hats on when it comes to education. **Whether it is America's Most Literate Cities ranking Plano as number one in educational attainment,** or the fact that **23 Plano schools have received the prestigious National Blue Ribbon Schools of Excellence honor awarded by the U.S. Department of Education,** Plano's school system has a lot to boast about.

Now only that, but **every year the award has been presented (1992-2009), Plano's school district has been selected for a "What Parents Want Award" by SchoolMatch.** SchoolMatch is one of the nation's largest school selection and consulting firms. According to SchoolMatch, only 16 percent of the nation's school systems have been designated for this honor.

Primary and Secondary Education...

- #1 in Educational Attainment – *America's Most Literate Cities,* January 2009
- #11 Best Place to Live for Colleges – U.S. College Search, January 2006

- 14 of the Top 100 High Schools in America (Dallas-Fort Worth-Plano-Arlington area) – *USNews.com,* 2010

LIFESTYLE

As an area with a real estate market on the rise, a successful job force and a seemingly poverty-proof economic model, Plano is a desirable place to live, no matter your cultural heritage. More and more people are moving to Plano and contributing to its diversity in the arts and entertainment.

If living in a community surrounded by aesthetically pleasing surroundings is of high importance to you, know that **AmericaTheBeautiful.com named Plano one of the 10 most beautiful cities in the country.**

Or how about equal rights in the workplace between genders? **Ladies' Home Journal said that Plano is the 9th-best city for women to work.**

Want to raise a family? **U.S. News & World Report said Plano is one of America's top 10 cities to grow up in** and **Best Life Magazine said Plano is the 26th-best city to raise a family.**

Is healthy living something you're striving for? Stay in good physical shape with a community that will keep you accountable. **Men's Health Magazine said Plano is the 9th-most healthy city in the country.**

Everyday Life...

- #9 Best City for Women to Work – *Ladies Home Journal,* 2008
- #9 Healthiest City – *Men's Health Magazine,* 2008
- Top-10 Most Beautiful City in America – *AmericaTheBeautiful.com,* 2008
- Top-10 City to Grow Up – *U.S. News & World Report,* 2009
- #26 Best Place to Raise a Family – *Best Life Magazine,* 2008
- Top-100 Best City to Raise a Family – *MSNBC.com,* May 2008

Dating and Relationships ...

- #6 Most Postings Online of Any Metro (Dallas-Fort Worth-Plano) – *FindMapping.com,* January 2010
- #9 Best Place For Singles (Dallas-Fort Worth-Plano area) – *Forbes.com*, June 2008

PART I

BUYING AND SELLING REAL ESTATE IN THE PLANO AREA

CHAPTER 2

TOP TIPS FOR PLANO AND NORTH DALLAS AREA BUYERS

GET YOUR FINANCING FIGURED OUT

Before knowing what homes to consider, you need to know how much you can afford, and that comes down to the monthly payment amount. Between an array of loan products and constantly changing lending guidelines, confusing or insufficient online mortgage calculators, variable interest rates and credit score surprises, most buyers are looking in the wrong price range (too high or too low), and every buyer can really benefit from the information and guidance of an exceptional loan officer. Ask your REALTOR® for a referral to a mortgage lending specialist with at least five years' experience. Based on your preferred monthly payment, income, and credit scores, the mortgage specialist will review all your loan and down-payment options and write you a "Pre-qualification letter" stating what purchase price you can afford. In most cases, the seller's agent will require this letter in order to consider your offer. A "Pre-approval letter" (as opposed to a pre-qualification letter) requires more labor on your part to provide the lender with additional paperwork and verification. In the Plano and North Dallas market, submitting the pre-APPROVAL letter positions you as a much stronger, more serious buyer in the eyes of the seller because it shows that financing issues will be far less likely to arise.

At one time, using mortgage brokers specializing in residential loans was a great option to capitalize on obtaining some of the most competitive rates because of access to large quantities of wholesale lines of loan products; however, this has dramatically changed in recent times as the lending climate continues to trend towards more and more regulation. This, in turn, has forced many lending sources to abandon wholesale products once made available to third party brokers, and consequently, the brokers are now far and few because access to large varieties of competitively priced loan products is now very limited. While direct, national lenders (i.e. Wells Fargo, Chase and Bank of America) tend to focus exclusively on their own products, many have become competitive in recent times depending on the type of loan product. Even some local and regional retail bank operations or specialized mortgage brokers are now focusing more energy in the mortgage arena and can provide decent loan products and rates despite once being too busy with other facets of the business and once offering very limited mortgage options. One other possible avenue that is sometimes worth checking into is your local credit union (if you have an affiliation with one of course).

When shopping for the best rate for your family, be sure you are comparing 'apples to apples' as rates can change daily from lender to lender. Also, think twice about switching away from a lender who invests precious time to give you advice and guidance. These people are usually far more valuable than saving an eighth of a point on your rate. They're also the ones who will be upfront with their fees. Anyone can quote you a lower rate, but the fact is that some lenders drop the ball and can cost you money or delay your closing, and in Texas, this could potentially put a buyer in default of the sales contract (Speak to an attorney for further information regarding the dangers of being in default of contract). Because poor lenders can prove to be quite costly (no matter what great rate was quoted), the rule of thumb is to always go with someone with whom you feel comfortable, who has your best interests in mind, who is a good trusted advisor, who takes the time to explain your options, who will see the loan all the way through, and whose rates are reasonable. Take note that 'Reasonable' rate always trumps 'Best' rate when there is a certain level of service provided. When it comes down to choosing your lender, it is no time to mess around with someone who might make it work. It's critical to have someone who will get the job done.

DO NOT USE INTERNET LENDERS, out-of-region lenders, or any lender who was not referred to you unless you like last-minute surprises. Typical surprises used to be unexpected rate hikes the day before your closing when it is too late to react. Anyone can talk, but not everyone can deliver; furthermore, if there are issues with the loan, you want to have peace of mind knowing you or your REALTOR® can get face to face with the lender to fix the problem. There's nothing worse for a buyer or seller than getting to the settlement table with no sign of the funds and no sign of the lender (or a lender who is asleep in California during the 9 a.m. settlement in Dallas, Texas).

Be sure your loan officer explains how loan locks work as this may vary from lender to lender. Some lenders may have special incentives such as a float-down option whereby your locked rate can actually be adjusted should a major reduction in interest rates occur after your lock and before the closing.

Finally, when your loan officer asks for additional paperwork, be sure to provide it immediately. Your lender cannot control what the underwriter requests and when it is requested. The bottom line is that no matter who the loan officer is, if you are late to submit documents to the lender, your settlement might also be late. Keep all monthly statements updated as they come in because the lender will probably need to have the latest statements on hand. Also, a recent trend is the verification of credit scores a few days before settlement which simply means DO NOT APPLY FOR NEW CREDIT OR MAKE LARGE PURCHASES

PRIOR TO PURCHASING YOUR NEW HOME! The following checklist will help you to gather most information lenders will require:

LOAN APPLICATION CHECKLIST

- ❑ Borrower's Information
- ❑ Social Security Number
- ❑ Driver's License or other photo ID
- ❑ Home address(es) for the past two years (plus landlords' addresses if renting)
- ❑ Insurance- Name and phone number of your agent. Include member number if issued

Employment/Income

- ❑ W-2's for the last two years
- ❑ Employment information for the past two years, including employer, job title, tenure and employer's address
- ❑ Paycheck stubs for the last 30 days
- ❑ If self-employed or commissioned: Tax returns with schedules for the last two years, year-to-date profit and loss statement and balance sheets
- ❑ Veterans: Certificate of Eligibility- If you are a veteran or active duty
- ❑ Copy of divorce decree and proof of child support income if it is to be considered as part of income for credit purposes

Assets/Bank Statements

- ❑ Most recent statements from banks or other financial institutions. Include bank name, address and account number, plus the balance for each checking, savings, retirement and asset accounts. Include all pages
- ❑ List of assets and their values, including cars, stocks and real estate

Debts

- ❏ Addresses of other real estate owned and the applicable loan information including the name and address of the lender

Refinance Information

- ❏ Copy of Deed
- ❏ Copy of homeowner's insurance
- ❏ Copy of your last mortgage statements (1st and 2nd)

Note: The above information is usually required by your lender for each borrower listed on the loan application. This is a general checklist and is meant to be a guide, not a definitive list. Additional information may be required by your lender.

USE A REALTOR®

Most, if not all, of the buyer agent commissions are paid by the seller on the buyer's behalf, so for a buyer, the help of a real estate professional is extremely inexpensive and in many cases free. A good buyer agent will help you find the right home in the right area, guide you away from big mistakes, point out red flags in a house or in a deal, navigate you through complicated contracts and paperwork, negotiate a better deal for you, and help you with assembling your team of professionals (inspectors, lawyers, lenders, etc.). Some buyers think they will save money by not having an agent. Think again. The seller has agreed to pay a certain commission rate to the listing agent (seller's agent), regardless of whether or not the buyer is represented. If the buyer has no agent, the listing agent will keep the entire amount, and you the buyer will miss out on the benefit of professional advice and representation.

Beware of agents who offer you part of their commission as a "buyer rebate". This is often a sign they are a struggling real estate agent with little or no value to differentiate themselves from the good agents, and as a result may not be competent to represent you. Think about it, if they are so quick to give away their income, imagine how easy they will roll over with YOUR money when it comes to negotiating. The differential in these two amounts are usually not even in the same ballpark, and 9 times out of 10, a good, competent agent will save you significantly more money than one who rebates in hopes of capturing clients. Remember, as with most things in life, you get what you pay for.

When selecting an agent, ask for a referral. People generally only refer their friends to someone who will do a great job...it's their name on the line. Chances are the agent will want to do an excellent job so that same friend will continue to refer other friends. It's brilliant, yet not rocket science. It's called working by referral, and smart buyers should take advantage of that.

Be sure your agent really knows more than just one specialized geographic area and that you feel comfortable together because this really is a partnership situation.

Many buyers and sellers are unclear of the differences between agents, REALTORS*, and brokers when referring to an individual person. Simply put, real estate agents are licensed sales people. Brokers are also licensed to sell but are held to a higher standard of knowledge and education when it comes to licensing. All can help people buy and sell real estate. Brokers can also manage other real estate agents or start their own brokerage. In Texas, most will be referred to as either an Associate Broker or a Managing Broker. Most practicing agents and brokers opt to follow certain ethical standards and join the National Association of REALTORS*. So to clarify, both sales agents and brokers can be a REALTOR*. For the purpose of this book, I may use some of these titles synonymously but will most frequently use REALTOR*.

START EARLY

Most buyers purchase a home that does not match their original criteria 100%. If you start looking too late, you might buy the wrong home. It makes sense to start looking and exploring long before you are ready to buy to give yourself time to learn and think about what you see (most times 3-4 months in advance is good). The criteria for your next home will likely evolve and change as you look at homes. Meet with a good REALTOR®, and discuss your criteria. Then spread out a map and ask which areas have historically held value and which have not. Finally, and most importantly, determine how much commuting you are willing to invest each day. In the Metroplex, we speak in terms of time, not distance. I always tell clients new to the area that they will usually pay more in one of two ways: 1) On the front end when paying more for a home, or 2) On the back end when spending precious time each day commuting to and from work. It is often times a tradeoff for Plano home owners. In some cases, buyers are fortunate enough to live close to work or to travel against traffic. Keep these things in mind.

Your REALTOR® should immediately start sending properties matching your criteria; these days, it is almost exclusively done via email/internet. Sort through the listings, and pick the ones you like the most. When you have time, drive by these homes and see what you think about the neighborhood, the shopping, the work commute and the overall appearance of the home as compared to the listing photo as pictures can be very deceiving. You will find neighborhoods you never knew existed. Remember too that you are not just buying a home but rather a piece of the neighborhood, with surroundings that can affect the home you are thinking of purchasing. Look out for things you like or don't like and don't be afraid to vocalize them to your REALTOR®. At this juncture, exploring the geographic areas in which you may have interest is a productive and even fun part of the process, and you can do it whenever spare time unexpectedly presents itself. If, while driving around, you see a "for sale" sign in front of a property that piques your interest, tell your REALTOR˚ about it, and see if he can obtain further information. If it is listed, your REALTOR˚ can cross-reference to determine why it didn't make your established search list. If it is a 'For Sale By Owner' (FSBO), be sure to let your REALTOR˚ know immediately. Despite having to do twice the work, many good REALTORS˚ will be happy to interact with FSBOs and most FSBOs will agree to cover the cost of the buyer broker fee. Interestingly, over 86% of FSBOs eventually list with an agent; however, until that time, it is critical your REALTOR˚ makes the initial contact to eliminate any confusion or misunderstanding over obligation to pay the buyer broker fee.

Feel free to continue the home search online if you wish, especially if supply is low and there are few choices. 'Out of the Box' searches can sometimes pay off. Realtor.com, HomesDataBase.com, or Ebby.com You may find homes of interest that do not meet your original criteria and even decide to alter your original parameters…No problem. Inform your REALTOR˚ of these criteria changes if you wish, and he will send you more homes to consider.

If you see a home you absolutely love, call your REALTOR˚ and tell him you want to see it ASAP. No harm in looking, and if it is the perfect home, maybe it makes sense to move a little earlier than you planned.

MOVE UP IN THE DOWN MARKET

This is the most profitable time in the history of the North Dallas area to sell your current home and purchase a more expensive home. Here is a very simplified example: Let's assume the average price of a home in the Plano area has dropped 10% over the past 18 months. So if you own a home that would have been worth $400,000 in the previous market, you may only get $360,000 for it now or $40,000 less than you hoped. However, you should be able to purchase your next home at a 10% discount also, so you get a $600,000 home for $540,000, which is a $60,000 savings. In total, you took a $40,000 loss and a $60,000 gain which gives a net result of being $20,000 ahead. It gets better though. In some areas, the lower-priced homes depreciated less than the higher-priced homes. So if your $400,000 home only depreciated 5%, but the $600,000 home depreciated 15%, then you would lose $20,000 on your current home and gain $90,000 on your next home, for a $70,000 positive net! Compare this to moving up in a rapidly appreciating market, when any appreciation on your lower-priced home is wiped out by the price increase of your next home. You are actually taking a loss on the transaction. Keep in mind that getting a bargain on the higher-priced home does not necessarily mean negotiating a big reduction off the list (or "asking") price, because the list price most likely has already been adjusted downward to the right price.

KNOW YOUR CRITERIA

Here is a list of criteria for you to think about:

- ☐ Price range
- ☐ Detachd/Twnhme/Condo
- ☐ Number of bedrooms
- ☐ Master down (Y/N)
- ☐ Number of bathrooms
- ☐ City
- ☐ School district(s)
- ☐ Acreage
- ☐ Age of home
- ☐ One story or two story
- ☐ Lot type (corner/cul-de-sac)
- ☐ Flat lot (Y/N)
- ☐ # Garage spaces
- ☐ Commute time to work
- ☐ Fireplace (wood/gas)

- ☐ Fenced yard (Y/N)
- ☐ Sq ft
- ☐ Exterior (brick/stone/stucco)
- ☐ Community pool (Y/N)
- ☐ Golf course community (Y/N)
- ☐ Short-sale
- ☐ REO/Foreclosure (Y/N)
- ☐ "Fixer-upper" (Y/N)
- ☐ Deck (Y/N)
- ☐ Pool (Y/N)
- ☐ Gated community
- ☐ Granite Counters
- ☐ Flooring (wood, ceramic tile, carpet)
- ☐ HOA Dues

Tell your REALTOR® everything you want in your next home. If your search results in too many homes to choose from, you can add to your criteria. If not enough homes match your criteria, you can make your criteria less specific. Generally it's best to start your search as broad as possible.

UNDERSTAND DOM AND PRICE/SF

DOM is "Days On Market". This number is important because the longer the home has been on the market, the more likely the seller's mindset or position has shifted. Sometimes this can translate into opportunity for buyers because it can be an indicator of how motivated the seller might be. Reports printed by your REALTOR® from the NTRES (North Texas Real Estate Information System), North Dallas Multiple Listing Service (MLS) have two kinds of DOM. The first, DOM, means "Days on Market/MLS". Listing agreements between broker and seller can be terminated and new agreements signed or agents can be fired and hired, and this number will reset to zero each time one of these scenarios occurs, so this number is somewhat meaningless. CDOM, "Cumulative Days on Market" is more helpful because it is the total number of days the property has been on the market regardless of short breaks in listing agreements. However, it is good to note that this number will be reset to zero if the property is taken off the market for at least 30 days. In this case, you can ask your REALTOR® to run a report on the property address to see the complete MLS history, including all price reductions.

Once you identify a home you like, how do you determine if it is priced correctly? Look up the homes that have sold recently in the same subdivision and find those of comparable quality to the home you like, considering overall condition, upgrades, lot size, etc. Your REALTOR® may be able to assemble a "Sales Price per Square Foot" or "Comps" ($/SF) analysis for each of these, to get an idea what the home you like should sell for.

.Ask your REALTOR˚ to print out and help you analyze a detailed "CMA" report for the properties in which you are interested. This report will automatically summarize critical information for you. Pay little attention to SP/LP% (percentage of list price that a property sold for) on this report. This calculation is only helpful when understanding trends and relationships to original sales price and CDOM. There can be a lot of timing strategy involved in what to offer based on the timing and amount of seller price reductions. A good REALTOR˚ will help you interpret anything of significance with this figure.

UNDERSTAND SHORT SALES AND FORECLOSURES

Short Sales

A "short sale" is a situation in which the seller owes more on the home than it is worth, and does not have the funds to come up with the difference at closing. In Texas, the seller has to disclose that it is a short sale and it will be advertised as such in the MLS. The key point I tell all my buyers who are looking at short sale properties is that patience is the key. You might get a good deal from a short sale but it can also take longer to get an approval compared to an owner-occupied deal. Usually when we are looking at short sales, we will submit an offer on a short sale property but continue to keep looking as we wait for an answer from the bank.

When an offer is made, both buyer and seller typically sign a "Short Sale Addendum" which outlines the terms/timelines of receiving approval, doing inspections, etc. Once an offer is accepted by the seller, the listing agent submits it to the seller's lender for approval (along with a laundry list of other items). In rare circumstances does this approval happen quickly; in fact, most often it takes several months, and even then, the answer might be "no".

So it is possible to get a good deal on a short sale, but the lower the offer or the lower the agreed upon price in relation to true market value, the less chance that the lender will approve it. This is because the bank wants to recover as much of their money as possible. Buyers may get a good deal, but they rarely get the 'deal of the century' that some buyers think they're getting with short sales. If you want certainty or have strict timelines about when (or if) you will be able to actually occupy the property, setting your heart on a short sale can be extremely frustrating and a risky proposition. If you have a flexible timeline, perhaps you wish to enter into a short sale situation.

If you decide to consider short sales, be sure to set a deadline for receiving bank approval and/or be sure you have another exit strategy if needed. A good REALTOR˚ can help you understand these complexities and some of the pitfalls involved. But also keep in mind that because of the lengthy process, the seller often times only has one shot at a short sale and wants a buyer who is willing to ride it out with them. The truth of the matter is that as the buyer, you are at the mercy of the bank(s) and the person negotiating with the bank on the seller's behalf. This is often the listing agent or an attorney. As a buyer, you really want to know who is negotiating, how many banks and loans are involved, which banks are involved, and whether or not the seller has the rest of the package prepared for the bank. The listing agent will try to keep you waiting by giving you hopeful updates, but often the process drags on indefinitely. Should you find another home while you are waiting for bank approval, be absolutely sure you can get out of the short sale contract before purchasing another home—do not make this mistake as it could prove to be costly. You should have a "Release Agreement" signed by both parties. Consult your REALTOR˚ and legal counsel there are any doubts whatsoever.

Short sale buyers should consider structuring the deal in such a way that the appraisal and home inspection occur only after title examination and/or the creditor's approval is complete in order to reduce financial risk if the deal falls apart. Because delays are likely, buyers should not lock in their mortgage interest rates until bank(s) approval is received; otherwise, it can be costly to get that rate lock extended. On the other hand, buyers who do not lock in an interest rate may experience a higher one once the bank approval is finally received. There are no guarantees with short sales; however, there is a saying that tends to hold true: "There is nothing short about short sales." Finally, keep in mind that it is difficult, and perhaps impossible in most cases, to get money for repairs. Most short sales are offered in "As-Is" condition.

Foreclosures

If a homeowner stops making mortgage payments, the bank will eventually foreclose on the property. In Texas, the foreclosure process involves auctioning the property on the courthouse steps on the 1st Tuesday of each calendar month, just as it was written back in the olden days. The bank holding the 1st Trust (the biggest stakeholder in the property) sets the minimum bid. Often that minimum price is higher than any bidder is willing to pay. In other words, the minimum bid is higher than market value. When this occurs, the bank essentially takes ownership of the property and lists it for sale with a real estate agent. In a sense, it is as if the bank is the winner of the foreclosure auction and now actually owns the property.

You may have heard the terms "REO" or "Foreclosure". Despite meaning two different things, most agents and buyers use these terms synonymously. But technically speaking, a foreclosure is the process viewed from the courthouse steps, and an REO is a bank owned house that was acquired through the foreclosure process. REO stands for "Real Estate Owned."

Banks approach pricing in several ways. Some purposefully price under market to create quick interest and bidding wars—they let the market dictate the price. Others will price the property a little on the high side, hoping to recover the amount owed. In North Dallas the latter tends to be more of the trend, and then the bank will drop the price substantially every few months until it sells or incrementally every 3-4 weeks until it sells. The strategy is to understand the value of the property (see below) and make offers at or below that value regardless of the current list price. In some cases, knowing this value will tell the buyer to hurry with the offer before another buyer beats them to the punch, and in these cases, it's not unheard of to pay more than list (asking) price to secure a desirable REO.

Asset managers are usually assigned these properties to make decisions on behalf of the seller (the seller may be the asset manager's bank or another bank). In a stable market such as Plano, bank asset managers tend to enjoy countering the offer at or near the original asking price no matter how low the offer; however, if the offer is within 3-5% of the asking price, they are more likely to accept rather than counter. Banks do have special formulas that determine how low they will go (their 'floor'). Like with most sellers, that bottom line tends to change as the days on market increase. Most listing agents are not privy to how low the bank will go. If a property sits for an extended period of time, buyers can sometimes luck out on presenting low offers, but you have to make the offer at the right time, usually just prior to the property coming off the REO market and into the hands of an auction house. Since agents and buyers do not know when that will take place, don't hesitate to re-offer if you have already been turned down.

UNDERSTAND HOW TO DETERMINE THE TRUE VALUE OF A PROPERTY

A home is worth whatever a buyer is willing to pay and a seller is willing to accept in a non-distressed situation. The best source to estimate the true market value of a property is an experienced, busy REALTOR®, because he is working with buyers and sellers in the current real estate market and has access to the best data (from the MLS and local real estate association). He will also correctly adjust for quality and feature differences.

The second best valuation sources are experienced, busy appraisers. They have access to the same data, but they work for banks, not buyers and sellers. In addition, they are constrained by inflexible appraisal rules which do not allow them to consider some relevant information and comparable properties.

Inexperienced REALTORS˙ and appraisers can be wildly inaccurate. Websites like Zillow.com calculate market values without the input from human experience or judgment and they use incomplete data from county tax records. The "value" found in the county tax records is only useful in certain jurisdictions and with professional interpretation. While based on recent sales data, taxed assessed value is calculated for the purposes of property tax assessment. A sales to taxed assessed value analysis can be extremely useful with proper interpretation and statistical integrity; however, it is only one 'piece of the puzzle' when determining value. These methods can be virtually useless depending on the jurisdiction's method for determining the tax assessed value. In Dallas County, this number is updated every year with consistent measures of valuation. This consistency is the key to successful use of this method.

ASK TWO KEY QUESTIONS IN A COMPETITIVE SITUATION

Even in a challenging market it's possible to find yourself competing against another buyer for a low-priced property (see also "Understanding Short Sales and Foreclosures" above). Sometimes competing against others to buy homes is what makes the market challenging. The listing agent is prohibited from disclosing details of any offers received but may disclose the existence of other offers depending on the listing agreement. In a multiple offer situation, the listing agent will usually ask both/all buyers to return with their "best and highest offer". Once these best/final offers are received, a good REALTOR˙ will review the offers and discuss the pros and cons of each with his seller client so the seller can select one buyer with whom to negotiate a final agreement with acceptable terms.

When considering your offer price, ask yourself, "If we lose this property at this price, will I regret not offering more?" If so, you might want to increase your offer. Conversely ask yourself, "If we get the property at this price, will we regret paying that much?" If so, consider decreasing your offer. If you really want a property and are in a multiple offer situation, it is no time to play games. The winner will be the buyer who goes in goes in with a loaded gun—the offer must be merciless. Aside from the offer price, there are many strategies buyers can take to strengthen the offer. Some of these strategies include but are certainly not limited to the following: minimizing the number of buyer contingencies (protective clauses), proposing quicker timelines (or timelines that mirror the seller's needs), offering to pay for some of the sellers' typical closing costs (title policy of insurance, home warranty costs, etc...) purchasing the home "as-is", making a larger down payment or earnest money deposit. Discuss these strategies with your REALTOR®.

WALK THE NEIGHBORHOOD BEFORE MAKING AN OFFER

Before committing to purchase a home, take a few slow walks through the neighborhood at different times of day. Listen for barking dogs. Look at the neighboring homes to see how the surrounding homes are being taken care of with their maintenance and upkeep. Look for children playing if that is important to you (the law prohibits your REALTOR® from discussing "familial status"). Introduce yourself to a few neighbors, tell them which home you are thinking about, and ask them what they know. Neighbors love to talk and you might be glad you listened—they are usually a phenomenal source of information with a perspective that no REALTOR® can give unless he lives in that particular neighborhood.

CHAPTER 3

TOP TIPS FOR PLANO AND NORTH DALLAS AREA SELLERS

MAKE BUYERS FALL IN LOVE WITH YOUR HOME

Buyers keep looking until they fall in love. They are not looking for "a" home; they are looking for "the" home, their "dream" home. They are tired of seeing homes that are not ready for sale (more than 75%). They want a clean, fresh, move-in-ready, "Turn-Key" home. Most do not want to do even minor projects, despite what they say.

As a seller, it is critical to understand the mind of the buyer. Buyers do not buy homes; they buy the feeling they get when they are looking at a home. In other words, buyers buy emotionally, they buy with their eyes. They are not always using their brains to decide, they are using their hearts. And in good markets or tough markets, when a buyer finds the right home, they will fall in love, and that home will sell for the highest possible price.

We have witnessed a buyer considering two identical homes on the same street, in the same neighborhood, with identical lots, and pay

$15,000 more for the one that spent $950 preparing the home for sale. We have seen homes sit on the market for six months, then sell in 15 days (at a higher list price) after a few small adjustments to improve the buyer perception of the home. The old cliché holds true here: You don't get a second chance to make a good first impression, so don't wait six months and miss out on lots of great buyers.

If you want to sell your home for the highest price in the shortest amount of time, emphasize or add elements with which buyers will fall in love, and fix or remove issues that will cause them to hesitate. One of the most helpful tips that I give when it comes to the conditioning of a home is the hiring the services of a good home stager. Home staging has come around to mean a lot of different things to people but basically it is preparing the home with the mindset to maximize the spaciousness, flow and overall feel while minimizing any undesirable features.

There are a few investor types out there who truly decide with their brain, whose first priority is a *good deal* on a house (as opposed to buyers looking for the best home for themselves). As sellers, we want the buyer to choose our home as the *right home*--We are not looking for them to get a *good deal*, right? So unless you are desperate, ignore the investors for the most part. What we want is a buyer to come to your home, fall in love, and impulsively write an offer at (or near) your asking price. So we will concentrate on this type of buyer instead. In addition, the majority of buyers are this type anyway. To win over these buyers, enhancing the appeal and value as described above is critical. Once your home goes on the market, it's no longer your home. It's a product we are marketing to the masses. It's a product we are packaging for profit. Never forget that.

MAKE A PROFIT WHEN YOU SELL BY MAKING SMART INVESTMENTS

By making the right investments in your home, you will not only cause buyers to fall in love, but you will also almost always make a profit. While sometimes difficult to quantify, and depending on your neighborhood, your price point, and the size of your home, the following improvements will generally produce at least $2 or more in increased sales price for every $1 you invest. And anything that increases your price will also reduce your "days-on-market."

- ☐ **Granite countertops in the kitchen.** They are almost a necessity in the North Dallas area if you expect your home to sell for top dollar. You should be able to get them for $45 per square foot, installed. Go with a standard, lower-priced, nice looking choice such a St Cecila, a nice tan colored granite. For higher-end homes, consider Juparana Lapidus, and consider adding granite to the master bathroom as well. For homes under $225,000, consider granite-looking laminate countertops, or if there is an island in the kitchen, you can consider putting granite there only. Stay away from beveled edges. Regardless of type, stick with rounded / semi-bullnose edges, and you won't go wrong.

- ☐ **Stainless steel appliances.** You should be able to get a refrigerator, oven, microwave, and dishwasher for under $2,500. If your current appliances are white or cream color, this is especially important. Black appliances may be okay if they are fairly new. Often, these appliances can be purchased as a package for further savings…be sure to ask!

- ☐ **Replace old carpets.** If they are over five years old, they will not look new when cleaned, unless they are very good quality. New carpet also helps a home smell new. Use a good mid-range carpet, and be sure to use top-grade or thickest pad available—the pad is very inexpensive and can transform the feeling of the carpet to a higher quality.

- ☐ **Remove wallpaper.** Buyers today strongly dislike wallpaper, except for a very subtle pattern in the powder room.

- ☐ **Refinish dull and scratched hardwood floors.** Shining floors make a stunning impact on buyers.

☐ **Paint.** Go with a light beige on the inside. It makes the home look more expensive and makes white trim "pop". White trim, including crown molding and chair rail should have a bright white semi-gloss paint. All outlet covers and switch plates should be bright white to match the trim (no cream colored covers). Painting your front door and shutters black is often times an easy and effective formula for sharpening the appearance of your home. I would suggest going to your local Home Depot or Lowes to purchase the shutters because they tend to be very inexpensive and look much better in most cases, while painting shutters can be time consuming and easy to screw up. Shutters can be purchased starting around $30 per window (pair) for standard louvered type shutters.

☐ **Hardware.** Sometimes you can create a fresh new look with simply adding some new door hardware and cabinet hardware in kitchens and baths. Coupled with fresh paint, new hardware can really make a stellar presentation and a great first impression with the buyers!

☐ **Light Fixtures and Ceiling Fans.** This one is missed a lot of times but this is one that I see that has significant "bang for the buck" when it comes to resale. Updating light fixtures in the front porch area, entry and formal areas usually scores major points with the buyers. I also recommend not overlooking the powder bath downstairs or the master bedroom. In these key areas, upgrading to a nice oil rubbed bronze or satin nickel-finish light fixture or ceiling fan has been known to help many of my sellers attract the very first buyer who sees their home with these upgrades and makes an offer to purchase on the spot!

This advice is subject to modification based on the specifics of your home, and over time as buyer tastes evolve. I recommend getting the advice of a staging consultant who works with real estate agents. Many interior decorators specialize in preparing homes for buyers. It could also be very helpful if your REALTOR* holds a staging designation. This would be an "Accredited Staging Professional" or ASP.

Fixing problems is always better than offering an allowance, because to make up for the problem you will have to reduce your price more than it would have cost you to fix it. I always advise against allowances simply for the fact that you are advertising a "known defect". It usually comes out ahead for my sellers when they go ahead and address the issue (worn carpets, chipped counters, bright wall colors) and get them fixed, then they can start advertising it to their benefit versus a negative!

DO THESE EASY THINGS

Here are a list of low-cost, easy improvements which will pay for themselves many times over:

- ☐ **Clean every inch of your home.** Get help if you need it. When I say clean, I mean "Q-Tip* Clean."
- ☐ **Spread new mulch.** Use dark brown "triple-shredded stained bark." The stain keeps it looking better much longer. I have used Scott's treated bark that is guaranteed to last a year and it is worth the little bit extra to get a nice mulch that is going to last while the house is on the market. These can be found at any Lowe's or Home Depot.
- ☐ **Plant many, many flowers.** More than you think you need. Flowers may be the single best investment you can make to sell your home. Reds and yellows always attract the human eye, so keep this in mind when attempting to accentuate a feature in your home, your yard, or on your deck. Annuals are curb appeal and you can't have too many!
- ☐ **Remove clutter.** Remove personal pictures. Remove everything from horizontal surfaces except a few decorations. With the help of your REALTOR*, a few select items can later be added. I

usually advise my sellers to de-personalize and de-clutter their homes in anticipation of their upcoming move and suggest packing up unused or out of season items and putting them in an attic, storage building or even just simply out in the garage. Remember the buyers are coming to see your home-not your trophies!

☐ **Remove window treatments.** Leave blinds, but keep them open at all times unless the neighboring house is an eye-sore. Heavy draperies and valances take away from the room and shrink the size of a living area. Many times, simply taking the window treatments down in an area visually opens up and I have seen it appear to double the size of a room with this one trick.

☐ **Clean your windows.** While this may seem obvious, you would be surprised how many people forget to do this. I ALWAYS recommend removing the screens as well. The easiest solution is to ask your REALTOR® for referral to a good, inexpensive window washing company. This should be done immediately prior to placing the home on the market for sale, and the window company can even remove all the screens so you don't have to. Leave all screens in a storage area (in the attic or garage) for the future buyer—they will want them but will rarely notice the missing screens when visiting your home. They will, however, notice the bright, vibrant colors from your trees outside and your windows will absolutely sparkle. This may sound corny, but I think this is one of the most effective and cheapest tricks in preparing your home for sale.

☐ **Remove basketball goals, play sets, and tree houses.** These will turn some people off, and no one will ever say "I would have bought that home if only it had a basketball goal." If you have a flat driveway they can install one themselves. Especially remove trampolines. They make many mothers nervous.

USE TEMPORARY STORAGE CONTAINERS

Many sellers have had good experiences using temporary storage containers (such as PODS or Pack-Rat) to store clutter while preparing their home for sale. Some sellers end up using them for the entire move, often in combination with hired labor. As of this writing, a 16-foot container (holds approximately 4 rooms) was $59 for drop off and pick up, plus $199/month for secure, climate-controlled storage, plus a second $59 at final drop off and pick up. The other alternative is hauling material to and from a storage location, which is less expensive, but more work for you. Also, many area storage facilities offer great incentives such as $1 for the first month (with no minimum stay!).

GET YOUR IMPROVEMENTS PERMITTED AND INSPECTED

If you have made any structural changes to your property that were not permitted and inspected, it will very likely be addressed by the buyers' home inspectors. That will make most buyers nervous, and even if they are not concerned, they will use it as a negotiating lever. As a result, it is almost always better to get the home inspected prior to listing and make any necessary repairs, I especially like to recommend a pre-listing inspection for a home older than 15 years since a lot can happen with these older homes. The inspections are inexpensive and fairly quick. This way too if the inspector does find some concerns you can address them without risking losing a buyer under contract. If you have questions, call the county and ask them anonymously.

PRICE YOUR HOME PRECISELY

The price you want or need means nothing to buyers. Yes, making smart investments and properly preparing your home for sale will definitely increase the value, but if your asking price is too much above that value, it will not sell. In fact, because the market is much more price-sensitive than most sellers realize, you may not even get any showings.

Do not make the mistake of thinking, "I'll price it high, because the buyer will make a low offer, and we'll meet in the middle." That is not how it works. Buyers very rarely make low offers, at least in the first 30-45 days a home is on the market. Buyers generally do not like conflict and typically do not want to upset or offend sellers. Neither do their agents, because they hope to work with the listing agent many times again in the future. The buyers have the data, they know what the comparable properties sold for, and if your home is overpriced they assume you will only accept offers close to your list price. Rather than argue about it, they will just ignore your home.

I am not suggesting that you under-price your home to motivate buyers to come see it. Your well-prepared home is motivation enough, and you deserve every penny you can get from the sale, right? An *accurately-priced* home will sell just as quickly as an under-priced home (in fact, under-priced homes look suspicious to buyers). But price cannot be an obstacle either. If your home is prepared correctly, the fair-market value for your property will be near the top of the range of the comparable homes that have sold recently. List your home at no more than two percent above fair-market value, and that is enough "negotiating room" for most buyers to feel like they "won."

Other major pricing mistakes sellers commonly make would include justifying their high price by saying:
- "I can't go up, but I can always bring my price down."
- "It only takes one buyer."
- "Let's just test the market" *

*Caution: Only test the market with the guidance of a good REALTOR® and BE SURE to have a pre-determined price adjustment plan in place based on activity levels. Seller must not lose the 'Golden-Time,' this is the first 2-3 weeks on the market when 80% of the showings occur (See "Sell your home quickly" section below for a better understanding of this).

Price It Right—IT'S CRITICAL!

UNDERSTAND HOW BUYERS FIND THE HOME THEY PURCHASE

You have prepared your home for the market and priced it realistically. Now you need to market it effectively. In order to do that, you need to know how buyers in the Plano area find the home they purchase. Almost every buyer searches for homes on the internet, but except for a small percentage, that is not how they find the home they actually purchase.

The vast majority of North Dallas area buyers (approximately 84%) become aware of the home they actually purchase through a real estate professional. This is because most buyers purchase a home different from the criteria they originally defined as they go through the process, and good REALTORS' help clients adapt their searches accordingly and help find homes often overlooked otherwise. Good REALTORS' also search outside the box as well as seeking appropriate properties from other REALTORS' with whom they have established relationships in an effort to find suitable properties before they are even on the market. This isn't always possible, but a good agent is always looking. So sellers and listing agents would be smart by not only marketing to buyers, but by marketing to the REALTOR' representing buyers. Easier said than done, because brokers get so bombarded with emails and flyers that they just end up deleting or throwing them away. The key here is to realize that 10% of the brokers sell 80% of the property. Knowing who these brokers are and how to get them to pay attention to your home can prove to be very beneficial. To accomplish this, your REALTOR' should have great relationships established with many other agents. It's great if the agent is well thought of amongst his peers. Cooperative agents bring buyers to see each other's listings and ask to return the favor when appropriate.

About four percent of North Dallas area buyers become aware of the home they purchase **through a friend** who lives in the same neighborhood as the home being sold. The best way to make this fact work for you is to call your neighbors and invite them to come to see your home, then ask them if they know any friends or relatives that might want to live in the neighborhood. They will be especially curious to see your home if you have made significant improvements to prepare it for sale.

Six percent of North Dallas area buyers find the home through spotting a **"for sale" sign** while exploring neighborhoods. To maximize this traffic, have a high-quality sign, preferably one hanging from a professionally installed post. A better sign is more noticeable, and it adds to the perception of quality of your home. Also, skip the brochures in front of your home. Most of them get picked up by neighbors anyway, and real buyers use them more to eliminate your home than to schedule a showing. If interested in the home, most buyers will call their REALTOR˚, or if unrepresented, will call the number on the sign. You or your REALTOR˚ can sell your home more effectively than a brochure out front.

While fewer than four percent of buyers do actually find the home they purchase **through the Internet,** do not ignore this one. Be sure your REALTOR˚ will be marketing the property on Realtor.com, *homesdatabase.com,* as well as the websites of the other real estate firms in the area. Depending on the property and location, you may also want to re-list your home on Craigslist every three days so it does not get too far down on the page. Definitely list it on Zillow.com and Trulia.com (two of the most popular real estate web sites), and if you search you will find at least 30 other real-estate related sites on which to place it. While the percentage of purchasers through the internet is small, it is important to note that the National Association of REALTORS˚ reports that 87% of home buyers have used the internet as an information source and 77% have actually driven by and viewed homes they have seen online. Despite the fact that most buyers use a REALTOR˚ to purchase, an internet presence has become essential.

Do not invest in print advertising, either in the newspaper or the real-estate-related magazine you see in the grocery store. They are very expensive, and statistically they generate almost zero results.

Finally, **I advise against open houses**. The North Dallas area is not an open-house oriented market. The chance of selling your home this way (less than 1%) is not worth the safety concern of having unrepresented strangers exploring your home. There are some exceptions to this; on occasion it does make some sense. It is usually driven by market conditions. Sometimes rapid market conditions warrant an open house upon entry to the market place. Consult your REALTOR® to see if it makes sense in your situation.

These statistics come from extensive experience with buyers and sellers in the greater North Dallas area as well as NAR studies. You may find statistics that vary slightly from those above regarding how buyers find homes; however, findings reported from study to study are fairly consistent, so the numbers above are a good representation for you to get the idea.

SELL YOUR HOME QUICKLY

Brokers set up searches in the Multiple Listing Service (MLS) for their clients; if done effectively, homes that come on the market meeting their buyer's criteria get sent to the buyer automatically. So when your home is activated in the MLS, it will be emailed to hundreds and in some cases, thousands of potential buyers all at the same time. Some of these buyers just started looking, so even if they see and love your home, they are not ready to make a decision. They need to see more homes first, and might not have their financing figured out. However, the majority of buyers has been looking for a while and is ready to buy immediately when they find the right home. These buyers are the key to success, and you have one chance at them. They will see the listing and look at the pictures and the price and decide whether or not to schedule a showing to see your home. If they decide "no", they will never see your home again. If they decide to come see your home, they will decide to either buy it, or not. If they decide "no", they will never see your home again. If you do not sell your home to one of these ready-to-buy buyers, you may be in for a long wait, because every buyer who sees your home from then on will be a "new buyer" who is not ready to buy yet.

If your home is prepared right, priced right, and marketed right, you should be able to sell it quickly, in any market, to one of these "ready-to-buy" buyers in less than 30 days. And the faster you sell your home the better price you will get. Here is why: if a buyer walks into your home and falls in love, and the home has been on the market only a few days, they will think, "If we love it, someone else will love it too. We can't let someone else get it first. So let's make an offer today, and let's make it close to asking price. We are not going to let a few thousand dollars get between us and our new home."

After your home has been on the market 30 days, this sense of urgency among buyers is gone. Buyers start saying "Hmm, if this home is so great, why hasn't anyone else bought it yet? I wonder what's wrong with it." Or, "We like it, but it's been here this long already. It'll be here for a while longer. Let's keep looking in case we find something better." Not good for you. Again, this is the 'Golden Time', the first 2-3 weeks on the market with 80% of the showings occur.

If you over-price your home you will get less in the end, because buyers will ignore it until you fix the price, and by then you will have missed all the "ready-to-buy" buyers. Do not have the attitude of "I'll wait for my price". The longer your home sits, the lower it will go. After 90 days buyers will think you are desperate, and in many cases, they will start to "low-ball" you.

Selling a home is a pain. But, you have the choice of: (1) experiencing that pain, at the beginning, for the short amount of time required to get your home ready the right way, or (2) trying to avoid pain at the beginning, and experiencing pain for six months (or more) of price reductions and showings. Constantly having your home ready for showings is stressful. Especially if you have kids or pets.

You have one chance to get the best price in the shortest amount of time. Do the work, be realistic, and get it over with.

HIDE THE PETS

We all love our pets. But buyers do not like pets. In my experience, 70% of buyers will not consider buying your home if they see you have a cat. Too many people are allergic or have friends or relatives who are. Thirty percent of buyers will not consider your home if they see you have a dog. To a lesser extent, it is the same for hamsters, ferrets, rabbits, turtles, etc. So, as much as possible, take the pets out of the home during showings, and hide the evidence left behind (pet food, bowls, litter boxes, and beds). For the average home, this effort will increase your sales price by over $5,000, and reduce the days-on-market by 50%. It's worth the trouble.

MAKE PRICE ADJUSTMENTS QUICKLY BASED ON SHOWING TRAFFIC

Insufficient showings mean your home is overpriced. In our market, here is a good rule of thumb: If you get three or fewer showings in the first 20 days, the market is telling you your home is overpriced by at least 10%. If you get between 4 and 12 showings, you home is 4% to 7% overpriced. If you get 12 or more showings in the first 20 days, but no offer, your home is about 3% overpriced. For higher-priced or very unique properties, you should expect slightly fewer showings, but the conclusions remain the same. Adjust your price immediately. The longer your home is on the market, the lower the eventual price will be. Again, it is always smart to predetermine these adjustments.

BE SMART ABOUT WHAT OFFER YOU ACCEPT

It is very difficult for a seller to back out of The Regional Sales Contract, so think carefully before signing on the dotted line.

While circumstances vary, I generally advise not to consider contracts that are contingent upon the sale of a home that does not already have a contract on it. The buyer may not have properly prepared their home for sale, and/or may be unrealistic about asking price. Sometimes a seller will accept such an offer while retaining the right to continue marketing his property, and while reserving the right to a "Kick Out" clause. This would give the buyer a 48-hour notice when another offer is received to either terminate their offer or drop the contingency. This will not help much because the NTREIS (MLS) will require you to list your property as "Contingent with a Kick Out", which will significantly reduce your showings to the tune of 90%. In the case where the buyer's home is already under contract, it should depend upon how good the contract is. Have your REALTOR® contact the listing agent for the buyer's home. If everything looks solid, you should feel good about moving forward.

Make sure the buyer's financing is in good shape. Certainly ask for a pre-approval letter, but I also recommend having your REALTOR® ask permission to contact the buyer's lender to see how much research the lender has really done.

For homes below $250,000 it is more common for buyers to ask the sellers to contribute to the buyer's closing costs. This is also referred to as 'Closing Cost Assistance' or 'Seller Subsidy.' Be sure to account for this when deciding whether or not to accept an offer. For instance, a buyer may offer $250,000 and ask for $5,000 in seller subsidy. The net result from the seller's eye is a net offer of only $245,000. Keep that in mind, and negotiate accordingly. The buyer often needs this money to purchase your home because they do not have enough cash to cover both the down payment and closing costs such as inspection, appraisal, loan origination, etc. The risk to the seller is that the home must appraise for the total amount, including the closing costs. If it does not, the buyer will ask you to reduce your price to the appraised value (still including closing costs), and if you refuse they might be unable to close.

IF BUYING AND SELLING, GO FOR A SIMULTANEOUS CLOSE

If you are both selling and buying a home, the timing is important. If you sell your home before you find the next one, you will end up moving twice, once into a temporary location, then later into your new home. If you buy your new home before you sell your current home, you will end up paying two mortgages for a while (which also requires the approval of your lender). However, with a smart strategy, you might be able to sell and buy on the same day. This is not always possible, but it is certainly ideal.

The key is to work on finding your next home while preparing your current home for sale. With the right advice from a great REALTOR®, and a realistic price, you should be able to get a contract on your Plano area home within 30 days. If you have done your homework on the buying side and there is enough inventory to support a good choice for you and your family, you will already have a few top choices for your next home. If so, go ahead and get your top choice under contract, contingent on the closing of the existing contract on your home. While not always agreeable to the seller of the house you wish to buy, it is certainly worth attempting. If not, negotiate a longer closing date on your current home to give you more time, and get to work finding the right home. In either case, you should be able to arrange the same closing date for both homes.

If you do not need the cash from your current home in order to purchase the next home, and your lender approves you for a loan on your next home while you still own your first home, it can be very convenient to close on your new home a week or so early to make the move easy.

Most sellers will try to schedule the closing of their current home in the morning on the closing date. Then they get that title company to wire the proceeds to the next title company in order to close later that day on the home they are buying. In other words, the title company agent represents the transaction, not buyer or seller. This title company will have more control over the satisfying the legal timelines and can rush couriers to the courthouse and anything else needed to disburse funds in a timely manner. Discuss options with the escrow officer at the title company.

No matter how much you prepare, keep this important fact in mind: although most real estate closings happen on time, they can be delayed for a dozen different reasons. This is especially true with REO properties. Stay calm, and prepare in advance. When choosing a moving company ask them how much it will cost you if they have to hold onto your belonging for an extra day or more (see the "Storage Container" section above for a different strategy). With REO purchases, ALLOW AN EXTRA 15-30 DAYS on your lock period. While REO sales aren't as time consuming as short sales, delayed settlements are the norm. If you have a loan lock expiring the day after the settlement, you may be in big trouble. Experienced lenders and REALTORS® should realize this and properly guide you. On REO purchases, I always make it clear to the buyers that they should not, under any circumstances, have the loaded-up moving truck in the settlement company parking lot because there is always a chance that keys will not be exchanged the day of settlement.

GET AN EXPERIENCED, FULL-SERVICE REALTOR® AND LISTEN

Not all REALTORS® perform equally. Ten percent of area REALTORS® are responsible for over 80% of all sales in the Plano area. These REALTORS® average far less time on the market than the other 90% of the REALTOR® pool.

A tough real estate market is a "professional's market." The sellers will really benefit by having a full-service REALTOR® to help do everything properly so the home will be the one buyers choose. "Limited service" brokers do not have time to help you get everything right, and trying to sell your home by yourself will leave you helpless and frustrated. In the North Dallas area, 92% of For Sale By Owners eventually commit to using an agent. This should tell you something. Go with someone who is good—someone with skill, integrity, and a strong marketing plan. The right agent does this every day and will give sellers a distinct advantage in the market place and will increase the sellers' net walk away dollars far more than the couple of percent FSBO's attempt to save.

A busy, experienced agent is by far the best qualified person to calculate an accurate, fair-market-value for your home. He works with buyers and sellers all the time and has his finger on the pulse of the market. Good agents have ongoing, productive relationships with other good agents and can often times get their colleagues to bring their suitable clients to your home.

Find a great REALTOR° and listen! He might upset you in the beginning when telling you the truth about your home, the market, and what the market is saying about your home, but he also knows that it is better than upsetting you every day for six months while your home sits unsold.

A good REALTOR° knows how to negotiate the best price for you. He will prove it to you by sticking to his commission rate when you meet him. If he does not believe in himself enough to charge his full fee, then you should not believe in him either. Just tell him to get to work and earn it. Real estate brokerage is like any other business. You get what you pay for, and paying less will cost you more in the end.

PREPARING FOR A SHORT SALE

If you should determine that a short sale is in your best interest, there is a process to increase overall chance successfully completing this type of sale. (See Buyer Tips section for more on Short Sales). For a short sale approval, the two most important aspects are having a Purchaser and having a Ratified Contract.

Prior to obtaining the Purchaser or upon obtaining the Contract, you must put together a short sale package. This should be forwarded to the Short Sale Lender's Loss Mitigation Department for review and decision on the debt relief requested.

The short sale package must contain the following:

1. *Your Hardship Letter:* This is the seller's letter to the bank outlining your current financial difficulties that are creating the need to sell at this time and why the Lender should grant the debt relief requested. Make sure that it is signed, and that you include all of current troubles with your finances, whether it be a high interest rate on your mortgage, accumulating bills, loss of employment, divorce, or whatever.

2. *Written Authorization:* A notarized, written authorization is required for either the agent or attorney to discuss/negotiate the short sale on the seller's behalf with the Lender.

3. *A fully ratified Sales Contract, including any addenda.*

4. *The Purchaser's Loan Pre-Approval Letter*

5. *A copy of your executed Listing Agreement.*

6. *Seller's last two pay stubs for (if you have a regular-pay job).*

7. *Seller's last two months' bank statements for primary checking and savings accounts.*

8. *Seller's last two years' tax returns.*

9. *A short statement (signed) from the seller listing monthly income vs. monthly expenses.*

10. *The last mortgage statement from each mortgage/credit line on this property.*

Once you have all of that together, it needs to be forwarded to the Loss Mitigation/Short Sale Department of the lender(s) involved. At that time, your attorney should open up a case file, rush-order the title exam, and create a Draft Settlement Statement showing exactly what the Lender stands to net from the sale, and that should immediately be forwarded to the Lender.

CHAPTER 4

55+ COMMUNITIES: INSIDE INFORMATION FOR MATURE ADULTS

WHY MOVE TO PLANO AND THE SURROUNDING AREA?

Texas has recently become one of the top retirement destinations in the county, beating out Arizona and California and closing in on Florida. The Lone Star State boasts a sunny climate, a lower cost of living and less volatile weather patterns than other retirement destinations, and as such, its popularity has grown rapidly over the last several years. In response, the state is aggressively seeking to improve its accessibility to relocating retirees and now runs a website (*www.retireintexas.org*) devoted to promoting Texas as the new destination of choice. The Texas Department of Agriculture has also instituted a certification program, the GO TEXAN Certified Retirement Community Program, which accesses and certifies communities based on their desirability as retirement destinations.

Plano and the surrounding area north of Dallas is particularly attractive for older Americans and retirees from all over the country are now calling it home. The healthy job market and robust economy has drawn in many young families and so, in addition to the reasons stated above, older adults are also moving to be closer to family. Plano was ranked by CNN Money magazine in 2006 as the 11th best place to live in the United States, in recognition of the area's high-quality living standards, industry, and top educational institutions. Adults 65 and over comprise 4.9% of the regions total population of 241,991.

COMMUNITIES FOR OLDER ADULTS

There are many communities in Plano and the surrounding area that cater to older adults. These communities can be divided into three categories: Active Adult Communities, Continuing Care Retirement Communities and Retirement Rental Communities. Most of the Active Adult Communities allow residents to purchase their homes; however, some of the communities listed below rent or lease their properties. A minimum age requirement of either 55 or 62 may apply to some communities.

ACTIVE ADULT COMMUNITIES (55 AND OVER)

Americans are living longer, healthier lives. As the baby-boomer generation reaches retirement age, Active Adult Communities continue to gain in popularity. As the title suggests, these developments emphasize activities and amenities such as fitness centers, cooking classes, golf outings and pools. Some developments are designed to be self-contained communities and include everything from grocery stores to doctors' offices, restaurants to walking trails.

Active Adult developments may either offer homes for purchase or rental options. A common feature of these communities is low-maintenance housing – lawn care and exterior building maintenance are often included in homeowners' association (HOA) fees or monthly rental fees.

ACTIVE ADULT COMMUNITIES IN PLANO AND SURROUNDING COMMUNITIES

Conservatory Senior Living

Municipality: Plano

Description: Conservatory Senior Living offers resort-style retirement living in one and two bedroom suites.

Types of Homes: Apartments

Price Range: Call for Details

HOA Fees: N/A

Manager: Conservatory Senior Living

Nearby: I-75 and Highway 121, Dallas/Ft. Worth

Activities and Amenities: Fine Dining, Full-Time Social Director, Fitness Program and Wellness Classes, Movie Theater, Salon and Barber Services, Transportation, Pool and Spa, Arts and Crafts Studio, Game Room

Address: 6401 Ohio Drive, Plano, TX 75024

Phone: (972) 491-3100

Website: *www.conservatoryseniorliving.com*

The Plaza at Chase Oaks

Municipality: Plano

Description: The Plaza at Chase Oaks is an active adult community operated by Bristol Properties.

Types of Homes: One and Two Bedroom Apartments

 # Of Homes/Sites/Units: Call for Details

Price Range: $524 - $785 (Income Restricted)

HOA Fees: N/A

Manager: Bristol Properties, Inc.

Nearby: N. Central Expressway, Sam Rayburn Toll way, Dallas/Ft. Worth, Downtown Plano

Activities and Amenities: Business Center, Fitness Center, Pool and Spa, Library

Address: 7100 Chase Oaks Blvd, Plano, TX 75025
Phone: (214) 473-8778
Website: *www.plazaatchaseoaks.com*

Frisco Lakes

Municipality: Frisco
Description: Frisco Lakes is situated by a lake and golf course. It offers nine models of ranch-style homes, ranging from 1,301 square feet to 2,681.
Types of Homes: Two and Three Bedroom Ranch-Style Homes.
# of Homes/Sites/Units: 2,400
Price Range: Start at $149k
HOA Fees: $105/Month + One-Time $1,500 Capital Contribution
Developer: Pulte Homes/Del Webb
Nearby: Dallas North Toll way and Interstate I-35E, DFW International Airport, Stonebriar Centre, Lake Lewisville
Activities and Amenities: Fitness Center, Indoor and Outdoor Pool, Bocce Ball and Tennis Courts, Game Room, Golf, Arts Studio and Craft Center, Walking Trails
Address: 1011 Pasatiempo Dr., Frisco, TX 75034
Phone: (469) 362-3800
Website: *www.pulte.com/delwebb*

Villas at Country Lane Seniors Campus

Municipality: McKinney
Description: The Villas at Country Lane presents opportunities for owning and renting. It is part of Country Lane Senior Campus, which also offers rental apartments, a nursing and rehabilitation center, and a dementia care center.
Types of Homes: Two and Three Bedroom Duplexes
# of Homes/Sites/Units: Contact Site
Price Range: Call for Details
HOA Fees: $250/Month

Developer: Savannah Developers
Nearby: Highway 75, Historic Downtown, Stonebriar Mall
Activities and Amenities: Movie Theater, Fitness Center, Pool, Coffee Shop, Transportation, Library, Arts and Crafts Room, Bocce Ball Courts, Salon, Concerts
Address: 2491 Country View Lane, McKinney, TX 75069
Phone: (817) 371-0844
Website: *www.countrylaneseniors.com/villasMcKinney.html*

Wellstone at Craig Ranch

Municipality: McKinney
Description: Wellstone at Craig Ranch offers eight models of high-end condominiums ranging from 2600 to 3200 square feet.
Types of Homes: Condominium
# of Homes/Sites/Units: 200
Price Range: Start at $390k
HOA Fees: Call for Details
Developer: Wellstone Communities/FoxCor, Inc.
Nearby: Highway 121, Stonebriar Mall, Collin County Community College
Activities and Amenities: Wellstone Community Clubhouse, Hiking and Biking Trails, Transit System, Fitness Center, Business Center, Indoor track, Pool and Spa
Address: 6850 TPC Drive in McKinney, Texas 75070
Phone: (972) 540-2724
Website: *www.activeadultliving.com/TX/dallas_wellstone.htm*
www.adultliving.robson.com/

Robson Ranch

Municipality: Denton
Description: Robson Ranch offers 17 models of two and three bedroom homes ranging from 1305 to 3198 square feet.
Types of Homes: Single Family Homes

# of Homes/Sites/Units: Contact Site
Price Range: Start at $139k
HOA Fees: Call For Details
Developer: Robson Ranch
Nearby: I-35 W., Murchison Performing Arts Center, DFW
International Airport, University of North Texas
Activities and Amenities: Sports Club, Pool, Tennis Courts, Salon,
Restaurant, Wildhorse Golf Course, Clubhouse, Walking Paths, Creative
Arts Center
Address: **9501 Ed Robson Blvd, Denton, TX 76207**
Phone: (888) 988-3927
Website: *www.robson.com/*

CONTINUING CARE RETIREMENT COMMUNITIES

Continuing Care Retirement Communities (CCRC) are
developments that provide a continuum of care to residents from
independent living to skilled nursing. CCRCs offer the opportunity for
an individual to remain in one location for the rest of his or her life.

Upon first entering a CCRC, most residents move into an
independent living situation (a single-family home, townhouse or
apartment). Like Active Adult communities, CCRCs offer activities and
amenities such as restaurants, fitness centers, book clubs and on-site
health care. What makes CCRCs unique is that they also offer assisted
living and skilled nursing care to their residents, should the need arise.

Contracts are another distinguishing feature of CCRCs. Residents
must enter into a contract with a CCRC prior to moving in. Most
contracts include both entrance fees (some of which may be refundable)
and monthly fees. Some CCRCs also offer the ability to purchase a
home. The American Association of Homes for the Aging has described
three basic types of CCRC contracts:

- **Type A, Comprehensive** –Contracts are all-inclusive. Housing,
  community services and access to all levels of care are included in the price.

- **Type B, Modified**– Modified contracts provide housing, community services and a specified amount of long-term care, after which the resident must make additional payments.
- **Type C, Fee for Service** – Fee-for-Service contracts provide housing, community services and guaranteed access to health care at the going rate.

Because of the many different options involved with Continuing Care Retirement Communities, prices vary greatly, both between communities and within communities.

The Texas Register Division registers all Continuing Care Retirement Communities in the state.

The Legacy at Willow Bend

Municipality: Plano
Description: The Legacy at Willow Bend is a Life Care Community located on a 28-acre resort-style campus. Residents have the option of renting an apartment or a villa. Apartments range in size from 900 to 1,850 square feet. The villas start as large as 2,300 square feet.
Types of Homes: Apartments and Villas
Services: Independent Living, Assisted Living, Nursing Care, Memory Care
Entrance Fees: Call for Details
Monthly Fees: Call for Details
Nearby: I-75, Highway 121, The Shops at Legacy
Activities and Amenities: Fitness Center, Aquatics Center and Spa, Art Studio, Lounge and Café, Library, Card Rooms, Fine Dining, Salon, Dog Park, Theater, Transportation, Planned Social Programs
Address: 6101 Ohio Drive, Plano, TX 75024
Phone: (972) 468-6200 or (866) 953-4229
Website: *www.thelegacywb.org/Willow-Bend/index.php*

Edgemere

Municipality: North Dallas

Description: Edgemere is a Life Care Community with Tuscan-style architecture. The community is operated by Senior Quality Lifestyles Corporation and is situated on a verdant campus close to the big-city excitement and culture of Dallas.

Types of Homes: Apartments

Services: Independent Living, Assisted Living, Nursing Care, Memory Care

Entrance Fees: Call For Details

Monthly Fees: Call For Details

Nearby: Dallas North Toll way, W. Northwest Highway, Highland Park Shopping Village, Winspear Opera House, Dallas Museum of Art

Activities and Amenities:

Address: 8523 Thackery St., Dallas, TX 75225

Phone: (214) 625-9100 or (888) 658-4359

Website: *www.edgemeredallas.com/The-Neighborhood-Location-Map.asp*

Presbyterian Village (62+)

Municipality: North Dallas

Description: Presbyterian Village North is a Continuing Care Retirement Community situated on scenic 63-acre campus. Depending on the level of care needed, residents choose between single homes and apartments.

Types of Homes: Single Homes and Apartments

Services: Independent Living, Assisted Living, Nursing and Rehabilitation Care, Memory Care

Entrance Fees: Call for Details

Monthly Fees: Call for Details

Nearby: LBJ Freeway, N. Central Expressway, Kindred Hospital of Dallas, Texas Health Presbyterian Hospital, Harry Moss Park

Activities and Amenities: Wellness Center, Dining, Auditorium
Walking Paths, Rose Garden, Volunteer Opportunities, Weekly Worship
Services
Address: 8600 Skyline Drive, Dallas, TX 75243
Phone: (214) 355-9001
Website: *www.presbyterianvillagenorth.org*

The Forum at Park Lane

Municipality: Dallas
Description: The Forum at Park Lane is a Continuing Care Retirement
Community owned by Five Star Senior Living. It is located on a seven-
acre tree-lined campus and offers a choice of one and two bedroom
apartments ranging from 600 to 1,400 square feet.
Types of Homes: Apartments
Services: Independent Living, Assisted Living, Nursing Care, Short Term
Assisted Living Care
Entrance Fees: Call for Details
Monthly Fees: Call for Details
Nearby: North Central Expressway, Southern Methodist University,
Texas Health Presbyterian Hospital Dallas, North Park Mall
Activities and Amenities: Fine Dining, Wellness Program, Social and
Recreational Activities, Spiritual Activities, Transportation,
Address: 7831 Park Lane, Dallas, TX 75225
Phone: (214) 369-9902
Website: *www.theforumatparklane.com/*

RENTAL RETIREMENT COMMUNITIES

Rental Retirement Communities may offer independent living
arrangements, assisted living arrangements, memory care, nursing care, or
any combination of thereof.

Preston Place

Municipality: Plano

Description: Preston Place is an independent senior living community situated on twelve landscaped acres of land in one of Plano's older neighborhoods. The community is owned by Spectrum Properties and offers apartments ranging from 650 to 1,440 square feet.

Type of Units: One and Two Bedroom Apartments

Services Offered: Independent Living

Nearby: Dallas N. Toll way and N. President George Bush Turnpike, DFW International Airport

Activities and Amenities: Transportation, Planned Activities, Pool and Spa, Crafts Room, Health and Wellness Programs, Additional Services Offered a la Carte

Address: 5000 Old Shepard Place, Plano, TX 75093

Phone: (972) 931-1336

Website: *www.spectrumprop.com/prestonplace.htm*

Franklin Park at Canyon Creek

Municipality: Plano

Description: Franklyn Park at Canyon Creek is an independent living community featuring Tuscan-style architecture. The community offers apartments ranging from 785 to 1,664 square feet.

Types of Homes: One, Two and Three Bedroom Apartments

Services: Independent Living

Entrance Fees: Call for Details

Monthly Fees: Call for Details

Nearby: N. President George Bush Turnpike, Independence Parkway, University of Texas-Dallas, DFW International Airport

Activities and Amenities: Gourmet Dining, Glass skywalk, Fitness Center, Wellness Program, Library, Transportation, Theatre, Activity Director, Chapel, Grand Ballroom, Greenhouse, Spa and Salon, Pool

Address: 440 Independence Parkway, Plano, TX 75075

Phone: (469) 467-2262
Website: *www.franklinpark.org*

Sunrise of Plano

Municipality: Plano
Description: Sunrise of Plano is a senior living community owned and operated by Sunrise Senior Living.
Types of Homes: Apartments
Services: Independent Living, Assisted Living, Memory Care
Entrance Fees: Call for Details
Monthly Fees: Call for Details
Nearby: Dallas Parkway, Rosemeade Parkway, Lewisville Lake, Presbyterian Hospital - Plano
Activities and Amenities: Dining, Bistro, Sunroom, Landscaped Gardens, Walking Paths, Beauty and Barber Shop, Social and Educational Programs, Transportation, Wellness Program
Address: 4800 West Parker Road, Plano, TX 75093
Phone: (972) 985-9181
Website: *www.sunriseseniorliving.com*

Horizon Bay

Municipality: Plano
Description: Horizon Bay is an assisted living and memory care community owned and operated by Horizon Bay Retirement Living.
Types of Homes: Studio and One-Bedroom Apartments
Services: Assisted Living and Memory Care
Entrance Fees: Call for Details
Monthly Fees: Call for Details
Nearby: Dallas Parkway, Rosemeade Parkway The Shops at Willow Bend, Arbor Hills Nature Preserve, Presbyterian Hospital - Plano
Activities and Amenities: Dining, Transportation, Walking Paths, Tearoom and Parlor, Craft Room, Spa, Fitness Room, Beauty Shop, Social and Recreational Programs, Educational and Cultural Programs

Address: 3000 Midway Road, Plano, TX 75093
Phone: (972)-473-7400
Website: *www.horizonbay.com*

Esperanza of Carrollton

Municipality: Carrollton
Description: Esperanza of Carrollton is owned and operated by Esperanza Senior Living. Residents choose between apartments designed for independent or assisted living. There are also specially designed assisted living apartments and care plans for those with Alzheimer's and dementia.
Types of Unit: One Bedroom and Studio Apartments
Services Offered: Independent Living, Assisted Living, Memory Care
Entrance Fees: Contact Facility
Monthly Fees: Contact Facility
Contract Type: Contact Facility
Nearby: Highway 121, I-35E, Dallas/Fort. Worth
Activities and Amenities: Library, Activity Center, Salon and Barber Services, Dining, Laundry Service, Transportation
Address: 1029 Seminole Trail, Carrollton, TX 75007
Phone: (972) 395-3553
Website: *www.esperanzaseniorliving.com/carrollton*

Atria Carrollton

Municipality: Carrollton
Description: Atria Carrollton is a senior living community owned and operated by Atria Senior Living Group.
Types of Units: Apartments
Services: Independent Living, Assisted Living, Memory Care
Entrance Fees: Call For Details
Monthly Fees: Call For Details
Nearby: I-35E, N. President George Bush Turnpike, Trinity Medical Center

Activities and Amenities: Chapel, Computers, On-site Physical Therapist, Activity Director, Transportation, Café, Pets Welcomed, Retreats/Temporary Stays,
Address: 1825 Arbor Creek Drive, Carrollton, TX 75010
Phone: (972) 862-8700
Website: *www.atriaseniorliving.com*

The Lodge on Preston Ridge

Municipality: Frisco
Description: The Lodge on Preston Ridge is located on a five acre landscaped campus. Apartments ranging from 414 to 514 square feet are available to accommodate individuals seeking independent or assisted living arrangements.
Types of Homes: Studio and One-Bedroom Apartments
Services: Independent Living and Assisted Living
Entrance Fees: $2000
Monthly Fees: $1995 to $3895
Nearby: Highway 121, County Road. 66, Collin County Community College
Activities and Amenities: Transportation, Wellness Center, Planned Activities, Dining, Walking Paths, Gardens
Address: 5850 Ohio Drive, Frisco, TX 75035
Phone: (972) 668-4100
Website: *www.thelodgeonprestonridge.com/*

Atria Richardson

Municipality: Richardson
Description: Atria Richardson is senior living community located in a quiet, residential neighborhood. The community is owned and operated by Atria Senior Living Group
Types of Units: Apartments
Services: **Independent Living, Assisted Living, Memory Care**
Entrance Fees: Call for Details

Monthly Fees: Call for Details
Nearby: I-75, Richardson Regional Medical Center, University of Texas-Dallas
Activities and Amenities: Activity Director, Transportation, Café, Pets Welcomed, Retreats/Temporary Stays,
Address: 1493 Richardson Drive, Richardson, TX 75080
Phone: (972) 231-3313
Website: *www.atriaseniorliving.com*

The Wellington at Arapaho

Municipality: Richardson
Description: The Wellington at Arapaho is a senior living community owned and operated by Capital Senior Living. The community offers studios and apartments ranging from 318 to 892 square feet.
Types of Homes: Studio, One and Two Bedroom Apartments
Services: Independent Living, Assisted Living, Respite Care
Entrance Fees: Call for Details
Monthly Fees: Call for Details
Nearby: N. Central Expressway, President George Bush Turnpike, Richland Community College, Spring Creek Forest Preserve
Activities and Amenities: Transportation, Social and Recreational Programs, Library, Beauty and Barber Shop, Fitness Room, Walking Paths
Address: 600 West Arapaho, Richardson, TX 75080
Phone: (469) 330-2800
Website: *www.wellingtonatarapaho.com/*

PART II

PLANO AREA
CITIES AND TOWNS

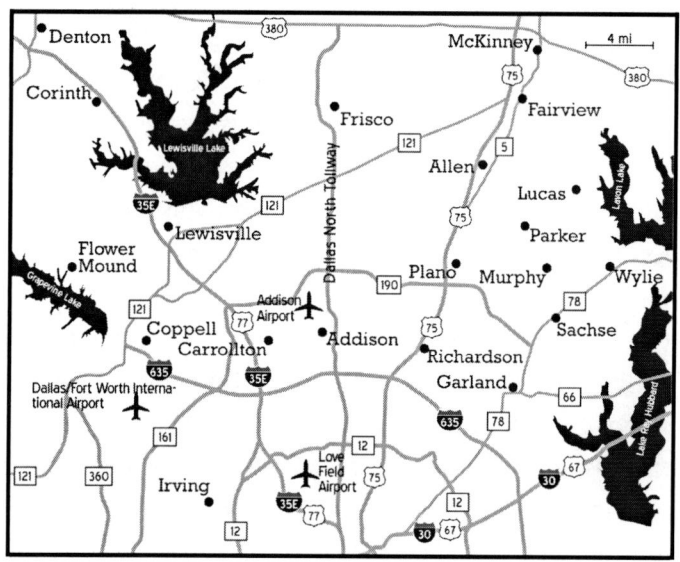

CHAPTER 5

PLANO

Named in 1850 for the vacant terrain surrounding the area, Plano means "plain" in Spanish. The community was formed in the early 1840s, with most of the early pioneers migrating from Tennessee and Kentucky.

In 1846, William Foreman bought land and settled northeast of Plano and erected a sawmill and gristmill. It was the popularity of these services that started the development of the community. Foreman believed the town needed a proper name, and after recommending Fillmore, after the U.S. President, and Foreman, after the town's founder, Plano was agreed upon.

In the 1850s, growth of the town was steady, with businesses, schools and churches established in the area. However, the arrival of the Civil War halted progress from 1861-1864. Progress picked back up after the war ended when men who fought in the war returned, and new residents from the North and South moved in to start a new life. In 1872, the completion of the Houston and Texas Railroad helped drive continued growth into the town, and in June 1873 the city was incorporated. However, in 1881 much of the city was destroyed by a fire, although many early buildings survived and are still standing. While Plano was mainly a farming community through most of the 20th century, by the 1960s the expansive growth of Dallas influenced the town's economy and helped turn Plano into one of the fastest-growing cities in the U.S.

SURROUNDING COMMUNITIES

Considered one of the largest Dallas suburbs, Plano covers a total area of 71.6 square miles. Since the city is locked in by surrounding communities, Plano has virtually no room for expansion. Therefore a great deal of crossover exists between Plano and the towns that it borders. These towns include:

Frisco:

Located Northwest of Plano, Frisco is a rapidly growing Dallas suburb that serves as a bedroom community for many professionals working in the Dallas-Fort Worth Metroplex. In 2007, Forbes Magazine named Frisco the 7th-fastest growing suburb in the U.S.

The Colony:

Developed in 1969 as a "dream city" modeled after Dallas, The Colony is Northwest of Plano. With a total of 15.7 square miles, there are large pockets of undeveloped area in The Colony that make it perfectly positioned for future growth.

Carrollton:

Settled in 1842 as an agricultural community, Carrollton was named by *Relocate America* as one of "America's 100 Top Places to Live" for 2006. It was also chosen as the 15th "Best Place to Live" by *Money Magazine* in 2008. Carrollton is located in portions of Dallas County, Denton County and Collin County.

Richardson:

Located in both Collin and Denton Counties, Richardson is home to the Telecom Corridor, which is made up of a high concentration of telecommunications companies. In 2009 it was voted by *Business Week* as the 2ⁿᵈ "Best Place to Raise Kids in Texas." It is bordered mainly by Plano and Dallas.

Murphy:

Situated halfway between Plano and Wylie, Murphy is two miles south of the famous Southfork Ranch, made famous by the TV show *Dallas*. While the community is focused on maintaining its country-living atmosphere, Murphy is just 20 miles from downtown Dallas, giving it easy access to all the amenities of big-city living.

Parker:

As the renowned location of Southfork Ranch, home to the famous TV family The Ewings, Parker has a total area of just 5.2 square miles. The community is located Northeast of Plano and is part of Collin County. Today, the town is still enjoying growth, with many new neighborhoods offering large lots and open space.

Allen:

Located North of Plano, Allen's population has grown tremendously in recent years, with its population jumping from 40,000 in 2000 to 77,644 in 2007. Developed in the 1840s when immigrants arrived in the area in search of free land, it is the site of one of the last conflicts between Native American Indians and the early settlers.

McKinney:

Second in population to Plano, McKinney was listed as the nation's fastest-growing city from 2000 to 2003, and again in 2006. Named after Collin McKinney, signer of the Texas Declaration of Independence, in 2008 McKinney was ranked by *Money Magazine* as number 14 for "Best small cities in the U.S."

Addison:

The Town of Addison is actually incorporated as a city and has a total area of 4.4 square miles. Settled as early as 1846 by Preston Witt, the community gained a name in 1902 when the first cotton gin opened. Today the town enjoys commercial growth and attractions like The WaterTower Theater, The Cavanaugh Flight Museum and Kaboom Town, one of the largest 4th of July fireworks shows.

Coppell:

Located Southwest of Plano, Coppell was settled by French and German immigrants in the 1840s. Originally named Gibbs Station, it was renamed in 1890 after George Coppell, an engineer who was responsible for bringing the railroad to the town. Today, with its close proximity to DFW Airport, and a growing commercial base of warehouses and transportation centers, the town is thriving.

Irving:

Originally settled in 1889 as an area called Gorbit, and then changed to Kit in 1894, the town was incorporated in 1914 and is thought to be named after literary author Washington Irving. The town is home to the Las Colinas area, one of the first master-planned communities in the U.S. It will also be home to the new Irving Convention Center, planned to open in November 2010.

Lewisville:

As part of Denton County, Lewisville is located west of Plano and is one of the oldest incorporated cities in the Dallas-Fort Worth Metroplex. Incorporated in 1925, the city was historically a small, rural town until the early 1970s when the population began booming, mainly due to its close location to the DFW Airport and The Vista Ridge Mall. One of

North America's earliest Paleo-Indian sites is found in the city, dating back to 1100 B.C.

Garland:

Just a short driving distance to most attractions in the Dallas-Forth Worth Metroplex, Garland is a thriving community Southeast of Plano. Settled in 1850 and created as a community in 1874, Garland was named after Attorney General Augustus Hill Garland. In 2008, the city consisted of approximately 218,577 residents and now boasts such attractions as the Hawaiian Falls Waterpark and the Firewheel Town Center, an outdoor mall with more than 100 businesses.

Flower Mound:

Named after a 12.5 acre mound covered by wild flowers, and considered a ceremonial site of the Wichita Indians in the early 1800s, this suburban mid-size city enjoys close access to the DFW Airport and the Dallas-Forth Worth Metroplex. The town prides itself on its SMART growth plan, designed to manage the rate and character of development in the community. Flower Mound was rated as one of the "Top 10 suburbs to live in Dallas-Ft. Worth" by *D Magazine* in 2008.

REAL ESTATE

Known for its wide open spaces and affordable real estate, whether you're looking for a single-family home, townhouse or condominium, the real estate market in Plano has something for everyone. Reports show that last year the Dallas/Fort Worth Metroplex added the most jobs of any U.S. metropolitan city. Therefore, this strong job growth is driving more people to Plano and keeping the value of the community's real estate strong. Plano truly is a great place to call home!

EDUCATION

Plano Independent School District serves most of Plano, with grades 9-10 attending a high school and grades 11-12 attending a senior high school. Some portions of Plano are also served by Lewisville Independent School District, Frisco Independent School District and Allen Independent School District. There are 70 public schools in Plano, as well as 16 private schools and two campuses of the Collin County Community College District. SMU-in-Plano, a branch of Southern Methodist University, is also in the area.

TRANSPORTATION

Plano is one of 12 suburbs in the Dallas area that is part of the Dallas Area Rapid Transit (DART) system. The Red Line of the DART light rail project has stations in Downtown Plano and Parker Road. Plano is also served by bus lines. As the first city in Colin County to adopt a master plan for roads, Plano is served by several major roadways and freeways. Central Plano is bordered to the north by SH 232, to the east by U.S. Highway 75, the south by President George Bush Turnpike, and the west by Dallas North Tollway. Plano is also convenient to the Dallas-Fort Worth International (DFW) and Love Field airports.

ARTS & RECREATION

From outdoor hiking to exploring the arts, Plano boats a wide variety of interesting things to do and see. Just some of them include:

- *Interurban Museum:* Home to one of the original electric trains that ran through Plano, this museum features interesting exhibits on the history of transportation in the area.
- *Arbor Hills Nature Preserve:* Offers vast areas of natural beauty for walking, jogging, hiking and other outdoor activities in a 200-acre park located on the western border of Plano.

- *ArtCentre of Plano:* A renovated historic downtown building features plays, musical performances, local artists and national shows.
- *Heard Natural Science Museum and Wildlife Sanctuary:* This 289-acre property features nature trails and live animals, as well as indoor exhibits showcasing fossils, local wildlife, Indian artifacts, rocks, minerals and seashells.
- *Heritage Farmstead:* This 1891 Victorian farmstead is listed on the National Register of Historic Places and features a million-dollar restoration of a 12-room, turn-of-the-century farm home complete with gardens, farm animals and antique farm equipment.
- *Southfork Ranch:* Get up close and personal with the most infamous Texas TV family: the Ewings. Tour the Ewing Mansion and grounds made famous by J.R. and the family.

SHOPPING

Plano boasts more than 70 shopping centers for shoppers of any style and budget. Around town and in the historic downtown, shoppers can find boutiques, specialty stores, one-of-a-kind shops, antique stores and galleries. Nearby are other popular malls, such as The Shops at Willow Bend, Galleria Dallas, NorthPark Center, Valley View Mall, Collin Creek Mall Stonebriar Centre, Allen Premium Outlets, The Village at Fairview, The Firewheel Mall and Highland Park Village.

CITY OF PLANO CONTACT INFORMATION

Website: *www.plano.gov*
City Hall: (972) 941-7000

PART II: PLANO AREA CITIES AND TOWNS

PLANO POPULATION GROWTH

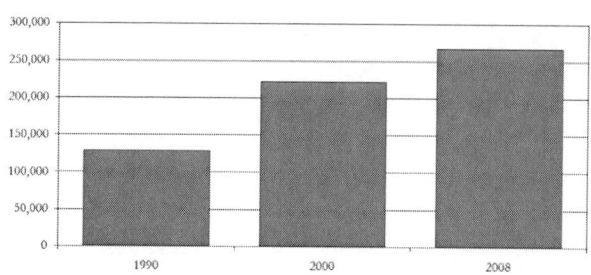

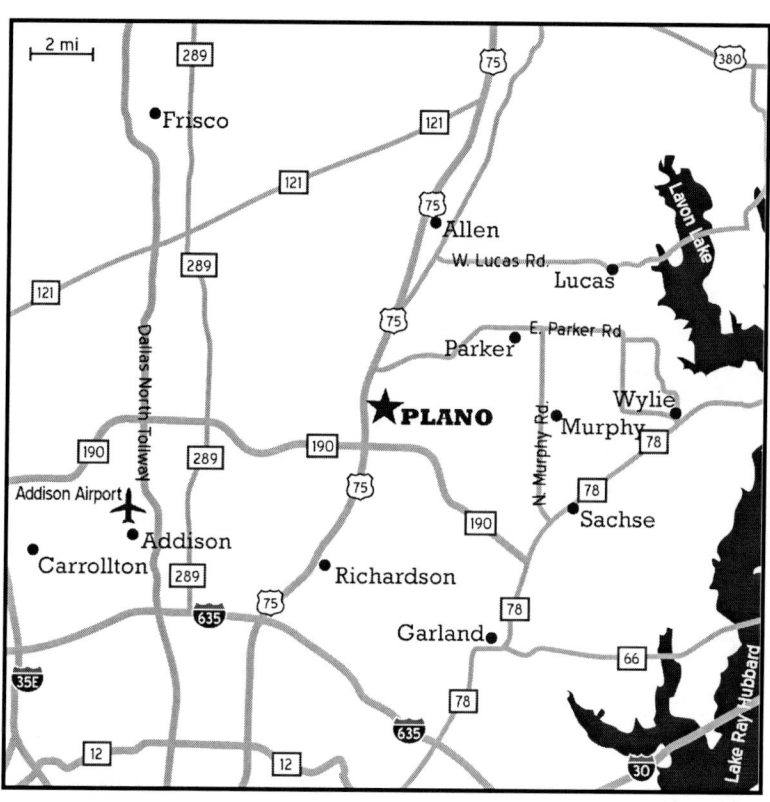

CHAPTER 6

FRISCO

Settlers first came to Frisco while traveling in wagon trains along the Shawnee Trail, an early route used to drive cattle north from Austin. In 1838 the trail become a north-south road, which opened northern Texas to trade, and was named Preston Trail, and later, Preston Road.

However, it wasn't until the introduction of the railroad that really gave birth to Frisco. In 1902, a line of the St. Louis–San Francisco Railway was built through the area, and a watering hole needed for steam engines was placed about 4 miles west. A community began to develop around this train stop and by 1904 the residents chose to name it Frisco City, in honor of the railway. Later the community's name was shortened to Frisco.

Frisco soon became a thriving town and served as a center of trade for the surrounding farms. In 1908 it became an incorporated city and the first municipal government was formed. By 1910, Frisco had a population of 332 pioneers and by 1950 the town had grown to 736 residents. Steady growth continued and in the 1990s the town's population exploded to 21,400 residents in 1997. Today Frisco's population is nearly 88,529.

Today Frisco continues to be one of the fastest-growing towns in the United States. Serving as a bedroom community for many people who work in the Dallas-Forth Worth Metroplex, the city is dedicated to preserving its environment, and has received the designation of "Tree City USA" since 2003 by the National Arbor Day Foundation, as well as the National Arbor Day Foundation Growth Award in 2007 for the third consecutive year.

With Preston Road still serving as one of the major north-south roadways in the city, many retail establishments and restaurants line the route. Frisco also boasts a high number of retail properties, such as Stonebriar Center, which is a huge 1.6 million square feet of retail featuring over 165 specialty stores-store shopping mall. Frisco Square is also a new mixed-use development that is positioned as the area's new downtown. Encompassing as much as 4.4 million square feet, Frisco Square offers office, retail, multi-family and municipal facilities on 147 acres and is the new chapter in Frisco's growth. Frisco also is home for the new Pizza Hut Park which hosts the regions FC Dallas Soccer Team. Along the North Dallas Tollway you will also see the magnificent Dr Pepper Ball Park which is home for the Frisco Roughriders the minor league expansion club for the Texas Rangers professional baseball club. Rounding out these wonderful sports venues is the brand new Dr Pepper Star Center which is the practice home to the Dallas Stars National Hockey League Team. Lastly the City of Frisco scored a major boon for the area in the Museum of the American Railroad which will bring over 36 vintage railroad pieces and call Frisco home in 2011.

CITY OF FRISCO CONTACT INFORMATION

Website: *www.ci.frisco.tx.us*
www.visitfrisco.com
City Hall: (972) 292-5000

FRISCO POPULATION GROWTH

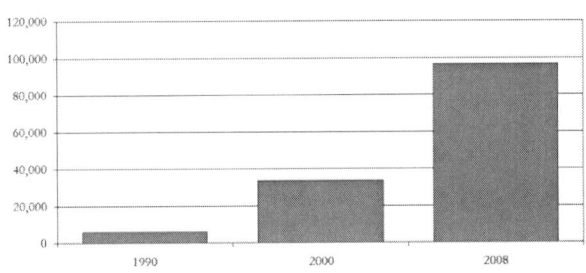

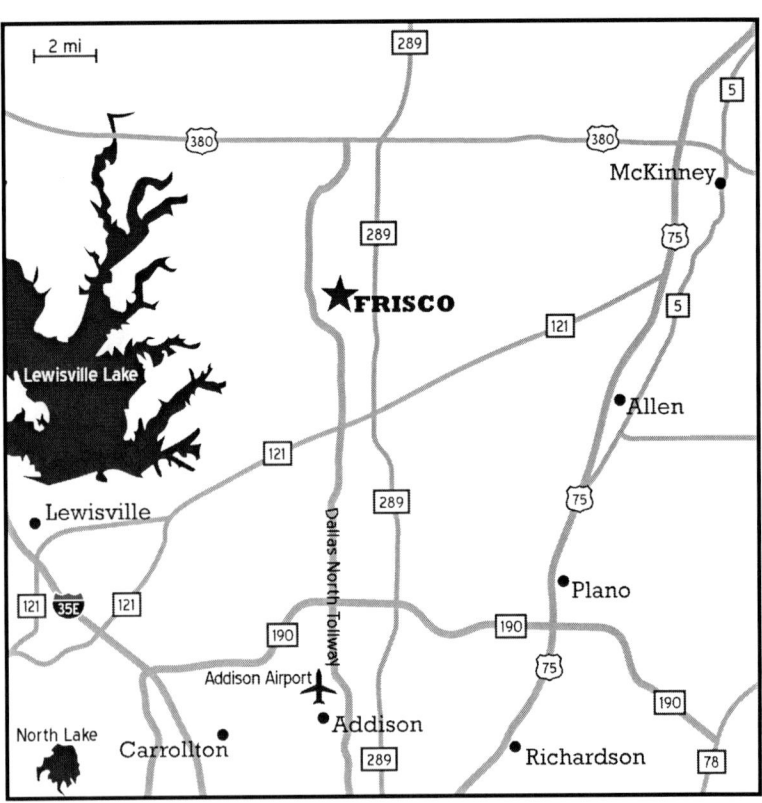

CHAPTER 7

ALLEN

The land that is now the city of Allen was originally inhabited by Caddo and Comanche Indian tribes. As early settlers arrived in the region, these tribes moved further west and were relocated to the Indian Territory north of the Red River. Immigrants of European descent moved into the area in the early 1840s. During that time a stage line ran from Bonham through McKinney to Allen and Plano, and crossed Rowlett Creek where SH 5 now crosses. Allen was also part of the Peter's Colony Land Grant from the Republic of Texas to the Texas Emigration & Land Company.

In 1872, the Houston and Texas Central Railroad (H&TC) was built, which laid out the original township of Allen. In 1918, the H&TC built a combination freight/passenger depot in the Allen Central Business District. It has been reported that Texas' first train robbery actually took place in Allen on February 22, 1878.

In 1908, the Texas Traction Company (Interurban) constructed the Interurban line through Allen as a stop on its route from Denison to Dallas. However, in 1915 a devastating fire destroyed most of the business district between the Interurban tracts, as well as the railroad. When the Interurban closed in 1948 the population of Allen declined to 400 in 1950. In 1952 the town was officially incorporated and in 1960 the construction of US 75 helped drive the city's growth once again.

Today, Allen's close proximity to the Dallas-Forth Worth Metroplex makes it a popular northern suburb. According to a 2007 census, the city had 77,644 residents. The Allen Independent School District has 15 elementary schools, 3 middle schools and 1 high school. The Allen Event Center, a 7,500 seat multi-purpose arena, was built in November 2009, and the city also offers ample recreation, shopping, dining and cultural opportunities. Allen prides itself on being a wholesome community that offers something for everyone. Allen also just opened up the brand-new Village at Allen in conjunction with the City of Fairview for a unique collection of anchor stores: JC Penny, Macy's and Dillards along with the flagship restaurant Ocean Blue by the world-known marine artist Wyland. Allen also boasts a great collection of shopping and restaurants in the new Watters Creek in Montgomery and the exhaustive collection of brand-name outlets at the Allen Premium Outlet Mall.

CITY OF ALLEN CONTACT INFORMATION

Website: *www.cityofallen.org*
City Hall: (214) 509-4100

PART II: PLANO AREA CITIES AND TOWNS

ALLEN POPULATION GROWTH

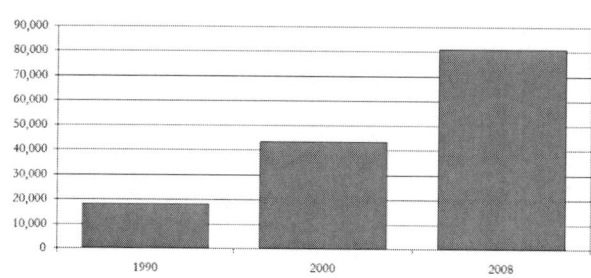

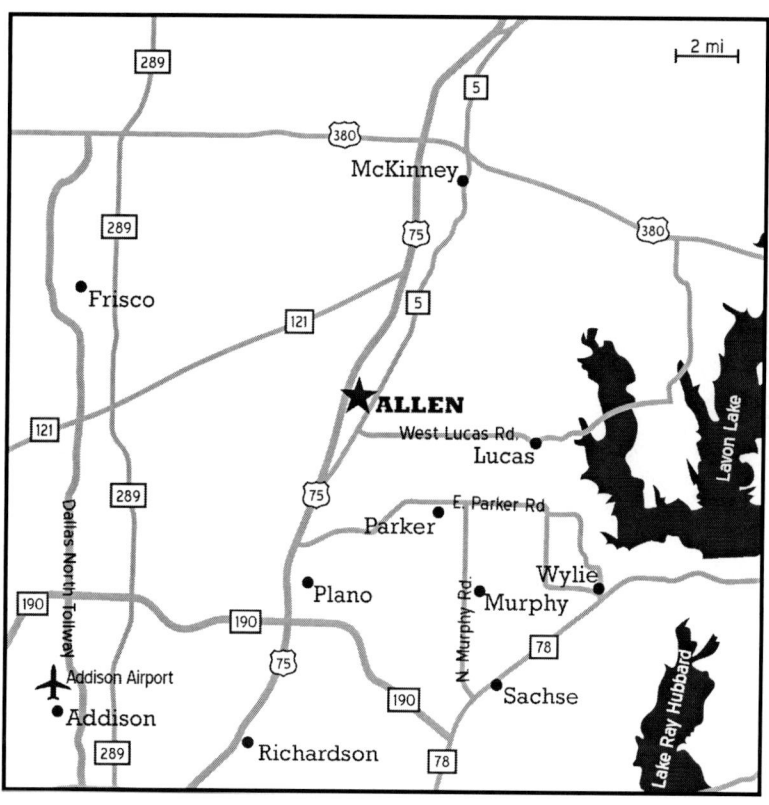

CHAPTER 8

MCKINNEY

As one of the oldest towns in North Texas, and the county seat of Collin County, McKinney was founded in 1841 when the first settlers arrived from Kentucky, Arkansas and Tennessee. Named for Collin McKinney, who was one of the 60 signers of the Texas Declaration of Independence, the city served as the main commercial center for the county for the first 125 years of its history.

Located just 30 miles north of Dallas, and close in population to Plano, today McKinney is a thriving community that offers a quaint, small-town feel. With a population of about 119,000 residents, McKinney has been ranked one of the fastest-growing cities in the United States. In 2008, the city was ranked 14th on *Money Magazine's* list of "Best Small Cities in the United States." And moved up to 5th best city on their list in 2010, which shows the attractiveness of this city. McKinney prides itself on its low crime and also the tremendous downtown with 19th Century buildings restored to house shops, restaurants and boutiques. There is even a new performing arts center in the 1875-built former courthouse building in downtown McKinney. Defense contractor Raytheon has a huge 3700+ workforce division in McKinney along with many other businesses in the medical, technology and financial services areas.

In recent years, McKinney has gained national media attention for the construction of LEED (Leadership in Energy and Environmental Design) and sustainable buildings. Just some of these structures include an office building, elementary school and automotive dealership.

McKinney has a total area of 58.5 square miles and is served by US 75 and US 380. The city is also bordered by State Highway 121. For education, the community is served by the McKinney Independent School District, although western McKinney is currently zoned to Frisco Independent School District and southern areas to Allen Independent School District.

McKinney boasts a vibrant Main Street downtown that is part of the National Trust for Historic Preservation. It offers over 100 unique shops and more than a dozen restaurants. The downtown also features events like ArtWalk, held in May, and other cultural attractions in the town include: McKinney Performing Arts Center, Chestnut Square Historic Village, Heard-Craig Center for the Arts and the North Texas History Center.

CITY OF MCKINNEY CONTACT INFORMATION

Website: *www3.mckinneytexas.org*
City Hall: (972) 547-7500

PART II: PLANO AREA CITIES AND TOWNS

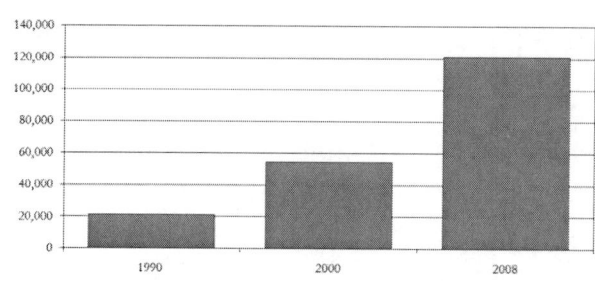

MCKINNEY POPULATION GROWTH

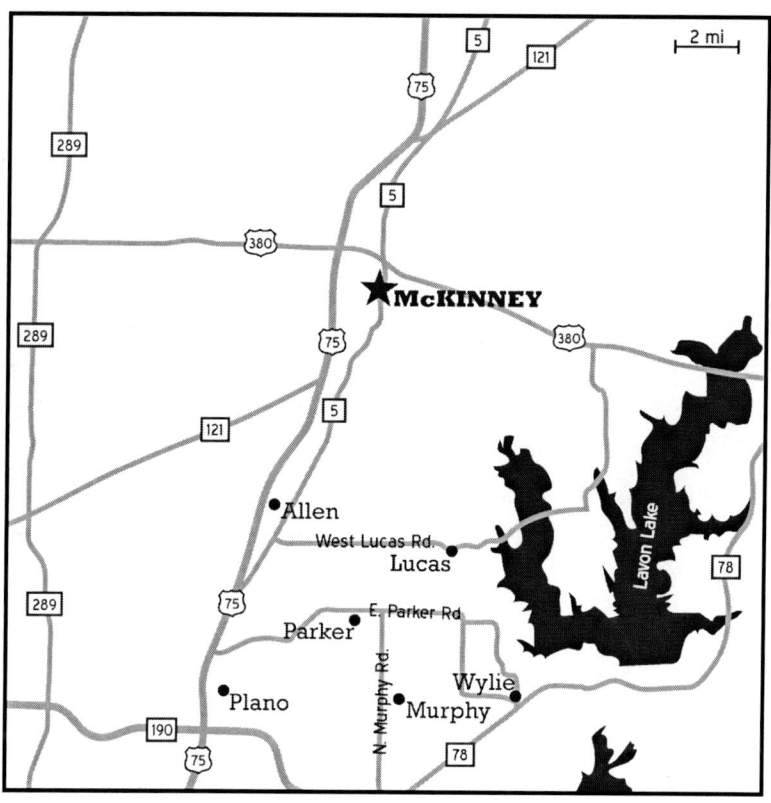

CHAPTER 9

RICHARDSON

Settled in the 1840s by pioneers arriving from Kentucky and Tennessee, Richardson was originally home to the Comanche and Caddo Indian tribes. The earliest settlers of European descent lived in an area later named Breckinridge, after the Vice President of the United States from 1857-1861. Made up of just a general store, blacksmith shop and an inn, the town was situated on land that is now Richland College.

After the Civil War, the area to the northwest of Breckinridge became the new center of activity, and when land was donated for expansion, the community was named after E.H. Richardson, the man responsible for building the railroad line from Dallas to Denison. Richardson was chartered in 1873 but it wasn't until 1924, when the Red Brick Road was built, that it increased in population. After World War II, the city experienced another surge in population and by 1950 it had approximately 1,500 residents.

Today Richardson is a bustling community with around 100,000 residents and is known as a prime location in the telecommunications industry. With more than 5,000 businesses within the city's 28 square miles, it was ranked as the 18th by *Money Magazine* as a "Best Place to Live in the United States" and 4th "Best Place to Live in Texas." Committed to ensuring a suburb quality of life for its residents, Richardson hosts several special events each year, such as Huffines Art

Trails, the Wildflower! Arts and Music Festival and the Cottonwood Art Festival, an award-winning exhibit of more than100+ artists and craftsmen from around the country. For outdoor recreation, the city boasts numerous parks, such as the 417-acre Breckinridge and the 58 acre Crowley, as well as more than 40 miles of trails and walkways. Richardson is also one of the densest high-tech areas in the nation, with Telecom Corridor, where Nortel (among other companies) houses its U.S. headquarters. The city, just north of Dallas, is also home to four DART rail stations and lots of new luxury condominium, apartment and town home developments.

CITY OF RICHARDSON CONTACT INFORMATION

Website: *www.cor.net*
City Hall: (972) 744-4100

RICHARDSON POPULATION GROWTH

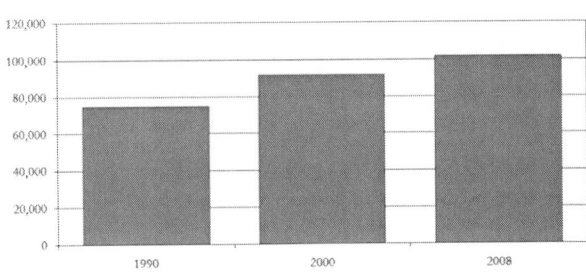

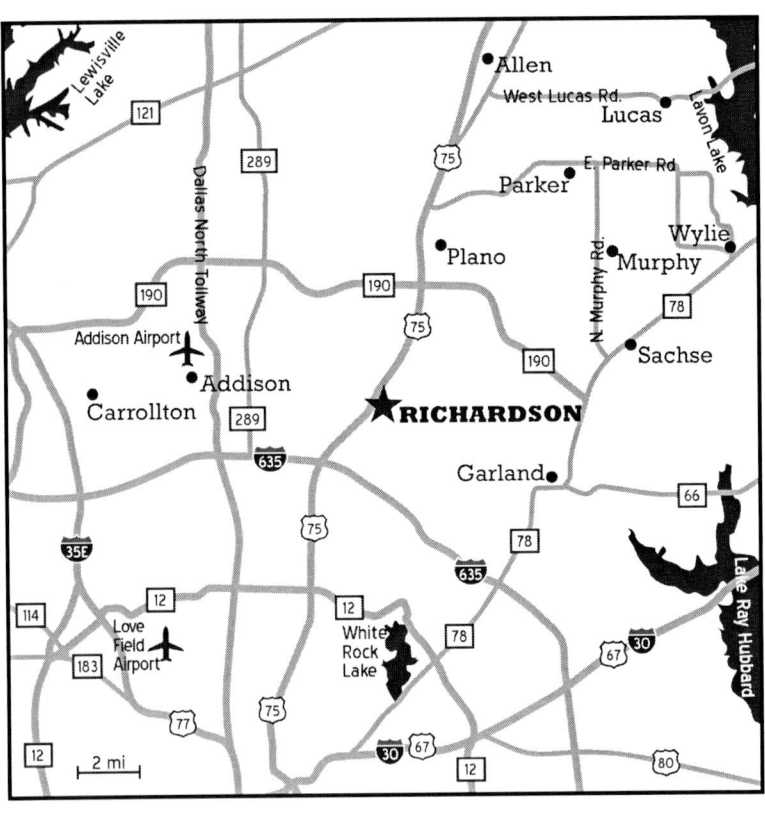

CHAPTER 10

ADDISON

The Town of Addison was settled around 1846 when Preston Witt built a home near White Rock Creek, a 30-mile creek in the Elm Fork Trinity watershed. In 1902 the community was named Addison, after the postmaster who served from 1908 to 1916. In 1902 the community opened its first industry: a cotton gin on Addison Road. In 1914, the Addison School Building was opened, which today is the site of the popular "Magic Time Machine Restaurant." The city incorporated in 1953 and in 1982 changed its name to "Town of Addison."

Modern day Addison is a far cry from the community it once was. The high growth of the 1980s has transformed it into a popular northern suburb of Dallas. The city prides itself on blending the diversity of a big city with the ambiance of a small town. In 2000 the city of Addison had a population of 14,166.

With over 170 restaurants, 22 hotels and many prestigious shops, the Town of Addison offers a wide range of opportunities for dining, lodging and shopping. In fact, it has been said that there is a restaurant for every 80 residents. The city is home to the Addison Airport, one of the busiest general aviation airports in the United States.

Some of Addison's most popular attractions include the Cavanaugh Flight Museum on the grounds of Addison Airport, the Mary Kay Museum and the WaterTower Theatre, the resident company of the

Addison Theatre Centre and every 4th of July Addison features "Kaboom Town" which is one of the premier fireworks displays in the all of Texas! For recreation, popular hotspots include the Addison Circle Park, the Iceoplex Skating Rink, 300 Dallas, as well as annual festivals like Taste Addison, the Out of the Loop Fringe Festival and Addison Oktoberfest.

For education, most Addison residents are zoned to the Dallas Independent School District, although some residents are zoned to the Carrollton-Farmers Branch Independent School District. The community is home to two private schools, Greenhill School and Trinity Christian Academy. Much of the housing attraction to Addison is with new multi-family "lofts," condos and townhome with access to Downtown Dallas in just a mere 10-15 minute drive.

TOWN OF ADDISON CONTACT INFORMATION

Website: *www.addisontexas.net*
City Hall: (800) ADDISON

PART II: PLANO AREA CITIES AND TOWNS

ADDISON POPULATION GROWTH

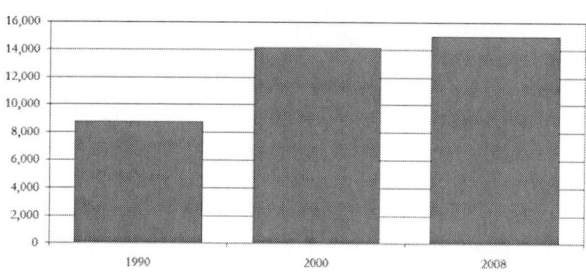

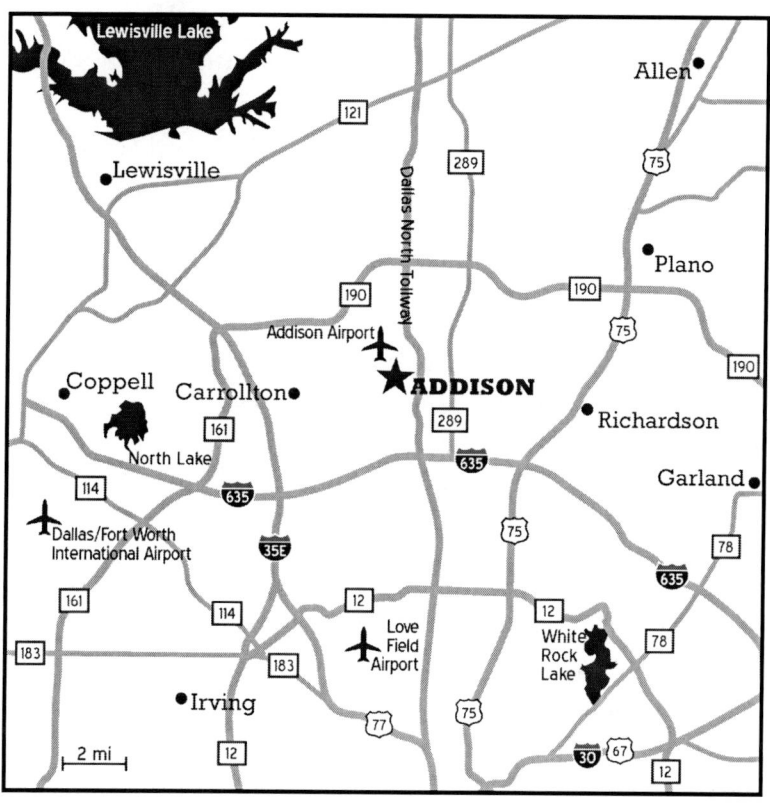

CHAPTER 11

CARROLLTON

The City of Carrollton was settled in the early 1840s by pioneers looking for prosperity and a better life. These settlers purchased land from The Peters Colony and planted crops, raised cattle and sheep, and built churches and homes. Historical texts tell of a settler who came to scout the area before relocating his family there. He was so impressed with what he saw that he brought a handful of soil home to show his family. Most of the early settlers were farmers, but other professionals, such as lawyers, doctors and preachers, also moved to the area.

In 1852, Carrollton was enjoying economic prosperity, with the Trinity Mils grain mill thriving. Around 1904 the brick manufacturing industry emerged in Carrollton, with The Carrollton Pressed Brick Company producing brick for some of the best-known structures in the area. The arrival of the railroad in the late 1800s helped change Carrollton from a farming community to a bustling business district. By 1908, there were three railroads using Carrollton as a way station.

Today, Carrollton prides itself on being a vibrant professional and residential community. With over 5,000 businesses calling Carrollton home, many residents are drawn to the area for its quality of life, good schools, abundant parks and safe neighborhoods. Carrollton is also home to Lucent Technologies Telecommunications Systems, ST Microelectronics Semiconductors, Halliburton Oil Field Products,

Hilton Reservations Hotel Reservation System, Budget Rent-a-Car Car Rental Reservation System, Chrysler Corporation Parts Distribution and Ford Motor Company Parts Distribution. In 2008, Money Magazine ranked Carrollton 15th as a "Best Place to Live" and Forbes Magazine ranked Carrollton 12th for "America's Best Places to Move."

Although Carrollton is less than 40 square miles in size, there are a wide variety of real estate options for buyers who need more space but still want a short distance to everything the Dallas-Fort Worth Metroplex offers. The city offers many types and styles of homes, with buyers able to get more for their money compared with other parts of the country. There is a good mix of established homes and new construction with a distinct advantage in giving the buyer more bang for the buck in Carrollton versus Plano which has driven growth to Carrollton.

CITY OF CARROLLTON CONTACT INFORMATION

Website: *www.cityofcarrollton.com*
City Hall: (972) 466-3000

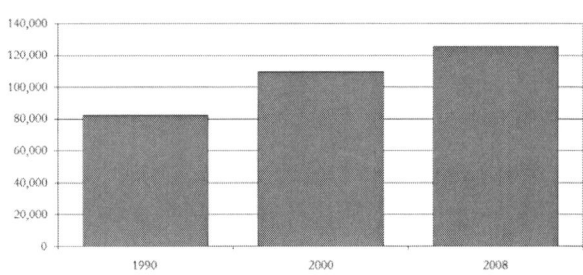

CARROLLTON POPULATION GROWTH

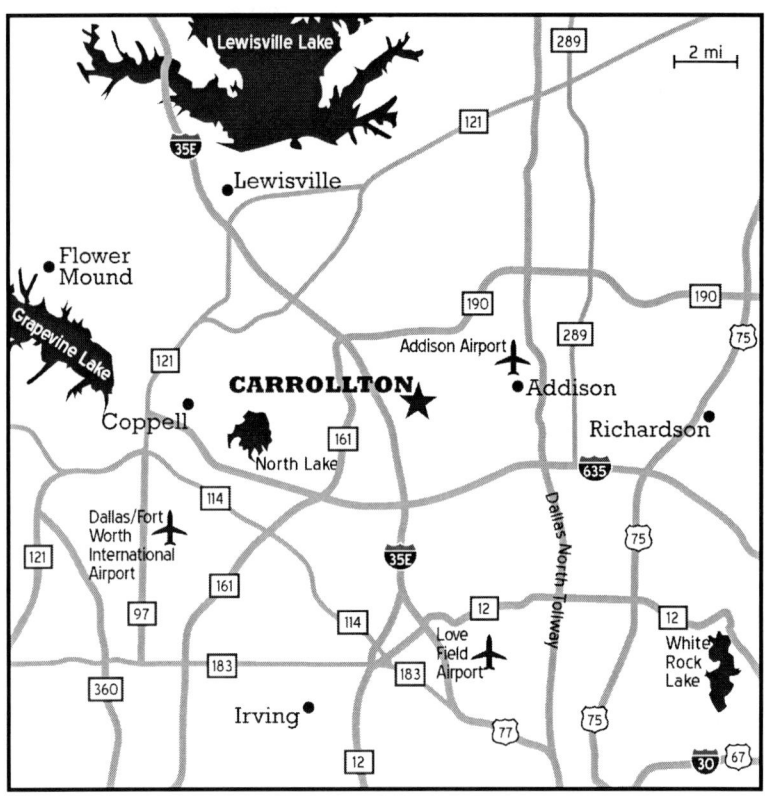

CHAPTER 12

COPPELL

Coppell began its transformation into one of Dallas' top suburban communities just a few decades ago, but for a century and a half prior it remained a quiet little farming community on the outskirts of Dallas. Beginning in the 1840s, German and French immigrants set up farms near the site of Grapevine Springs Park, where natural springs flow into Elms Fork on the Trinity River. Since that time, the community has undergone several name changes. Referred to originally as Grapevine Springs, the community changed its name to Gibbs in 1973 in honor of Barnett Gibbs, a Dallas attorney who later served as the Lt. Governor of Texas. Gibbs lasted only for a brief period; however, until the Cotton Belt Railroad came to the area and initiated the first great transformation.

The Cotton Belt Railroad built a depot in Gibbs in 1890 and named it Coppell for the engineer and railway investor George Coppell. Shortly thereafter, the community officially changed its name to Coppell. Growth was slow and steady in Coppell during most of the next century and topped off at just over 1,000 residents when the next transformation was brought on by yet another transportation hub, The DFW International Airport. The DFW International airport, the second largest airport in the country, was built in 1974 and partially lies in the City of Coppell. Its construction sparked the boom that changed the small farm town into the thriving, upper-middle class suburb it is today.

Coppell is home to Grapevine Springs Park, originally made famous by The Republic of Texas' President Sam Houston, who camped around the springs during negotiations with Native Americans in 1848. The federal Works Progress Administration designated the land as a park in 1936 and outfitted it with rock walls, walking paths and picnic areas that the city now maintains. The city has retained a strong sense of community even in the midst of rapid growth. Residents enjoy 116 acres of parks, community gardens, well-established churches, excellent schools and safe neighborhoods.

Coppell is conveniently located with easy access to two major interstates and two highways that lie right outside of the town limits. Due to its prime location, high quality of life, and robust economy it has recently become home to a growing number of major companies' manufacturing and distribution centers. The population of Coppell is 39,550, a nine percent increase over the last ten years.

The Coppell ISD was ranked as the #1 music program in the United States by the Music Educators Association in 2000. Also, all of the elementary schools in the Coppell Independent School District rate as "Exemplary" by the Texas Education Agency which is the highest rating a school can get. In addition, the athletic facilities of Coppell High School are among the finest in the nation. On-campus facilities include a 12,000-seat football stadium, an indoor football practice field house with one of the largest weight rooms on the high school level, a practice baseball field, a practice softball field, two gymnasiums, and a tennis complex. Off-campus facilities include an indoor swimming pool at the Coppell YMCA and a baseball and softball stadium located next to the Coppell Middle School West campus.

CITY OF COPPELL CONTACT INFORMATION

Website: *www.coppelltx.c2crm.com/*
Town Hall: (972) 462-0022

PART II: PLANO AREA CITIES AND TOWNS

COPPELL POPULATION GROWTH

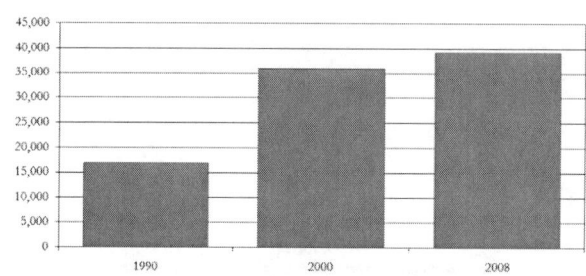

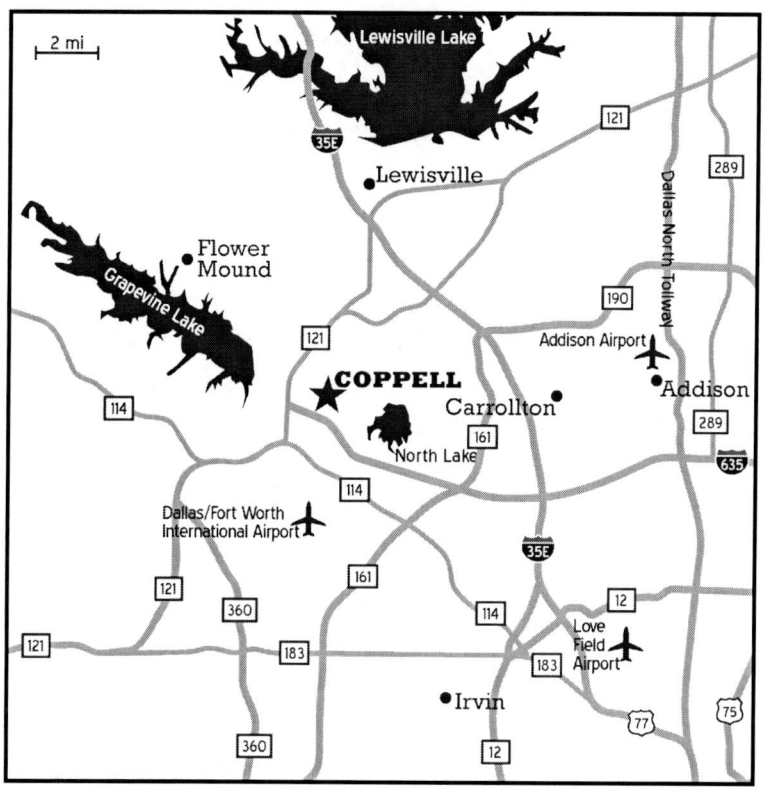

CHAPTER 13

IRVING

It is hard to imagine the diverse and vibrant Irving, Texas of today as a small collection of communities with a population barely totaling 200, but that is exactly how it started just over one hundred years ago. Settlers first arrived in the area in the mid-19th century. Upon arrival, they began forming the small communities that eventually became Irving: Sowers, Kit, Union Bower, Finley, Estelle and Bear Creek. In 1902, J.O Schultze and Otis Brown, surveyors for the Chicago, Rock Island & Gulf Railway, came to the area on business and ended up purchasing 80 acres of land they deemed ideal for the location of a new town. They named their intended town Irving and began their endeavor by selling lots of the land at public auction. Local historians believe the name Irving was chosen to honor Washington Irving, an author both founding families held dear to their hearts.

The new town quickly became a center for farming and poultry production, much of which was sold across the Trinity River in the Dallas markets. Otis Brown served as the community's first mayor and the town was incorporated in 1914. Since that time it has continued to flourish, annexing neighboring communities along the way, and is now one the most populous suburbs of the Dallas Fort Worth Metroplex.

Today Irving is a large, multicultural suburb that has just about as much to offer as neighboring Dallas. It is home to many large corporate businesses and four Fortune 500 companies, including: ExxonMobil, Kimberly-Clark, Fluor, Commercial, and Omni Hotel. Residents will find that shopping centers and ethnic and gourmet dining are available in abundance, as well as sporting, cultural and artistic opportunities. The Irving Arts Center, a ten-acre complex catering to the city's growing cultural and civic needs, offers a beautiful venue in which to enjoy the work of the performing and fine arts communities.

The City of Irving is one of thirteen cities included in the regions transit system, Dallas Area Rapid Transit (DART). As such, residents not only utilize the easily accessible highway and interstate systems, but also have the option of traveling via the extensive bus system and the Trinity Railway Express. In addition, construction is in the works for the new Orange Light Rail that will run through Irving to the DFW Airport and downtown Dallas. Corresponding with this project are exciting plans for the old Texas Stadium, which is set to become one the Metroplex's premier new developments.

Real estate in Irving caters to a wide range of budgets with everything from affordable single-family homes to million dollar estates. Las Colinas, a mixed-use community of more than 12,000 acres of land was the first of its kind in the country and is one of the largest master-planned developments in the Southwest. Residents will also find an array of educational opportunities. There are excellent preparatory and higher education facilities in the area, including the University of Dallas, North Lake College, and North Hills Preparatory School.

Irving's population has increased 5% over the last decade and now totals just over 200,000. The median age is 30.3, which is two years younger than the state's median age.

CITY OF IRVING CONTACT INFORMATION:

Website: *www.cityofirving.org*
City Hall: (972) 721-2600

IRVING POPULATION GROWTH

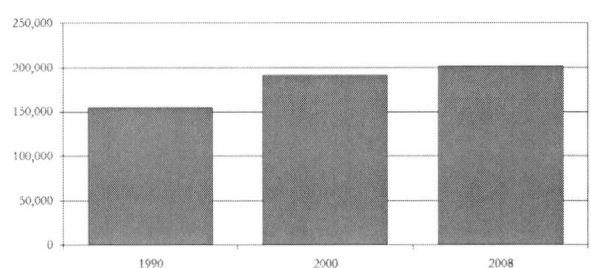

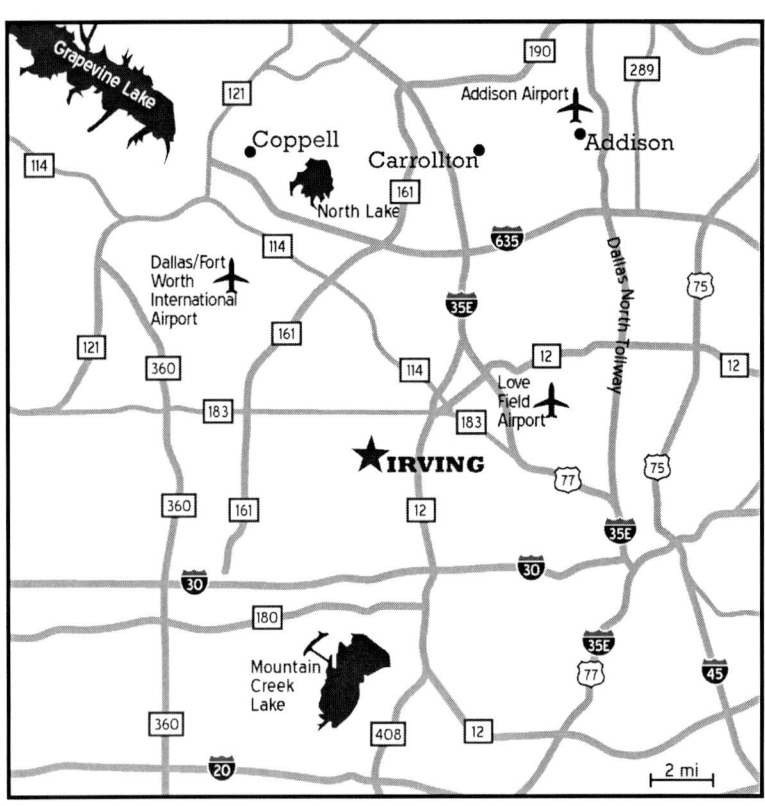

CHAPTER 14

LEWISVILLE

The area of Lewisville has been prime real estate for centuries. Not only is it one of the oldest incorporated cities in the Dallas Fort Worth Metroplex, it is also home to one of the earliest Paleo-Indian sites in North America, dating back to 1100 B.C. Just as Native Americans were drawn to the banks of Elm Fork on the Trinity River, so were the early settlers who began arriving in the first half of the 19th century.

The city's founder, Basdeal Lewis, purchased land from which to start a town in 1840 and named it Lewisville. The town, like most of its neighboring communities, was a small agriculturally based community, and had its own gristmill, cotton gin, livery stable, and feed mill. Growth was slow, but the town incorporated as a city in 1925. Shortly thereafter, the first automobile dealership opened and the first traffic light was installed. This traffic light, situated on Main St. and Mill St., remained the only one in the city until the 1970s, when the Dallas Fort Worth International Airport opened and Lewisville's population exploded. The city more than quadrupled its population during this short time period.

Lewisville is an ideal location for families. The community offers superb opportunities for career building, recreation, arts, culture and more. Residents work hard to maintain the city's small-town charm in the midst of rapid growth. At the same time, they also embrace the convenience and luxury of suburban life north of Dallas. The revitalized

Old Town Lewisville offers residents a chance to explore the city's history while perusing the many locally owned antique shops, clothing stores, and fine restaurants. Those interested in more modern settings appreciate the Lewisville Vista Ridge Mall. Vista Ridge Mall is one of the largest malls in the North Dallas area and offers patrons over 140 specialty shops and a 15-screen theater.

Recreational activities are an ever-important aspect of the Lewisville life-style. Lake Lewisville is a popular destination for families, singles, city-dwellers and outdoor enthusiasts who enjoy water sports, hanging out on the beach, biking, picnicking, and camping. The city also operates 23 parks, a Senior Center, two recreation centers, two libraries, numerous balls fields, walking trails, a skate park, a dog park and more. Other attractions include the Vista Ridge Amphitheater, Lewisville Center for the Creative Arts, private golf courses, and hundreds of dining options.

Lewisville is a member of the Denton County Transportation Authority (DCTA). The DCTA is currently working to expand the city's connection to the rest of the Metroplex with a commuter light rail that links to Dallas Area Rapid Transit (DART) commuter rails. In addition to good public transportation, the city boasts the lowest property tax rate in the Dallas Fort Worth area. Developments featuring town homes are increasingly popular in West and South Lewisville; but most of the new development is happening in East Lewisville. At just over 100,000, the population of Lewisville has jumped 30.7% over the last decade. The median age of a resident is 29.8 years, almost three years younger than the state's median resident age.

CITY OF LEWISVILLE CONTACT INFORMATION

Website: *www.cityoflewisville.com*
City Hall: 972-219-3468

PART II: PLANO AREA CITIES AND TOWNS

LEWISVILLE POPULATION GROWTH

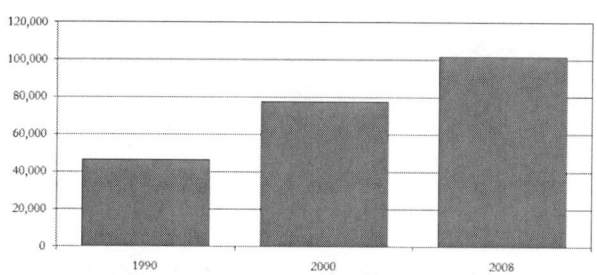

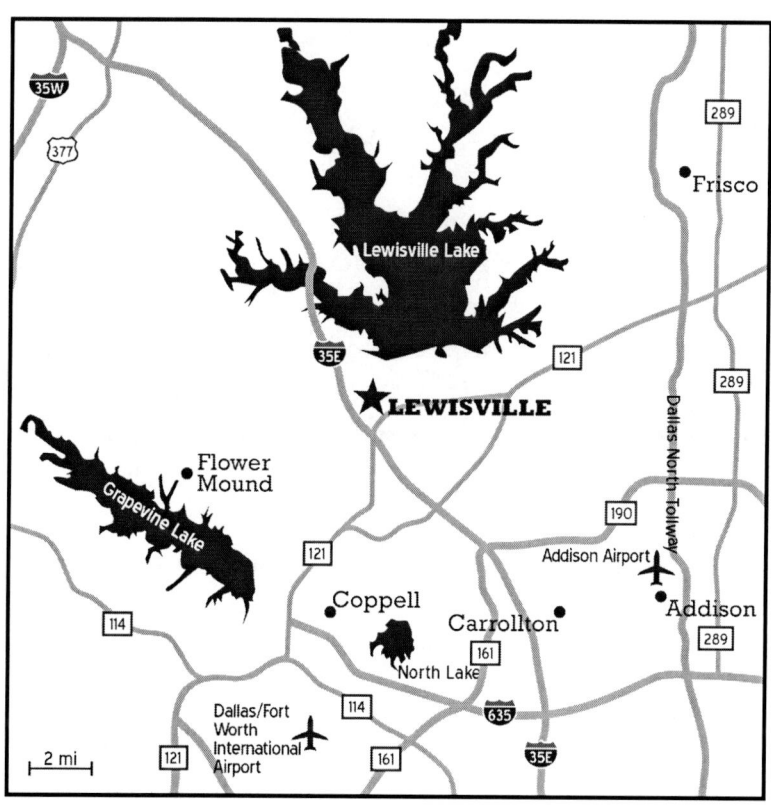

CHAPTER 15

GARLAND

Garland is the tenth-largest city in Texas and boasts a history as colorful as the state itself. Settlers began arriving in the area in 1850, but The City of Garland's story really begins in 1874 with a small community known as Duck Creek. Duck Creek consisted of a store, a corn mill, cotton-growing farms and a post office established in 1878. Change came quickly though when the Santa Fe Railroad and the Missouri, Kansas & Texas Railroad each built depots close by in 1886. Two new communities formed around the depots, Embree and a new Duck Creek, respectively. Initially the old Duck Creek post office moved to Embree along with many of its residents, but it wasn't long before new Duck Creek began aggressively competing for the old community's attention as well.

The competition between communities ensued for the next year until Congressman Joe Abbott was asked to intervene. Abbott passed a bill through Congress that relocated the post office to a spot between the two communities. The new location was named Garland, for Attorney General A.H. Garland, and the three original communities fused around it to form a new town. Garland was incorporated in 1891.

The City of Garland has had its share of drama throughout the course of its history. Thanks to a resourceful and committed citizenry, however, it emerges stronger from each new challenge. Two separate fires sparked the forming of the first volunteer fire department in 1889 and the municipal water and sewer system in 1923. The states refusal to provide affordable electric rates to support the new water system in turn initiated the drive to form Garland Power & Light, which is now the third-largest municipal electric system in the state. A few years later, the community was hit by a devastating tornado, but by the end of that decade new businesses were opening their doors and the area was on the road to recovery. Then in 1950, the city experienced a harsh drought that lasted for four years. In response to the drought, the city helped create the North Texas Municipal Water District. It was at this time that the area truly began to blossom and the population nearly quadrupled from 10,000 to more than 38,000 residents by 1960. It has continued to grow rapidly ever since.

Garland has become known as a big city with family-friendly environment and a small-town vibe. It has all of the accommodations of suburban and metropolitan life, while maintaining a hometown environment ideal for people in every stage of life. The city offers award winning recreational facilities, parkland, numerous retail and entertainment establishments, a championship golf course, elegant performing arts venues and public transportation routes on the Dallas Area Rapid Transit system. Some highlights are: the Firewheel Town Center, Bass Pro Shops on Lake Ray Hubbard, Historic Downtown Garland, Firewheel at Garland's Golf Park, the award-winning Patty Granville Arts Center, and the historic Plaza Theater. Garland also boasts a thriving business economy. The Garland Economic Development Partnership is a city initiative designed to actively attract and support new businesses interested in relocating to the area. A few notable businesses that call the city home include Raytheon, International Trucks and Kraft Foods. The fast food chain In and Out Burgers just put Garland in the news with their announcement of bringing their restaurant to the new Firewheel Mall, which will be the companies very 1st restaurant in the state of Texas!

Garland was number 67 on CNN Money Magazine's Top 100 Places to Live in 2008. It is noted for cultural diversity, excellent and innovative schools, safe and affordable neighborhoods and a variety of housing options. Sixty-four percent of the population owns a home and as of 2008 the median home price was $117,000. The population of Garland is more than 223,000, which makes it one of the largest cities in the Dallas Fort Worth Metroplex and the tenth-largest city in Texas.

CITY OF GARLAND CONTACT INFORMATION

Website: *www.ci.garland.tx.us*
City Hall: 972-205-2000

PART II: PLANO AREA CITIES AND TOWNS

GARLAND POPULATION GROWTH

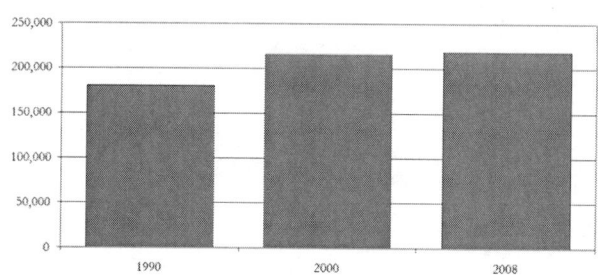

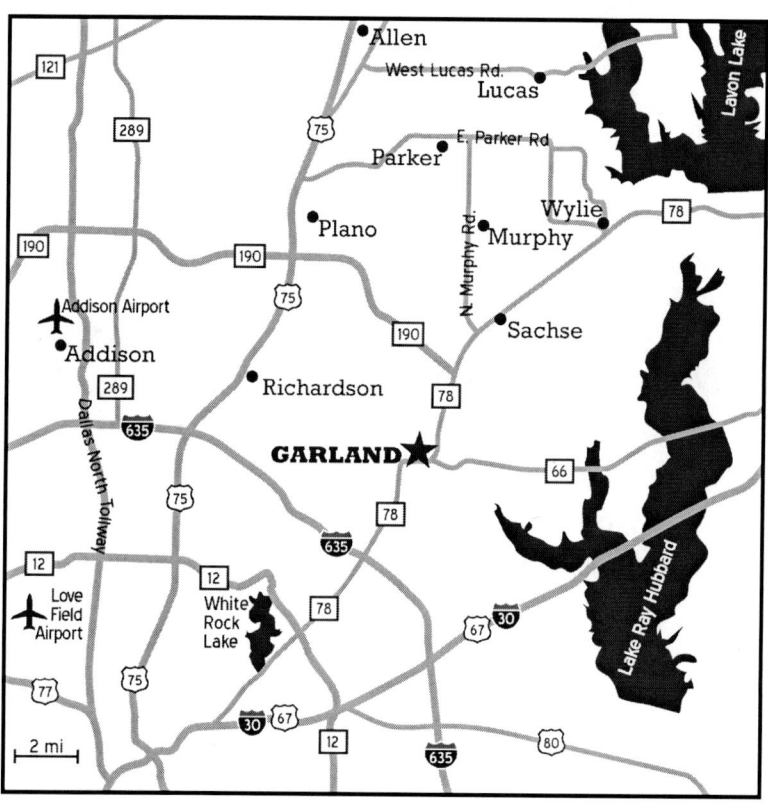

CHAPTER 16

FLOWER MOUND

As far back as 4000 B.C. the area that is now the Town of Flower Mound was inhabited by Native American tribes. In the 1840s, the region was settled by Europeans due to the Empresario Land Grants system. When Texas joined the union in 1845, the territory that would become Flower Mound was located in Fannin County, and later became part of Denton County in 1846. In the 1880s, Yoakley's Store was established and this historical business provided locals with a cotton gin, blacksmith shop, and Post Office for almost a century. The town remained sparsely populated until about 1961, when it was incorporated to avoid being annexed by nearby Irving. While in 1970 there were still only about 1,685 residents in Flower Mound, the town rapidly expanded as the area north of Dallas-Fort Worth International Airport grew more desirable.

Today the Town of Flower Mound strives to maintain a small-town atmosphere while embracing a dynamic economic development. Named after an actual mound that stands 50 feet above the surrounding countryside, it is known for its unusual 175 species of wild flowers that grows upon it.

With over 50,000 residents, Flower Mound prides itself on its SMART growth management system and conservation development projects to protect open spaces, natural habitats and vistas. Over $25 million dollars has been spent to provide the Lakeside Business District and the Denton Creek District with transportation thoroughfares and other improvements, and many new businesses have recently opened up shop thanks to the town's close proximity to the DFW airport and major roadways.

With its prime location along the north shore of Lake Grapevine, Flower Mound offers many recreation opportunities, such as boating, walking and golf. One of the fastest growing communities in the area, the town has one of the lowest property tax rates, and boasts sought-after planned communities like Bridlewood and Wellington, as well as excellent schools.

TOWN OF FLOWER MOUND CONTACT INFORMATION

Website: *www.flower-mound.com*
Town Hall: (972) 874-6000

FLOWER MOUND POPULATION GROWTH

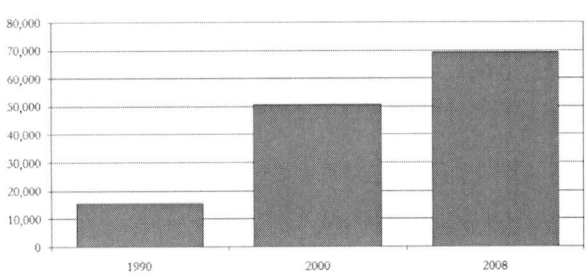

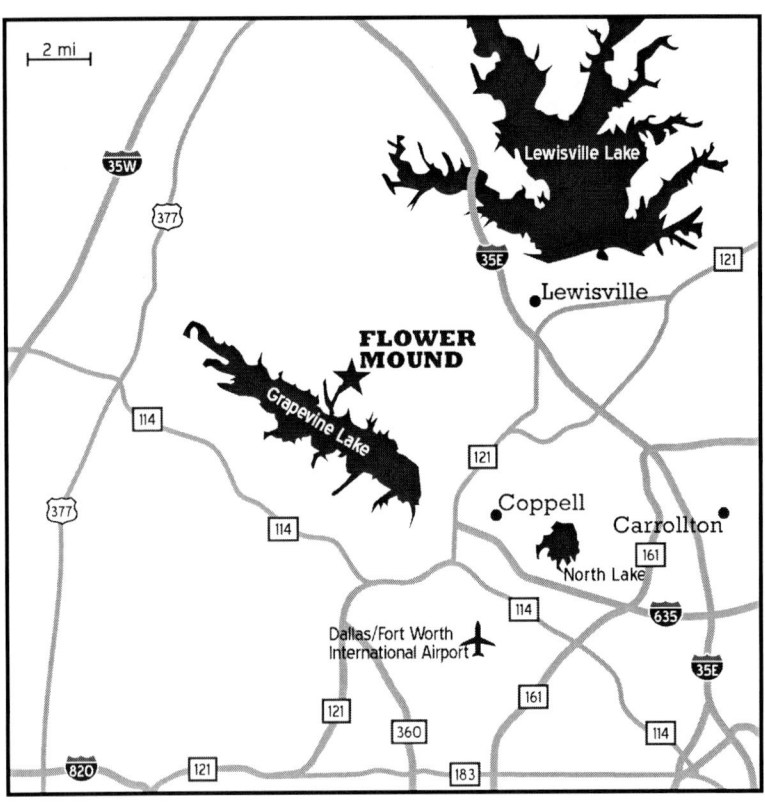

CHAPTER 17

MURPHY AND SACHSE

MURPHY

In 1846, the first settlers arrived in Murphy when they were lured by the offer of land grants from the Peters Colony. The original town site was located on land owned by C.A. McMillen, and was first called Old Decator and later renamed Maxwell's Branch. In 1888 the St. Louis Southwestern Railway reached the area and the town was given its current name, after William Murphy who provided land for the tracks and construction of the depot. Until the 1950s, Murphy was mainly a shipping point for famers and stock raisers. The city experienced a decline in population due to the Great Depression and mechanization of farming, and the population dipped to a mere 135 residents by 1961. However, by the mid-1970s the population escalated as businesses in nearby Plano and Richardson made Murphy a desirable community for commuters. In 2006, population in Murphy was more than 10,000 and growing. Large lots and new construction combined with its close proximity to Plano make this a great choice for the conveniences of the big city and the small-town feel.

Its border encloses just 3.8 miles, but its proximity to popular destinations makes it a hot spot to live. The City of Murphy is only 20 miles from downtown Dallas and about 30 miles from the DFW Airport.

The community is served by both the Plano Independent School District, as well as the Wylie Independent School District. The City of Murphy is committed to maintaining its country-living feel by offering fewer large lots for business development. Thanks to the opening of the President George Bush Tollway in 1999, Murphy has enjoyed rapid expansion as many new homes have been built in the past ten years. The city as rated #7 in the "Best Places to Live" survey by *D Magazine* in July 2008 and affords many opportunities for residents looking for single-family homes, condos and townhomes.

CITY OF MURPHY CONTACT INFORMATION

Website: *www.murphytx.org*
City Hall: (972) 468-4000

MURPHY POPULATION GROWTH

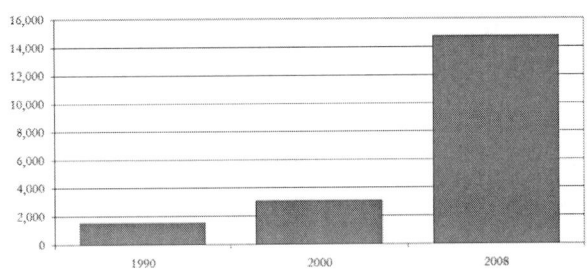

SACHSE

The City of Sachse was founded in 1845 when William Sachse acquired 640 acres in Collin County and erected one of the first cotton mills and gins in the county. In 1886, Sachse gave 100 feet of right-of-way frontage to the railroad, and in exchange the railroad built a depot and named the town after him. When the depot was constructed there was a misspelling on the signs, and the town was temporarily known as "Saxie." By the late 1920s, onions began competing with cotton as a major cash crop and the cotton platform located next to the railroad was transformed into an onion shed.

Today, Sachse is a rural community that is enjoying rapid growth thanks to the expansion of the North Dallas telecom corridor, as well as the President George Bush Turnpike. The city is located both in Collin and Dallas Counties and had approximately 16,200 residents in 2004. The Sachse residents that live in Collin County are zoned to Wylie Independent School District and residents that live in Dallas County go to Garland Independent School District. The City of Sachse is fostering the development of residential neighborhoods, as well as retail and commercial businesses along Highway 78, and looks forward to future growth while still maintaining its country living atmosphere.

For recreation opportunities, Sachse features the Woodbridge Golf Course, which is home to the Northern Texas Chapter of PGA America. The city also boasts numerous parks such as Bryan Street Park, Cedar Creek Park, Cornwall Park and Heritage Park. For cultural attractions, the Sachse Fallfest, an annual arts and crafts country fair, draws over 12,000 people. The Sachse Public Library sponsors preschool and summer reading activities for children, as well as various programs for all ages. Because of its close proximity to the Dallas – Fort Worth Metroplex, Sachse has easy access to all cultural activities the area offers, such as museums, theaters, and historical attractions. The community is primarily made up of single-family homes, ranging from $100,000 to $600,000.

CITY OF SACHSE CONTACT INFORMATION

Website: *www.cityofsachse.com*
City Hall: (972) 495-1212

SACHSE POPULATION GROWTH

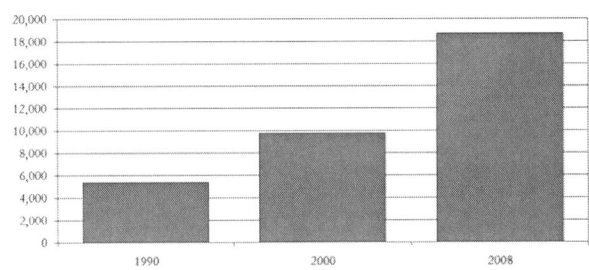

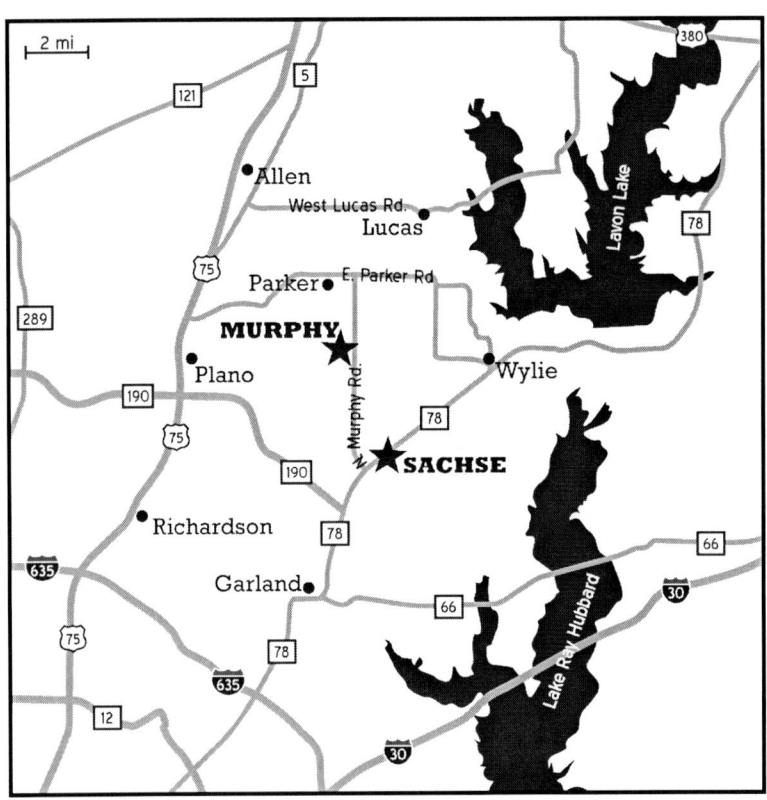

CHAPTER 18

WYLIE AND FAIRVIEW

WYLIE

Wylie is a growing city in the Collin, Dallas and Rockwall Counties of Texas. Located entirely within Collin County as recently as twenty years ago, this fast-growing city has expanded to include nearly 34 square miles of town.

Situated near both Lake Lavon and Lake Ray Hubbard, Wylie has been growing steadily in population since its founding in 1887. By 1890, there were hundreds of citizens and a schoolhouse was built, attracting even more residents. In the next few years several railroad tracks would be laid through the city, cementing it as a place for commerce and tourism. Before 1920, Wylie had garnered more than 35 businesses, a post office, several school houses and two banks to its fair city and a population of nearly 1,000.

The 2000 census found that Wylie had a population of just over 15,000, but the 2006 census saw that the population had skyrocketed to 32,142, a whopping 109% increase in population that caused Yahoo! Real Estate to call Wylie the 8th-fastest growing suburb in the country. Families love the city of Wylie for its community events, ranging from a summer concert series, a one-of-a-kind rodeo, traditional town festivals and holiday-themed celebrations for the Fourth of July, Thanksgiving, Christmas and more.

Every year, citizens of Wylie look forward to the city's annual Arts Festival in December that includes an arts and crafts booth, children's storytelling, a range of foods, a children's area, a cooking demonstration and live entertainment such as music and drama. The high point of the night is the lighting of the city Christmas tree that delights children and adults alike.

TOWN OF WYLIE CONTACT INFORMATION

Website: *www.ci.wylie.tx.us/index.jsp*
Wylie Chamber of Commerce: (972) 442-8100

PART II: PLANO AREA CITIES AND TOWNS

WYLIE POPULATION GROWTH

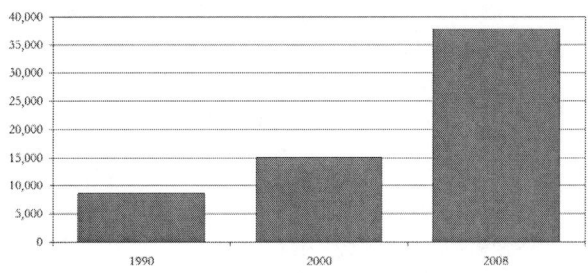

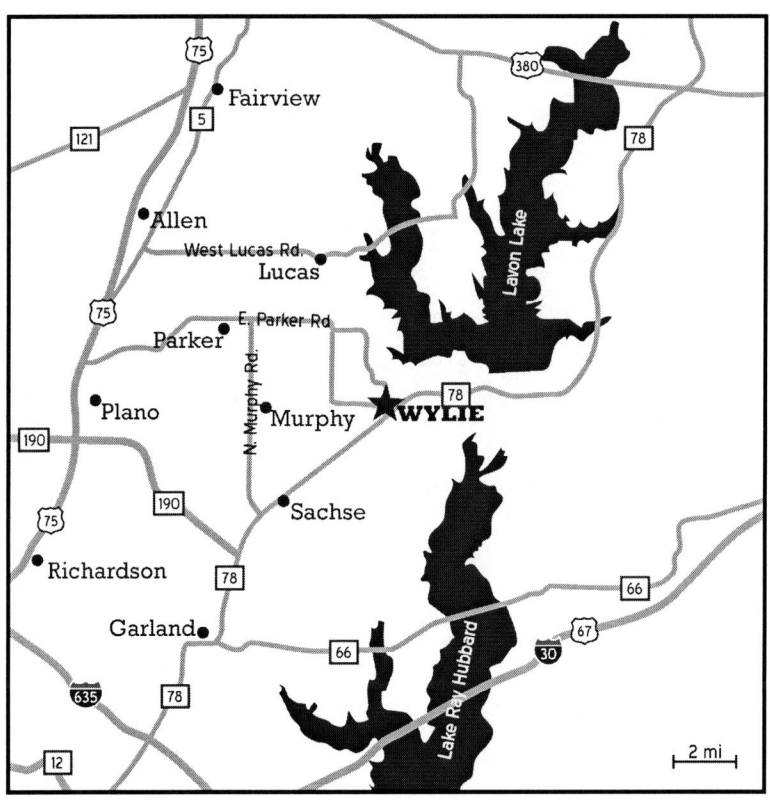

FAIRVIEW

Fairview is a budding suburb of the Fort Worth-Dallas metropolis located in Collin County.

Although Fairview is one of the youngest cities in Texas, it's one of the fastest-growing. Incorporated as a city in 1958 with only a meager population of 50, Fairview has grown to a robust citizenship of nearly 3,000 as of the 2000 census. Even though it's a meager population compared to such heavyweights as Dallas and Fort Worth, residents of Fairview contribute mightily to the state's economy. With an average income of over $110,000, this affluent suburb is a place in Texas where financial stability and success is not only encouraged, but expected. Fairview has enjoyed a boon of new construction from their recently opened Villages of Fairview Mall to brand new housing on large 1-acre or larger lots.

The town's motto is "Keeping It Country" but you'll find that a visit to Fairview is a visit to one of the best combinations of big city, fashionable living in a small-town, relaxed atmosphere. Just a few miles from several fine dining restaurants and upscale shopping, Fairview sits on dozens of square miles of relatively untouched Texas landscape. Walk through any of Fairview's several city-operated parks or stroll down Roadrunner Trail, a winding trail on a two-acre parcel of land that includes a range of foliage and wildlife. Or, keep it simple. Many residents like to sit back and watch the setting sun against the beautiful Texas countryside.

TOWN OF FAIRVIEW CONTACT INFORMATION

Website: *www.fairviewtexas.org*
Fairview Chamber of Commerce: (972) 562-0522

PART II: PLANO AREA CITIES AND TOWNS

FAIRVIEW POPULATION GROWTH

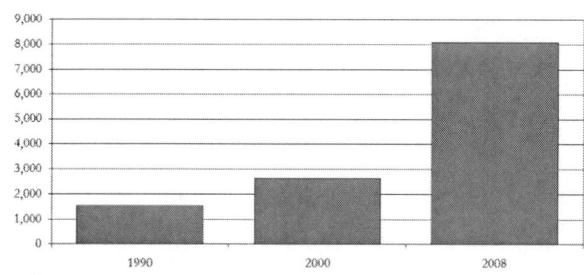

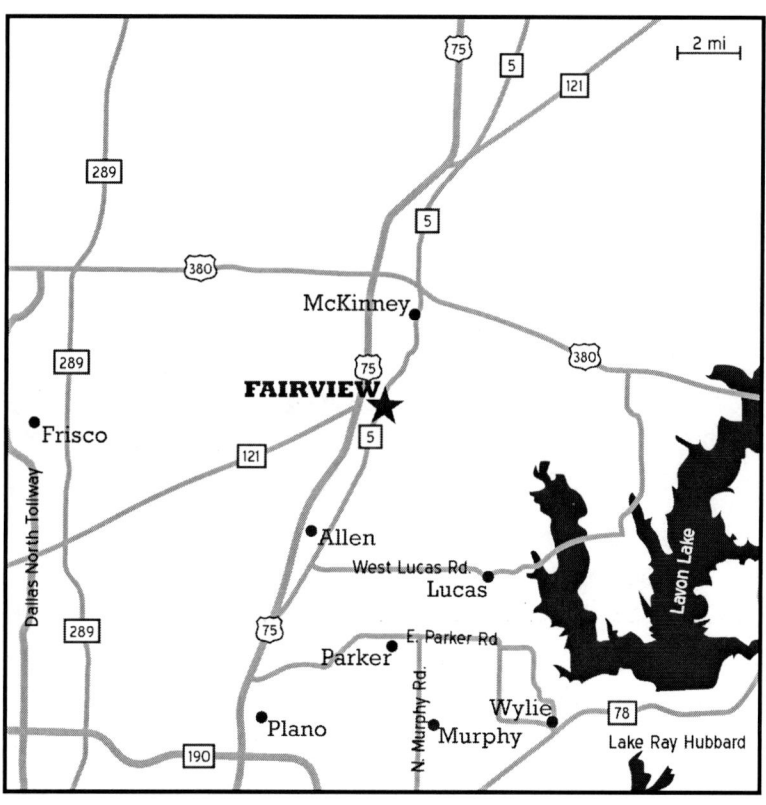

CHAPTER 19

PARKER AND LUCAS

PARKER

While it is one of the smallest cities In Texas, Parker is a probably one of the most recognizable, if even people don't know why.

Located in Collin County and a suburb of the Dallas-Forth Worth metropolitan area, Parker was home to the famous "Southfork Ranch" on the well known television series Dallas.

The 2000 census found that Parker had a population of 1,379 and a land area of only five square miles, but that doesn't stop it from attracting attention. In 2008, D Magazine named Parker the most desirable suburb in Collin County for a third year in a row. The magazine cited Parker's valuable education, low home prices, earning potential for professionals, ambiance and city safety.

The Parker community is one that is incredibly welcoming to families, new and old, as demographics show that nearly 85% of household populations are families. The average income for an individual was just over $34,000 and the average income for families was just over $110,000 making Parker one of the most affluent suburbs of Dallas. Parker offers a nice array of existing housing on acreage to large 4000+ square foot, brand-new construction. Parker also is known for horses, as a lot of the area residents own horses and boarding options are available nearby as well.

Safety is also a high priority for those in a place of leadership for Parker. An all-volunteer fire department has been protecting the city 24 hours a day, seven days a week since 1982 and a curfew ordinance is in effect, relegating that children aged 17 or younger be indoors between the hours of 11:00pm and 6:00am. This newly instituted ordinance has reduced juvenile crime greatly and helped the residents of Parker feel as though they and their family can be safe in this community.

TOWN OF PARKER CONTACT INFORMATION

Website: *www.parkertexas.us*
City of Parker: (972) 442-6811

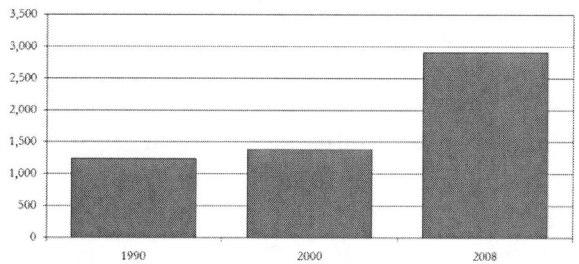

PARKER POPULATION GROWTH

LUCAS

The suburb of Lucas, adjacent to the beautiful Lavon Lake, is one of the most educated areas in its region, owing much of its prosperity to its high priority on getting young adults educated.

Less than 20 miles from larger cities such as Allen, Plano and Richardson, Lucas is a quiet, affordable suburb in north Texas with a density of only 435 people per square mile. According to the 2000 census, nearly 96% of its population of 2,890 residents had attained a high school education. Additionally, only four percent of Lucas' population was living under the poverty line, one of the lowest populations in the country. The per capita income for the city is slightly over $32,000 and the average household income tops $100,000. The correlation between a high graduation rate and a high earning potential cannot be ignored. The city of Lucas expects greatness and fosters growth like few communities in the country do.

With natural amenities such as Lake Lavon resting in Lucas' backyard, residents have come to deeply appreciate the abundant wildlife that the city offers. If you enjoy fishing, canoeing, camping or hunting, Lucas is where you'll find a piece of heaven on earth. Have your boat launched into the lake in minutes or ride a horse down the city's nine-mile equestrian trail. Large acreage home sites are prevalent in the area with most lots coming in at ½ acre or larger. So if you want your space- Lucas is the place!

TOWN OF LUCAS CONTACT INFORMATION

Website: *www.lucastexas.us*
Lucas Chamber of Commerce: (972) 562-0522

PART II: PLANO AREA CITIES AND TOWNS

LUCAS POPULATION GROWTH

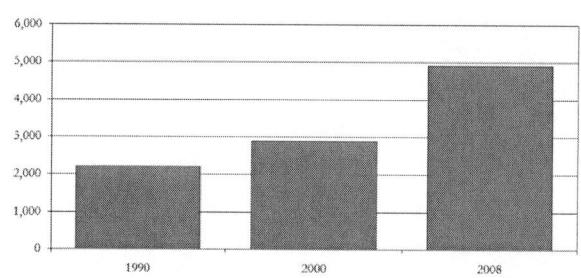

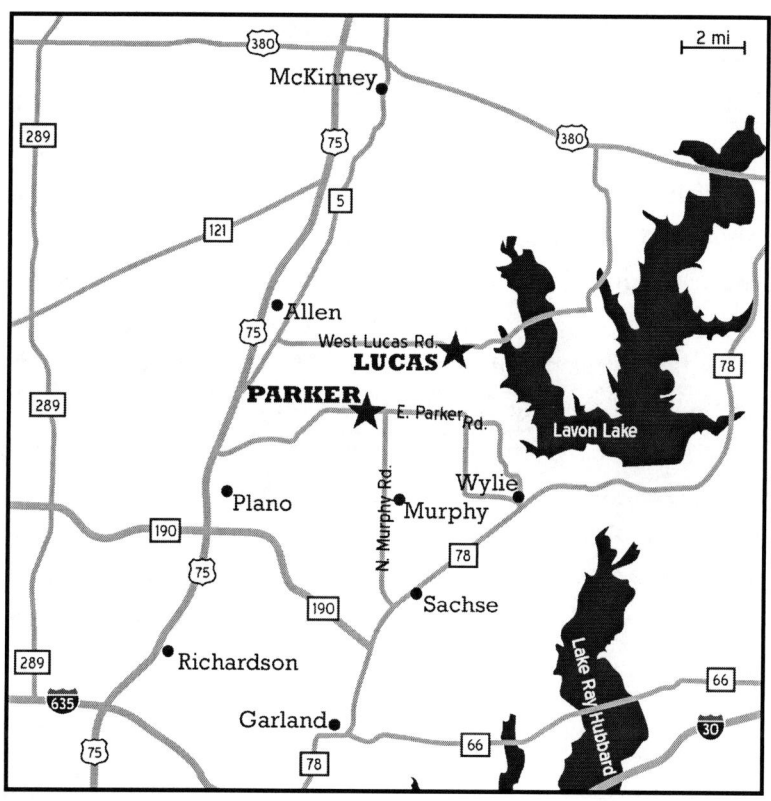

CHAPTER 20

ROWLETT

ROWLETT

Rowlett, which gets its name from the Rowlett Creek that runs through the center of town, is a major city that spans over both Dallas and Rockwall Counties. It is considered a bedroom community made up primarily of commuters that drive to neighboring towns for work.

Although it has only officially been a city since 1952, the city has blossomed into a large suburban area. The 2000 census found that Rowlett had a strong population of 44,503. The city is so affluent that homelessness is almost not present, with only 0.8% of the population living on the streets. Compare that with a national average of 3.4% of homelessness.

Education is also a priority for the Rowlett community as nearly 93% of its population 25 years or older has a high school education. Compare that with the national average of just 80% of adults earning a high school education or greater. Higher education is also encouraged as nearly one-third of all adults have attained a bachelor's degree from a four-year college or university. The national average is only 24.4%.

The city hosts special events all year designed to engage the entire town. For instance, every Easter, the city hosts what it calls an "Eggstraordinary Egg Hunt". Over 20,000 eggs are hidden all over Main

Street. Face painting, bounce horses, live music and photos with the Easter Bunny are also provided. There's also "Fireworks on Main" every July 3rd and "Movies on Main", a free series of movies shown to the entire town every fall.

Visit Rowlett and you'll find a family-friendly town that mixes the entertainment of a big city with the friendliness and community-oriented city-sponsored activities of a small town.

TOWN OF ROWLETT CONTACT INFORMATION

Website: *www.ci.rowlett.tx.us*
Rowlett Chamber of Commerce: (972) 463-CITY (463-2489)

ROWLETT POPULATION GROWTH

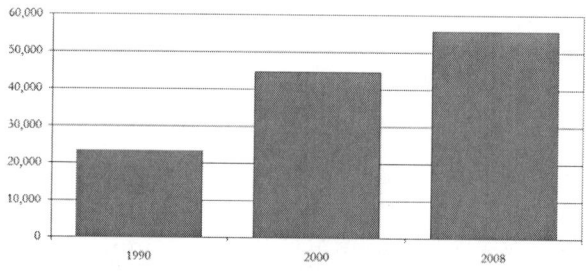

CHAPTER 21

CORINTH AND HIGHLAND VILLAGE

CORINTH

Corinth is a city in north Texas' Denton County and a part of the Dallas-Fort Worth metropolitan.

As the self-proclaimed "Gateway to Success," Corinth's growth is evident throughout. The city represents an attractive blend of enjoyable, family-friendly residential suburban areas within access to upscale commercial businesses and light industry, educational institutions and medical facilities, airports, major professional sports events, shopping centers and a variety of outdoor recreational activities. The city is within 35 miles of Dallas and many Corinthians make the drive regularly to go see America's team, the NFL's Dallas Cowboys or any of the number of museums, galleries or fine-dining establishments that the larger city has to offer.

The city of Corinth is, at its heart, a small town. As of the 2006 census there was a population of just over 21,000, prompting some to refer to the town as "The City in the Country." But Corinth takes pride in that. There's something to be said for the welcome respite that Corinth provides its residents. Whether it's taking a stroll through the town's 116-acre Community Park, picnicking with family after a hike through the city's dozens of nature trails or taking your boat out for an afternoon on quiet Sharon Lake or the ever-popular Lake Lewisville, Corinth has something to offer in terms of a relaxing and restful life.

Just because Corinth knows how to provide a peaceful life doesn't mean the city isn't industrious. The "Gateway to Success" wouldn't call itself so if it couldn't attract a number of businesses to function within the town's borders. Currently, 165 commercial ventures operate in Corinth with more coming every year. The retail climate has experienced a dramatic increase of 24 percent in sales tax revenue since 1990. More businesses coming to Corinth means more opportunity for jobs and a higher budget for local municipal governments to provide for its citizens. And Corinth knows how to answer more businesses coming to their fair city. Over 80% of Corinthians aged 16 years or older are in the labor force. Compare that to the national average of only 62% and you'll see just what kind of work ethic is fostered in this environment.

But it's not all work and no play in Corinth as city officials know how to provide a break for the hard-working citizens of the city. City-sponsored athletics leagues in softball, baseball, basketball, soccer, football and more operate throughout the year. The city also shows free movies in Corinth Community Park every Friday night from May until September. There are annual parties and festivals for nearly every holiday including Easter egg hunts in the spring, Fourth of July fireworks displays in the summer, a Thanksgiving parade in the fall and the lighting of the town Christmas tree every winter. Just because Corinth is a relatively peaceful place doesn't mean it's dull. There's something for everyone in this town, whether you're a businessperson looking for personal financial growth, a new family looking for a town to plant roots or a retired professional looking to enjoy the twilight of your life.

TOWN OF CORINTH CONTACT INFORMATION

Website: *www.cityofcorinth.com*

Town of Corinth Chamber of Commerce: (940) 498-3200

PART II: PLANO AREA CITIES AND TOWNS

CORINTH POPULATION GROWTH

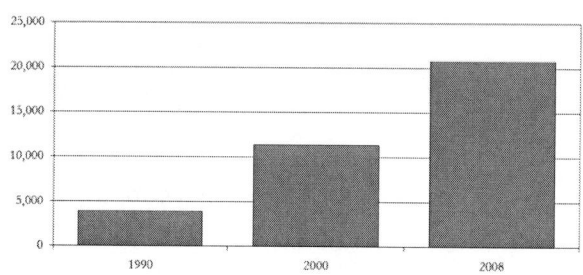

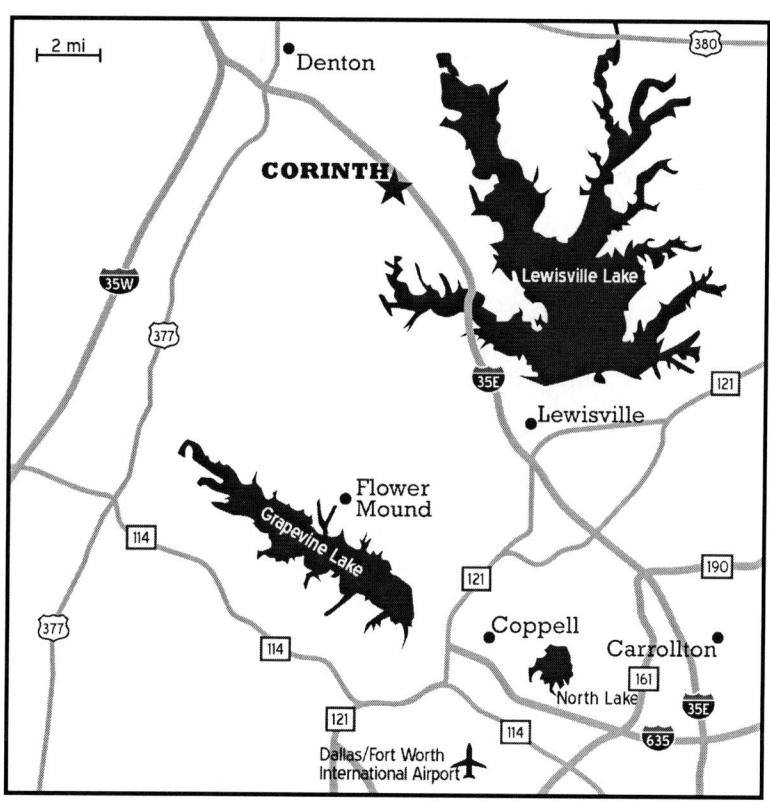

HIGHLAND VILLAGE

If you're looking for a suburb that values safety, look no further than Highland Village.

Voted the safest community in north Texas in the FBI's 2007 Uniform Crime Report, Highland Village is located in Denton County and on the southwest side of Lewisville Lake. The city is one of the fastest-growing communities in Texas over the last 30 years, boasting a population of only 3,000 in 1980, 7,000 in 1990, and a census estimate of 12,173 in 2000. Highland Village owes much of its appeal to its low unemployment rates, high value on high school and secondary education and high average income.

Nearly 75% of Highland Village residents ages 16 and older are in the workforce, compared to only a 61% national average. An industrious spirit drives the growth of employment in the town. Only 0.1% of families are below the poverty line in the city. Compare that with a national average of over 9% and you'll see why many hard-working people are moving to Highland Village.

The population of Highland Village is also very well educated; more than 54% of its residents have obtained bachelor's degrees and 98% have attained a high school diploma or equivalency certificate.

With such job growth in the city and a population that is extremely well educated, it's no surprise that Highland Village has one of the highest average incomes in north Texas with family households making an average of $105,109 and individuals making an average of $40,613.

TOWN OF HIGHLAND VILLAGE CONTACT INFORMATION

Website: *www.highlandvillage.org*
City of Highland Village: (972) 899-5131

HIGHLAND VILLAGE POPULATION GROWTH

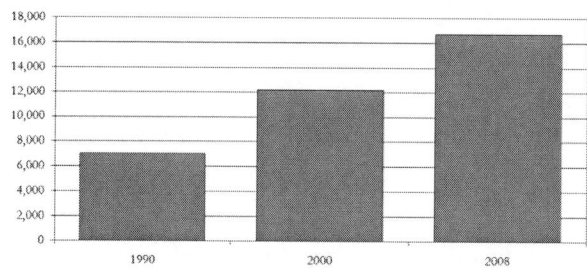

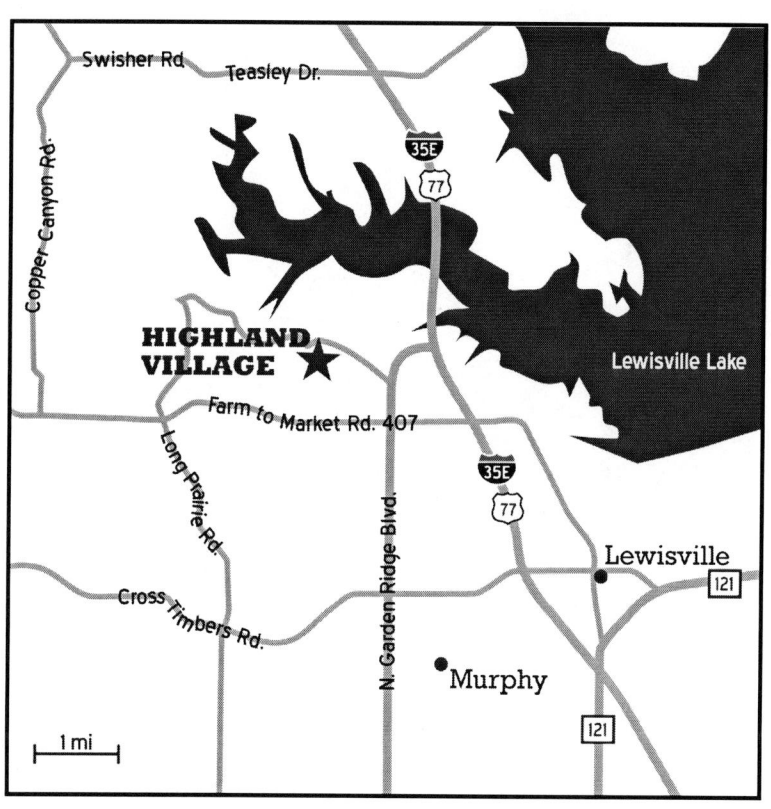

PART III

NEARBY DESTINATIONS

CHAPTER 22

VACATION FUN IN EVERY SEASON

Located in the Dallas-Fort Worth metropolitan region, Plano is in the perfect location for residents to visit all the city attractions, but is also only a drive away from the countryside. The affluent city has been rated as one of the best places to live in the country by CNN Money magazine; is known for its top achieving schools and comes complete with that famous Texas friendliness and a warm climate. What's not to love?

Plus, there's so much to do, and so close by. Known as the "Metroplex," or DFW, the portion of North Texas near twin cities Dallas and Ft. Worth is a busy, culturally rich and highly populated area. The greater DFW area boasts a population of over four million and is a hotbed of development. But beyond the construction and growth lies a region dense with museums, art, nightlife, world-class cuisine, natural beauty and that famous Texas charm.

HISTORY, MUSEUMS AND THE ARTS

For the history buff, a trip to **Grapevine**, one of the oldest settlements in North Texas, is imperative. With its historic Main Street, vintage railroad and historical museum, there are tons of learning opportunities. But Grapevine offers its visitors much more, including shopping, great dining and wineries. In fact, wine lovers can purchase one of several packages for their stay in Grapevine, and make the Texas wine scene the focus of the visit. For an all-inclusive look at what this historic town has to offer, visit Grapevine's Convention & Visitors Bureau Website, *www.grapevinetexasusa.com*. The site provides information on places to stay and a calendar of the numerous and enticing festivals and events that take place there throughout the year, including the Chocolate Festival, SummerBlast! and GrapeFest. Visitors may also want to visit the Grapevine Visitor Information Center, 705 South Main Street, Grapevine, 817-410-8136, before setting off to see the sights.

Visit the **Dallas Museum of Art**, 1717 North Harwood Street Dallas, 214-922-1200, *www.dallasmuseumofart.org*, for a stellar collection of more than 23,000 works from around the world, from many cultures and from ancient times to the present. The museum was established in 1903 as an outgrowth of the Art Committee of the Public Library and has since become one of the most well known landmarks in the area. Visit the art museum's Website for information on tickets, the regular collection and special exhibits and programs for children.

The Modern Art Museum of Forth Worth, 3200 Darnell StreetFort Worth, 817-738-9215, *www.themodern.org*, is dedicated to the collection and presentation of post-World War II art from around the world. The museum is home to more than 3,000 works of art, including pieces by Jackson Pollack, Susan Rothenberg, Andy Warhol and Robert Motherwell. Visit the museum's Website for more information about your visit, including listings of current exhibits.

For everything from Fort Worth history to dinosaurs, **the Fort Worth Museum of Science and History**, 1600 Gendy St., Fort Worth, 817-759-7500, *www.fortworthmuseum.org*, is the ticket. Among the museum's exhibits are the Native American Gallery, the Cattle Raisers Museum (a "museum within a museum"), a children's area and the

Energy Blast exhibit, which focuses on regional and traditional energy resources. The museum also has an Omni theater; ticket information and show times are available on the museum Website.

The **Irving Arts Center, 3333 N. MacArthur Blvd., Irving, 972-252-7558, *www.irvingartscenter.com*,** has theaters, classrooms, art galleries, reception and rehearsal facilities and a sculpture garden. In short, the center is all about the arts. Developed by the City of Irving Arts Board, the center was built to accommodate all levels of artists, from local beginners to world-renowned professionals. The arts center includes a 710-seat concert hall where visitors can catch a live show. Watch the center's calendar for special events, as well, such as children's performances. Families will also enjoy some of the arts programs offered at the Irivng Arts Center, like weekday story and art projects, weekend classes and summer art and theater camps.

In Southwest Dallas there is a truly unique museum that should not be missed. The **International Museum of Cultures, 7500 West Camp Wisdom Road Dallas, 972-708-7406, *www.internationalmuseumofcultures.org*,** is an anthropological museum featuring interactive videos from remote and varied parts of the world, including Africa and Southeast Asia, as well as authentic homes from the Lakota Sioux Native Americans and Papua New Guinea. The museum is open to visitors during weekdays and is available for private tours on the weekends.

OTHER ARTISTIC DESTINATIONS:

- The International Museum of Bowling in Arlington Texas - *www.bowlingmuseum.com*
- The Sixth Floor Museum at Dealey Plaza - *www.jfk.org/go/about*
- Dallas Museum of Nature and Science - *www.natureandscience.org*
- Old Red Museum of Dallas - *www.oldred.org*
- AT&T Performing Arts Center - *www.attpac.org*

restaurant, *www.elfenix.com*, has numerous locations in the North Texas area. Mi Cocina, *www.mcrowd.com*, is a local Tex-Mex favorite with many locations throughout the Metroplex.

There is no shortage of nightlife in the area and while Texas certainly has its share of Western-themed bars, cowboys and mechanical bulls, the DFW area is complete with a wide range of bars and clubs, including wine bars, jazz clubs, piano bars, sports bars, and relaxed cocktail lounges. A good bet for reviewing your choices in Dallas is Dallas.com's nightlife section, *www.dallas.com/nightlife*, which provides reviews of a long list of choices for your after dark options. In Fort Worth, check the Official Website of the Fort Worth Convention and Visitors Bureau for their nightlife section, *www.fortworth.com/visitors/nightlife*. The site provides a range of ideas for fun activities, such as **Hyena's Comedy Club**, *www.hyenascomedynightclub.com*, **Pete's Dueling Piano Bar**, *www.petesduelingpianobar.com*, and the **White Elephant Saloon**, *www.whiteelephantsaloon.com*, an authentic "Wild West" saloon. Other great locations include the Improv Comedy Club in Addison Texas(*www.symfonee.com/improv/addison/home/index.aspx*), The Martini Bar in Loft 610 in Plano, and The Shops at Legacy in West Plano

GET OUTSIDE

Itching to get back to nature for a jog, a hike or just a quiet stroll? **Arbor Hills Nature Preserve**, 6701 W Parker Rd., Plano, *www.plano.gov/departments/parksandrecreation/parks/Pages/arbor_hills*, is a 200-acre park complete with over two miles of paved trails, as well as unpaved pedestrian trails, a two-mile off-road cycling trail and three pavilions for picnicking. An interpretive trail marker system helps visitors locate points of interest within the park Wildlife lovers should stay on the lookout; the park is home to a wide variety of birds and other animals, as well as many trees and other plant life.

Fields of tulips, geraniums and the biggest collection of azaleas in the southwest are in store for visitors to the Dallas **Arboretum and Botanical Gardens**, 8525 Garland Road Dallas, Texas, 214-515-6500, *www.dallasarboretum.org*. Located next to White Rock Lake, the DeGolyer Mansion, a 1940s home that is listed as a Texas Historical Landmark. The arboretum also hosts special events, including spring afternoon seated teas, "Mommy & Me Mondays" and "Tiny Tots Tuesdays," and the "Twilight Tuesdays Concert Series." There are educational opportunities available as well, for children and adults alike, in the form of guided tours and research classrooms. The Dallas Arboretum Website provides all the specifics on everything the park has to offer.

Located in nearby McKinney, the **Heard Natural Science Museum and Wildlife Sanctuary**, 1 Nature Place, McKinney, 972-509-5253, *www.heardmuseum.org*, is both an outdoor sanctuary and a museum. Visitors will encounter numerous types of birds, insects and other animals that are local to the area, as well as learn about important measures in education and conservation that keep those species thriving. Visitors can set out on the trails to get up close and personal with nature, check out the museum exhibits or, of course, do a little of both.

PROFESSIONAL SPORTS

For the sports fan the North Dallas area offers a lot of professional sports options. From football, basketball, baseball, hockey and soccer, Dallas has it all!

Without a doubt, the **Dallas Cowboys**, *www.dallascowboys.com*, are one of the best-known sports teams in Texas and, in fact, in the country. The NFL team plays home games at the famous Cowboys Stadium in Arlington, an brand new, state-of-the-art venue with the world's largest HD video screens,100,000-plus-seater domed stadium, which is also used for other events such as concerts, religious events, motocross races and more. The Dallas Cowboys Website is a wealth of information for tried and true fans, and visitors alike, featuring detailed information on current team members, news updates and a full schedule and ticket information. The latest buzz is the upcoming Super Bowl XLV which will be played in the new Cowboy's Stadium in Arlington Feb 2011.

Basketball fans looking to catch the game are in luck. North Texas is home to, the **Dallas Mavericks**, who play at the terrific American Airlines Center in Dallas. *www.DallasMavericks.com*

You might not think hockey at first when you think Texas, and its warm climate, but the **Dallas Stars**, *www.stars.nhl.com*, are the city's official National Hockey League team. The team Website features stats, news, message boards and, of course, schedules and ticket information.

In the MLB, the **Texas Rangers**, *www.texas.rangers.mlb.com*, represent the Dallas-Fort Worth area and play in Rangers Ballpark, located in Arlington.

NEARBY HOUSTON AND GALVESTON

Houston

Roughly four hours from the DFW area, **Houston** is the largest city in Texas, and the home to Cowboys…but also astronauts. The bustling city is an excellent place to visit, but careful planning will help you get the most out of your stay. Before your trip, your first stop should be the Greater Houston Convention and Visitors Bureau Website, *www.visithoustontexas.com*. The site provides information on accommodations, special offers, an events calendar and all of the attractions you'll want to check out while in the Houston area.

While Houston has got absolutely everything—huge malls, world-class restaurants and museums to name a few—for many a stop at **Space Center Houston**, 1601 NASA Parkway, Houston TX, 281-244-2100, *www.spacecenter.org*, is the first priority. The official visitors' center for NASA's Johnson Space Center, Space Center Houston is home to various attractions that tell the story of human adventures into outer space. Visitors can even see astronauts training for their mission, as well as touch a moon rock and take a behind-the-scenes look at NASA. For hours, directions, ticket information, exhibits and other information, visit the space center's official Website.

Galveston

If you're looking for a beach getaway, **Galveston**, about a four and a half hour drive from the DFW region, is an excellent choice. The 32-mile island offers resort hotels, restaurants, shopping, art and entertainment and is perfect option for a romantic weekend or for a family vacation.

The island is also a great place to find history. Galveston was named for Spanish general Bernardo de Gálvez, who originally sent explorer Jose de Evia to chart the region from the Texas Coast to New Orleans. De Evia first named the spot Galveston Bay. The area grew and quickly became one of the busiest and largest ports west of New Orleans. But perhaps the area is best known for its most devastating event. On September 8, 1900, Galveston was struck by a ferocious hurricane known as the "Great Storm." More than 6,000 people died and a third of the city was completely destroyed. Although those who survived and stayed on in the port city were dedicated to persevere, Galveston suffered for many years until a revitalization effort in the 1980s made the city what it is today.

Your best bet for planning a visit is the official Website of the Galveston Island Convention and Visitors Bureau, *www.galveston.com*, which includes information on everything from performing arts to nature tourism to the best food and wine around. The site also includes a comprehensive list of various hotels, resorts, beach homes, bed and breakfasts and more places to stay on the island. Visitors may also want to check out the **Galveston Island Visitors Center** once they arrive, 2328 Broadway, Galveston, 888-425-4753.

AND MORE!

Looking for a thrill? Look no further than **Six Flags Over Texas**, 2201 Road To Six Flags, Arlington, 817-530-6000, *www.sixflags.com/overTexas*. Spend the day or the entire weekend screaming, laughing and eating your way through the 212-acre amusement park, which features every type of ride you can imagine, from the scariest of roller coasters to tame rides for tots. The park features a wide array of shows and concerts too, and if you want to cool off after a day in the sun, Six Flags Hurricane Harbor (*www.sixflags.com/hurricaneHarborTexas*), the largest water park in North Texas, is right across the street.

If exploring underwater worlds and exotic creatures is on the agenda, you must be headed to the **Dallas World Aquarium and Rainforest**, 1801 N Griffin StDallas, 214-720-2224, *www.dwazoo.com*. First you'll be greeted by the plants and animals of Borneo, as you enter through the Wilds of Borneo exhibit. Next, stroll through the aquarium, checking out the Orinoco rainforest exhibit, where birds fly freely through the trees and plant life, and manatees swim the waters. The aquarium portion includes fish species from all over the world, living in a specialized coral reef ecosystem. And don't miss the outdoor South Africa exhibit or the Mundo Maya exhibit and the avian species that live there, all the way from teeny tiny hummingbirds, to large birds of prey.

Located on 95 acres and featuring thousands of different types of animals, the **Dallas Zoo**, 650 South R L Thornton Freeway, Dallas, 214-670-5656, *www.dallaszoo.com*, is the ultimate zoo experience and a great day trip for the family. The largest zoological park in Texas, the zoo is most well known for its Children's Zoo and the Jake L. Hamon Gorilla Conservation Research Center. Visit the zoo's excellent website so you won't miss a single flamingo, elephant or cheetah! For those interested in renting space at the zoo, the Dallas Zoo also does events and parties, including weddings, birthday parties and corporate events. The Dallas Zoo just opened up an amazing 11-acre Giants of the Savannah exhibit which is the largest exhibit to open in the past 20 years at the Zoo. It features elephants, lions, cheetahs, giraffes and many other African species — truly worth a visit!

There is no shortage of animals in the region. Fort Worth has its own zoo, too. The **Fort Worth Zoo**, 1989 Colonial Parkway, Fort Worth, 817-759-7500, *www.fortworthzoo.com*, features 12 permanent exhibit areas, including the World of Primates, Raptor Canyons, Meerkat Mounds and Parrot Paradise, and, like the Dallas Zoo, offers rentals for birthday parties and other events. The Fort Worth Zoo also provides various education opportunities, including family programs and "Summer Zoo Camp."

You are in Texas after all, and you might want to check out the rodeo. For all the bucks and lassos, visit the **Mesquite Championship Rodeo**, 1818 Rodeo Drive, Mesquite, 972-285-8777, *www.dfwandbeyond.com*. The professional rodeo caters to families, and beyond the action at their Friday and Saturday night shows—which include a laser show, in addition to bull riding, steer wrestling and roping—families can enjoy face painting, a petting zoo and pony rides, not to mention the occasional rodeo clown.

Also a trip to the Fort Worth Stockyards is truly in order if you want a taste of Texas! It has an amazing assortment of restaurants, shopping, entertainment, and live concerts happening all year round!

PART IV

INTERVIEWS

In this section you will hear from 12 people (or couples) who live in the North Dallas area. You will learn how they chose the municipality in which they live, if they would make that same choice again, and why. Some of them are life-long residents who have seen their area evolve. Some moved from other parts of the country, and others moved from other areas within North Dallas. They will tell you who they think would like their town or neighborhood, and who would not. And finally, they will tell you what they do for fun!

The names of most of the interviewees have been changed to protect their privacy.

CHAPTER 23

HOWARD AND JENNY GRAY

PLANO

Can you tell me about where you live and how you ended up there?

Howard: That's a very interesting story. We were looking for a house and we didn't really find anything that we liked. The house that we ended up getting was one that we couldn't find the first day. Jenny ended up looking at it by herself and called all excited, and I dropped by later that day and we had to have it. We got a hold of a REALTOR, James, and he said there was a contract on it. We told him we very much wanted it. Jenny had dreamed about a house like this. She likes rock, and it has a large rock fireplace. James told us that we would be the first people he called if the contract fell through.

How long have you lived there?

Jenny: We bought the house at the end of April. We got married here in the house, in front of the fireplace that we loved so much.

Where are you from originally?

Jenny: I'm from West Texas and he's from Missouri.

Can you tell me about your neighborhood?

Jenny: The location is incredible. We have easy access to all the major highways and thoroughfares, basically to any major airport – it's 15 minutes to the airport.

Howard: We're right on a brand new toll road, so the location is absolutely, probably far and away the best location in the Dallas-Fort Worth area.

Jenny: The neighborhood is a young neighborhood. Very underdeveloped. The neighborhood has been kind of underdeveloped since we moved here.

Howard: There are eight houses that are being built right now.

Where do you go when you want to see a movie or go out to eat, or for other entertainment?

Jenny: We've got a couple of favorite neighborhood restaurants. We probably could find any type of restaurant that we would possibly want within ten minutes. We're in between two major shopping malls, very nice malls so that's great. Movie theaters, most anything like that, are there. We actually haven't been there, but there's the Dr. Pepper Ballpark, which is only five minutes away.

Tell me a little more about the area.

Howard: Plano, it's the most affluent city in the United States, and next to it is a town called Frisco, which, for its size, is the most affluent city of that size in the United States.

Jenny: It's a very up and coming area, it hasn't been too affected by the economy.

Howard: Even though we're in the city of Plano, we're actually in Denton County, which has much lower taxes.

Do you often travel to other cities?

Jenny: We go to Ft. Worth pretty often. We travel all over the Dallas-Ft. Worth area. I work in Allen, Texas, which is another neighborhood not too far away and he's had business clients in Los Colinas.

How's the traffic where you live?

Jenny: Actually, the traffic for me is just incredible. There's a major toll way that's just been built and it's a straight shot. I've never been caught in traffic. We've never had much of an issue here at all.

Howard: I actually go right into downtown, which is a heavy area that many people travel to and it is very rare that I get involved in a slowdown or a traffic jam.

Would you say that you have a good quality of life there?

Jenny: Absolutely. It's wonderful.

Howard: People are extremely friendly. People are out walking around and we meet a lot of people just being out in front of our house.

Is there anything else you think that people moving to the area should know?

Jenny: I think that what Howard brought up is really interesting – the fact that it is such an affluent area and the good thing about that is that people haven't had to suffer much because of the economy, so it's really positive here. You have all the perks and benefits of the city without having to live in the inner city.

Howard: Well, it's got everything really. It's extremely clean. Everything from the city and what they provide is fantastic – even though its government you can actually call them up and it's very friendly and eager to help. This area has pretty much everything you'd ever want within a very close distance. We love living here!

CHAPTER 24

TANA MOSSA

ADDISON

Tell me about how you came to live in Addison.

I've lived here since December a couple of years ago, I think since 2007. Basically I moved here because of what I do. I'm an in-home personal trainer. I wanted to be close to the toll way to be able to get to my clients quickly.

And have you found it easier to get around since you moved to Addison?

Definitely. And I'm close to downtown, too, and close to Frisco. It's definitely a good medium for where I need to be.

Tell me about Addison.

Addison is kind of small. There's not a lot to it, but if you want to go out and do stuff, we pretty much have everything here from clubs, different types of bars, to every restaurant you can think of. Whatever type of food you want, Addison has it. There are over 300 restaurants in this little area. And if you want to go downtown – and I go downtown a lot – there's always something to do. In 20 minutes you're downtown and you can enjoy the nightlife over there. Or it's 20 minutes over to Frisco and you can watch a baseball game down there.

What are the people who live in your neighborhood like?

I'd say I'm the youngest. I'm 28. There aren't many people, unless they rent, who are my age. There aren't many 20-year-olds who buy houses themselves. There are two married couples and an older guy who lives right beside me. The younger area would be Addison Circle. There are condos and apartments, and apartments tend to have the younger people, and condos tend to have the older.

Do you ever worry about crime?

No. No one messes with anyone here. I don't go to places where you would get into that kind of trouble. I left my door wide open on my birthday – I went out to have dinner with my family and I came home, and nothing happened. Nothing. I could have lost everything. I leave my door open a lot. Someone could just walk right in and take everything. I'm never worried about it.

How is traffic in the area?

Traffic can be weird. It just kind of depends on the time of day. You've got your normal rush hour traffic. Traffic isn't really a big issue on the toll way. Usually it's fine after six o'clock. So I try to plan around certain times. For the most part you're fine on the toll way, unless it's 5 o'clock.

Are there a lot of business opportunities in the area?

Luckily for me I'm connected with the right people. There are always opportunities; you just have to be able to really want to find them. The money's out there, you just have to meet enough people to help you, and it kind of depends on what you're doing. I don't think I could be an at-home personal trainer just anywhere in America. I could be a personal trainer still, but I'd be working in the gym and paying rent again. But there are always opportunities.

Do you do any outdoorsy activities near where you live, like running or hiking?

No. I am a former basketball player so running is one of those things I avoid. But it is out there. White Rock Lake is a place where a lot of people go. I have a lot of clients who do that. There are some places that people go to do the hiking thing, so it's accessible. There are a lot of country areas around here, too. A little past Denton has a few, but there's nothing specific that I can think of.

Are you happy in Addison? Do you ever think of moving somewhere else?

I do like Addison, I just wouldn't go for a condo again…because of the homeowner's association. I don't know anyone really who is a fan of a homeowner's association.

Do you ever consider buying something else?

Addison is weird. If I wanted to buy a house in Addison, I would have to spend a lot of money. So I would stick with a townhouse or condo here, unless the economy smiles on me.

Is there anything else you think someone considering the area should know?

I like everything. I'm kind of boring. I'm simple. I'm not hard to please. As long as there's a gym nearby me I'm happy. My gym is two minutes away.

Does Addison have a lot of fitness opportunities such as gyms?

In Addison there are probably three off the top of my head that are within three miles of each other and there's another one that's a high-class country club gym over here, too. And there's also an Addison gym, so there are actually five. I think the Addison gym is like five or 10 dollars a month if you live in Addison…or maybe it's free.

But I think, yes, with the food and the being close to everything, you can't really go wrong.

CHAPTER 25

JAN CAMPBELL

PLANO

Can you tell me a little bit about what brought you to the area?

Right now we are in Plano, Texas and we have lived here about 18 months. We came because my husband started a new job for a company here.

How did you pick your neighborhood?

The number one thing was schools. Plano has great schools and we made sure that the neighborhood had good schools. Here they have 9th and 10th grade as high school and 11th and 12th grade as senior high school, so in this case we made sure she would be going to Jasper High School and she would be going to Plano Senior High School. We are right on the corner between those schools.

Have you been happy with the schools so far?

Yes, the schools are excellent. They have good academics and music programs. We're not so much into the sports, but I think they're well ranked. They have a lot of activities in the schools that are ranked nationwide, like the academic decathlon, and a lot of the national organizations have chapters here in our schools.

Tell me more about your neighborhood.

We chose this neighborhood because of the location but what we found is that where we are tends to be a little bit older, so there are not many kids in our immediate area, but three streets over there are a lot of kids. Plano really has a good mix throughout, but generally the further north you go the newer the houses and the younger the families.

One thing is a lack of creative architecture and landscaping in these neighborhoods. Every house seems to look the same and everybody has their five shrubs all the same with their sidewalk in the middle so there's no variety here. Coming from California where we had all the different landscapes, it is so flat and brown here. That is my biggest disappointment.

But the housing is much cheaper. And the gas prices here are some of the lowest in the country. We travel all the time and Plano has some of the cheapest gas in the country. And this is a well educated area so you have a higher standard of living. You have a lot of corporate headquarters here so you get a lot of people in who have traveled, who have money and who appreciate the nice things culturally. So Plano has a great symphony. Dallas has a fantastic symphony, too. In Dallas everything is world class, but Plano has a great variety of superb cultural opportunities as well.

Is it easy to get out of town?

When you look at where I live I am smack dab in the mid of Plano. I can get to DFW in 25 minutes; I can get to Love Field in about 20 to 25 minutes. They have really been working on putting in a metro line, so you can do that and go to all the sporting events. My husband has gone on the metro to go down to the aquarium in Dallas. He can get down there in about 40 minutes. You've got good highway systems when there is not traffic. The bus system usually runs in lower income areas.

What are your favorite things about the area?

There is an abundance of churches and mission organizations, so we just got online and visited all the Baptist churches and then I visited all the ones within 15 minutes of our house, but there's every denomination, every group you could think of.

There is also extensive shopping. As someone coming from California, I can tell you, everything's here. We've got malls, everything from the higher end like Niemen Marcus to Penny's and Sears.

And they've got good restaurants. You can go to real high-end places in Dallas or on any of these streets along here; there is everything from fast food to little teahouses.

We have a great library system. We use it all the time and I'd say there's between eight and 10 libraries that I have access to and then in the summertime they have free movies for kids.

They have great walking paths. They're not all that aesthetic but they've got the triple-wide sidewalks and they literally go the entire length of Plano. Some places it's nice, some places it follows a creek. And attached to that are parks. Plano is a very pet friendly community. In my neighborhood, I would say easily 80 percent of the people here have pets and they're quite considerate. The city provides the poop bags and the neighbors I've encountered, they keep them on leashes. They're quiet, too.

Do you think the town provides good services to its residents?

They have a good recycling program, but I would say a relaxed recycling program, which is different than California. Here they provide you with a regular trash bin and a huge curbside recycling bin. It doesn't have to be sorted, so it's a relaxed set up.

They have great city athletic teams, youth teams, so if somebody's looking for children's sports programs...they have gymnastics, they even have a saltwater indoor pool. It's relatively cheap to go swimming or they have a city pass. I think a family can join for $140, or something in that range.

What do you think of the outdoor sights and sounds in your area?

Probably the most unique thing I've seen since I've been here is that starting in March they mow only the very edges of the median and city grass strips. In April, those fill up with wildflowers. It is the most amazing sight, it's beautiful. You've lived through five months of yuck and brown and winter and then, boom, it bursts open with blue flowers and red flowers and more. That's stunning to me. And when you drive through Texas in the spring it's just fields of bluebonnets and wildflowers.

The other thing, it's not obvious, but there's really a wide variety of birds here. Our neighbor has birdfeeders, and there's everything from cardinals and red-winged blackbirds to scissortail birds and birds of prey that come to feed. It's the north-south corridor for birds- and it comes right through the center of Texas. The corridor runs the whole length down into Mexico, the birds come through and we have a lot that have stayed all winter.

Do you think Texas is a nicer place to live than California?

There's no state income tax here. That' was nice to not have to fill that out.

The only other thing is that the water tastes bad in late summer and fall so we had to install a filter at the sink. As the lake level goes down the water tastes nasty so everybody puts a filter on their sink.

How is traffic?

Plano city streets are good. As far as traffic flow, unless there's an accident, the traffic moves at the speed limit. The streets are multi-lane. Of course you get your 8 a.m. and you get your 5 or 6 p.m. traffic. Plano is bookended: on one side is Interstate 75 and on the west side is the Dallas Toll Road, so when you get on those to go down to Dallas, you're going to have traffic, especially at rush hour times. A big challenge when you first move here is learning street names. While most streets run east/west or north/south the names sound similar. For example Plano Parkway, Park Blvd and Parker Rd are three east/west streets fairly close together.

CHAPTER 26

MARSHALL ALEXANDER

MURPHY

Tell me a little about how you ended up in Murphy.

We relocated from St. Louis, Missouri, for a job at UT-Dallas. We've been living here for a little over four years. Moving to Texas for us was good because we were looking to move up, and could get more home for our money here. That was nice. . But we chose Murphy because we heard that the Plano schools were excellent. In Murphy all of our driveways come from the front, so we are not an alleyway community, which I know for me was a big deal. It's also a newer community, with nice size backyards and a little bit of country living but with local conveniences.

Tell me more about Murphy and the type of people who live there.

Mainly professionals with families, but there is also a lot of ethnic diversity. Most are transplants from all over the country. Our neighborhood has homes from 1,800 to 3,800 square feet so it's a complete range of people, education and incomes.

Are there good activities for kids in the area?

We have nice parks within our subdivisions. There are plenty of kids' activities within a 5-10 minute drive. Currently for most of our recreational programs we go to Plano, Richardson or Wylie. There is plenty to do with your kids in Texas. In fact, we take one Texas vacation a year since there is so much to do and additional day trips with Murphy as our base. Also downtown Dallas has great arts district within a 30-minute drive or go a little further to Fort Worth for stockyard activities.

How is traffic?

Traffic isn't bad. Even if you're driving downtown say for a concert or something, if it's normally 30 minutes, in traffic it's about 45 minutes. We also have the DART, which is utilized by a lot of people for transport to downtown activities.

If you want to go out for dinner or coffee or drinks, are there places near home?

Recently they built Murphy Marketplace. There are coffee places, restaurants and stores which give residents several choices within our community.

Do you worry about crime?

No. Murphy is very safe. I left my garage door open while I was gone all day without any problems. The City government, fire and police departments are less than two miles from my home.

Do you ever think about moving anywhere else?

We truly like the Murphy area. If we do move there are several wonderful cities in Texas. Near a lake would be nice.

Is there anything else someone moving to Murphy should know?

Texas doesn't have state income tax which is great. Sales tax is about 8% but we do not have to pay tax on grocery food items.

Property taxes are a little high compared to Missouri, but we have amazing schools.

Murphy is growing fast, so there is a need to keep building new schools to avoid overcrowding.

Water can be a little nasty by the end of summer if it hasn't rained enough, so get a filter or a refrigerator with one built in.

But overall, the quality of life in Murphy is excellent; we have nice neighbors, developed good friendships, our home values are fairly stable, and it is a young growing community. We love it in Texas!

CHAPTER 27

ZACK AND CHERYL BAKER

HIGHLAND VILLAGE

Tell me about how you ended up in Highland Village.

Zack: A career transfer brought me to North Texas originally, and then Cheryl…

Cheryl: I moved here because it was cheaper than commuting from Chicago! I was in a long distance relationship so…we just followed Zack's job and we moved to Carrollton, and from there we moved up to Highland Village. We just wanted to get a little bit of a bigger house and a pool and yard and found the perfect house out here.

How would you describe Highland Village?

Zack: Well it's a bedroom community for Dallas. A lot of people who live here commute and work – it's kind of a neat mix because right in the area next to us you get into some areas where it's a little more rural – where people have big homes but also have 25 acres of property with horses and stuff, so there are a little more rural homes close to us. Also one of the larger lakes in Texas is here, Lake Lewisville, and Highland Park borders some of that. It has a little more of a small town feel, it really is a fairly small town.

So you like the small town feel?

Cheryl: Oh yeah. And it's close to Denton, which is a college town – University of North Texas – so there's music and plays and theater and art and stuff up there, and that's a 20 minute to a half hour drive, plus we're 40 minutes from downtown Dallas so that's really nice.

What do you do for entertainment?

Zack: We're small business owners, so frankly by the end of the workday we're not in much shape to do anything. And we're relatively low maintenance. We enjoy staying in and reading a book, or in the summertime just hanging by the pool, so we're not folks who need to do a lot of things to be happy.

Cheryl: Highland Village actually has some great restaurants because there's a great shopping area called the Shops at Highland Village which has some great restaurants.

Zack: Highland Village is a relatively young town, too and it's actually one of the safest…Safest City in Texas, it was voted.

So you don't worry about crime?

Zack: Not really, no. We lock doors when we leave just purely out of habit but we could probably go to the store or movies or whatever and not have to lock our door.

Cheryl: The police department here is really friendly and responsive. Each officer has an area that they patrol and if you go on vacation or something you can let them know and they'll check the house every day.

Can you walk and bike where you live?

Cheryl: There's a really nice hike and bike trail called the City Trail. It's really great, instead of our Wal-Mart having an auto shop, they have a bicycle shop and you can ride your bike down to the Wal-Mart.

Zack: I ride in charity rides, so when I go out and ride, I'm usually riding a pretty good distance, you know 30 or 40 miles, so it's not really riding up to the grocery store, but you could.

How's traffic in the area?

Zack: We're able to shape our appointments most of the time so we don't have to commute during the rush hour. If we worked in downtown Dallas and we had normal rush hour times, we wouldn't live here because it would be pretty much 45 minutes or an hour each way, and I don't have much patience to sit in that. So if you're going to work in Dallas, I would say this wouldn't be a good spot to be. Because of the lake we're on, there's really only one feasible route to go to Dallas. So yeah, traffic is an issue if you're going to drive between 7 and 9 and 4 and 6, but if you're not traveling during those times, it's not bad. I have a Thursday morning meeting at 7 a.m. that's about 20 miles from here and I can leave here at 6:30 and be there at 7.

How are job opportunities there?

Zack: Based on what we've read and what we know about other parts of the country, I would say we're fortunate here. I would say it's a significantly better market here than in other parts of the country and then, because it's a relatively high technology economy here – there's not a lot of big automotive manufacturing, old manufacturing – it's Texas Instruments and telecom companies and the folks in that "new economy" are the players. I think that because of that the opportunities are good compared to the rest of the country. Also, one of the things about Texas is the amount your dollar can buy vs. what you can get in a lot of other parts of the country. I think it bodes well if a company needs to move out of Washington D.C., say, and they want to move here, they can probably get the space for two-thirds of what they would pay in LA, for instance.

What else would you tell someone interested in moving there?

Zack: One thing that jumps to mind for me is the climate. We're in the first couple days of March and we'll be working outside this weekend in light sweatshirts. It's pretty hot in the summertime, and that' a downside, but nine months out of the year it's really nice compared with the rest of the country.

Cheryl: This year we got a lot of snow. I'm from Chicago and Zack is from Michigan so we didn't go anywhere, because people here don't know how to handle it, but it was beautiful!

Zack: When I was back in the corporate world, one of the things I liked about being here is you have Dallas Fort Worth Airport, which is a big airport that works fairly well and they you've also got Dallas Love Field. So you've got two major airports to fly out of or into on business, especially if you're a corporate person who flies a lot or a company looking to move here.

Another thing that just occurred to me is that where we live is just starting to get rural but even if you lived in Dallas, you're living in a metro area with all of the accompanying opportunities for recreation but you can live in downtown Dallas and you can drive less than an hour and you can be in ranch and farmland. And I don't think that's the way it is in the rest of the country.

CHAPTER 28

JIM BURNIE

COPPELL

Tell me about how you came to live in Coppell

I was in Farmers Branch and the house we were in was a corner lot and we had someone empty a pistol in front of a house around the corner, across the back yard. I had a three-year-old at the time and we decided it was time to move on. We did some research and between convenience to my wife's job in downtown Dallas and price point and quality of the schools, we found Coppell to be the best place for us. We found a partially built house in a new subdivision. And put an offer in. That was 12 years ago and we still love it here.

What are your neighbors like?

We have one of the most fantastic neighborhoods in the North Dallas area. We know a lot of friendly people. When people have tough situations, the neighborhood jumps together to help them out. A neighbor's house just got burned; within four hours of the fire supplies and clothes started showing up on their front lawn.

Families with young-to-teenaged kids live here. Older parents, who are already well into their career path, then they start their family later live here. It's not really a singles place, or a place for people looking for a nightlife. However, we do like to have fun. In our neighborhood we do a neighborhood happy hour once a month, and have each other for dinner, cocktails regularly.

What don't you like about living in Coppell?

Sometimes the parents can be a little overdramatic: we've got a lot of helicopter parents. And there are some challenges with the accountability of the children – they are borderline spoiled. They show a lot of attitude if confronted. There's a lot of entitlement for the younger kids because it is a very affluent area.

The schools are huge but are insanely overpopulated. However, they still manage the students well and doing well at Coppell opens a lot of doors nationwide as far as getting placement in colleges and such.

Another thing about my neighborhood is we're probably five minutes from DFW airport. It's convenient, but we get a lot of planes flying over.

Where do you go if you want to go out to eat, or for a drink or for other entertainment?

There's a lot of reasonably close restaurants, not only in Coppell but nearby in other towns. There's not a nightclub or bars, per se but there are plenty of bars and restaurants where you can have dinner and drinks.

Are there a lot of outdoors activities in Coppell?

There's a huge youth program. Any kinds of sports are available, from soccer to football to lacrosse. But there are also things like YMCA Adventure Guide for dads and kids. Adults I know participate in cycling clubs, running clubs and other group activities.

Do you ever worry about crime?

I would say the only crime I'd be worried about would be affluent kids looking to get in trouble: roaming the streets and being punks or getting into peoples' open garages or cars.

How are business opportunities in the area?

Opportunities here are excellent. It is a bedroom community so most people commute out. But Coppell was indicated on a recent survey on the news as having the lowest unemployment in the Metroplex. Part of it is if you're unemployed for any length of time you're out of here.

Do you ever think about relocating to somewhere else nearby? If you did where would you go?

We'd probably go to the Allen/Plano area because of the reputation of the schools and similar socioeconomic standards. If we moved farther away it would be probably Flower Mound just because it's slightly newer, there's more of a community downtown. They took a downtown area and rehabbed it and there's a square people hang out at. In Coppell there are a lot of parks but there isn't a downtown area specifically. Their working on it but it's a crossroads not a square. If you've got a square for people to go to for Independence Day or what-have-you, that's important.

Do you worry about Coppell growing?

We're built out. It's 98 percent built out. Yet every time I turn around I see another subdivision being built on a plot of land I didn't think was possible.

Do you feel that you have a good quality of life?

We have an excellent quality of life. We have excellent schools and the neighborhoods are safe and family oriented. We've been here long enough that if my daughter's screwing around I'm going to get a phone call. People keep each other in the loop for the most part. They say it takes a village – in its own way Coppell is that village

How often do you go to Dallas?

My wife goes daily because she works down there. We're 35 minutes away from downtown. Because I'm a financial planner and my practice is in Coppell, I go downtown probably a dozen times a year. If I go to Dallas it's probably for a special event, a sporting event or something. If I don't have a specific destination or a particular high-end restaurant I want to go to, I just stay up here.

CHAPTER 29

JON SAMPSON

FRISCO

Tell me about how you came to live in Frisco

I relocated for work. I came from Canton, Michigan and we've been here for 2.5 years. We live in a two-story, 4,900-square feet, 5-bedroom, 3.5-bath. We like it a lot; it's a very family-oriented community. It's much like Canton in that while it's a suburb of a major city it's pretty family-oriented.

What are your neighbors like?

It's very diverse. The neighborhood we live in is a lot of newer families. In our neighborhood it's mostly people who have been married 4-5 years. There are a lot of young kids, probably 10 and under. Most of the folks who live in Frisco work in corporate offices in Plano or Dallas.

What do you like about Frisco?

I would have to say my favorite thing about living here is the activities. The town of Frisco has a lot of family oriented events: concerts, or during summer they have festivals and things like that. It's close enough we can get to Dallas in half an hour to go to a concert. American Airlines Center is close and we can see a lot of concerts.

I would just say everything we really need is within 15 minutes of our house. Whether it's the mall, shopping or a place to eat -- everything is really close. A lot of parts of Frisco are not developed yet so we still have all types of animals such as cows and red tail hawks. It's not all built up. They do a good job with the parks and the landscape requirements of business to have green areas whether its shrubs, trees or grass. It's not a concrete jungle.

What don't you like about living in Frisco?

The taxes are higher here than in other areas. You pay for quality schools. That's the trade-off. The schools are great -- they have a great student to teacher ratio. But to pay for that we have high property taxes. If we were single, without kids, we would live elsewhere. You pay a lot to live in Frisco for someone without kids in the school system. But the taxes we pay for city schools are worth it.

Compare Canton, MI and Frisco.

They are very similar as far as the community and the activities for families. It's definitely cheaper to live in Frisco. We don't have state income tax, so that's a huge benefit. We picked this area because it was much like Canton. There are good schools in a small community. Everything is really close. The mall, Target Kroger are all no more than a mile or two away.

Where do you go if you want to go out to eat, or for a drink or for other entertainment?

We stay within Frisco. They have all the named chains. Outback, Olive Garden, those are all within close distance. We have a great minor league baseball team, the Frisco Rough Riders. They have a great facility, we love bringing the kids there. It's a great place to go. There's also the Texas Tornadoes, a minor-league hockey team right within Frisco.

Do you ever worry about crime?

No. I mean it's a very, very low crime area. I can't remember the last time there was any big crime. The crime that does happen tends to be breaking in to cars and stuff. As far as home invasion you don't really hear about that in our area.

Do you ever think about relocating to somewhere else nearby? If you did where would you go?

Probably McKinney. It's very similar to Frisco, but it's a little larger but a little more congested. The reason we didn't pick it when we moved here was the traffic. There are so many traveling between Dallas and McKinney. We settled on Frisco because it was an easy commute for me. I can get back and forth to work in Plano in 10 minutes.

Do you worry about Frisco growing?

It has grown. The city council and school board do a great job managing growth and making sure there are resources for all citizens. The city continues to build new schools to keep the student-to-teacher ratio around 1:25. They just opened another high school this year because the high schools were getting too large.

Do you feel that you have a good quality of life?

Absolutely. It's very low-key. You don't have to worry about crime. You don't have to worry about growth because the city has very solid zoning laws. You aren't going to have someone building something not appropriate for the area.

How often do you go to Dallas?

I would say probably about every other month. During summer we go to concerts in the city. We've been to Dallas Mavericks Games and Dallas Stars Games. Without traffic you can get there in 20-25 minutes. The one downfall of living in Frisco, you are going to get rush hour traffic in the morning going to Dallas or Irving but there are High Occupancy Vehicle lanes that make it a lot better. Still, it's not uncommon for folks to be tied up in traffic for a good hour or two.

CHAPTER 30

MARK FORT

MURPHY

Tell me about how you came to live in Murphy.

We moved to Murphy about ten years ago. We wanted to move out of large cities. We like the country environment and Murphy is a small, rural area. There's a horse ranch down at the end of the street, so it's very much a country atmosphere. Before we were in Murphy, I lived in Plano 35 years ago. Then we moved to Frisco, which is north of that – and Frisco was, at that time, kind of like Murphy is now. We lived there for about five years and in that time they built this mall and it became a thriving shopping megaplex. And it was taking me about an hour and 15 minutes to get to work, and we decided we wanted to get back into that country environment. The nice thing about Murphy is that it's surrounded by other towns and it's purely just a residential area.

Are you still commuting?

Actually, no. It's nice not to have to drive into an office anymore. When I have to work I basically just go upstairs to my home office. Most of us here are like that. It's a fairly small town, and most of the people are like myself; upper middle class, executives who like to work from home.

What are your neighbors like?

There is some variety clearly. I see a lot of diversity as far as nationality and age. But I think from a business perspective, I'd say it is upper middle class, because most of the homes in here, they start at $400,000 and go up to a million. So there are some folks here who are pretty senior level, in fact the CEO for Texas Instruments lives about a mile down the street. But there is a wide variety.

Where do you go if you want to go out to eat, or for a drink or for other entertainment?

We're not that far from any major areas. There's a thriving area near here called Allen, and there's a real nice, trendy shopping area. They've got a lot of really neat restaurants down there. Also, downtown Plano is about three miles from here, which has actually started to grow and have some neat night places. It's not that far at all.

What about outdoors activities in Murphy?

We've got trails all throughout Murphy and these trails wind all around through the residential community. Some of them lead you out to a shopping center, and the trails actually connect into the Plano trails. In theory, I've never tried this, but you could actually take them into the Dallas area. There are a lot of people in the evenings when it's cool, out walking their dogs, walking, jogging, rollerblading; it's a fairly active area. There's a community pool in the neighborhood we're in. Most of the homes have pools in them. There's a park with a pond. A lot of people go boating, and if you go a little farther north you get to one of the largest lakes in North Texas.

Do you ever worry about crime?

Not really. Nobody takes any chances. You read in the police bulletin that somebody broke into a garage and stole a bicycle, which typically indicates kids. I personally don't really worry about it. Everybody's got security systems and they're pretty high-end security systems. I don't think anybody has any fear. I just think a lot of people are taking a lot of precautions, which is a good thing to do.

How are business opportunities in the area?

I'm in the tech sector and I've been in it for 25 years and I've seen its up and downs. Prior to this, I worked for Nortel and it's really had its troubles, but a lot of people who were at Nortel have moved to Ericson and are working for other companies. I would say that the opportunities are scarce for the higher-end jobs, but I would say that I think that this area is a better area than most. I think it has held its own pretty well. We saw a lot of struggles from a lot of different people. There have been a lot of foreclosures in the Collin county area. I think that people are finally starting to see more income out there.

Do you ever think about relocating to somewhere else nearby?

We're happy where we are. We've lived in a lot of areas in the Dallas-Fort Worth Metroplex area and of all the areas where we've lived – Plano, Dallas, Frisco -Murphy is really the place we want to be. I wouldn't be happy living anywhere else.

Do you worry about Murphy growing?

Murphy can't grow like that. Murphy is primarily a residential area. The only thing I worry about in Murphy is that it might lose some of the country charm. There are a lot of residents that are very vocal with the city council, and a lot of us moved here to enjoy the horses the cattle, and to keep that sort of rural environment. One of the things that we see is that they're getting ready to widen one of the streets and we worry that they might get rid of the ranches. That is the one concern, that they might get rid of some of these ranches.

Do you feel that you have a good quality of life?

Yes, I think so. There's a lot going on, everything with the economy. I think it is a pretty good quality of life, with my work/life balance. It's not like I'm away from home. For the most part I'm with my family.

CHAPTER 31

LAURA MANOS

McKINNEY

How did you end up in the area?

We live in McKinney now, we've just moved here from Plano. We've lived here for eight months, and we decided to move to McKinney after starting a family. The cost of living in McKinney is just a lot more affordable than Plano. We wanted me to be able to stay home and raise my son and we got more house for the money and I was able to quit my job. The area's great for families.

What do you like about McKinney?

We moved to an area called Stonebridge Ranch and it's a big master-planned community. One of the big things they promote is back-to-community living. They do a lot of community functions. That was one of the things we loved about it. We are a young family and we're looking to interact with other young families so we were definitely looking for a very family-oriented area. The community offers a lot of amenities. There are a couple of pools.

Downtown is a historic area, so there's a lot of interesting history here. There's a lot of stuff like that in the area that draws you out of your home and once you're out, there are a ton of people to meet. When we bought our home in Plano, not a single person came to greet us when we moved in. I grew up in a neighborhood where when you moved in everyone welcomed you. When we moved to McKinney that's what we got. Ever since we've been here we feel very welcome, we feel very safe. I know my neighbors, I know who they are and I feel very safe with that. If I need something I can go to my neighbors.

Can you walk places near your neighborhood?

We're pretty active. We walk a lot. There are always people out walking. Outside of the neighborhood they've done an awesome job of creating trails that make you feel like you're going through park when you're really just on the outskirts of your neighborhood. It's very well landscaped. There's a Kroger a little more than a mile from the house. There's a Starbucks on every corner almost literally. I can walk to the aquatic center. We've got a jogging stroller and we can go out. It's close enough that if you wanted to walk you could, but if you want to run out in your car it's really easy. And it's far enough that you feel you aren't living next to Kroger.

Do you travel to nearby towns and cities for entertainment?

There's so much growth in this area. Right down the street between McKinney and Plano is Allen. And they're creating a lot of outdoor shopping areas. Some of these outdoor shopping areas have this very cool stuff. And a lot of the restaurants back up to this grassy area where they have live music. Lots of family friendly areas and lots of grassy areas so you can take your own picnic and you can sit out there and enjoy the atmosphere.

Is there any traffic?

My husband might have to deal with it a little. I don't anymore. Before I quit my job I drove an hour one way to work and traffic was terrible. On the way home I might average 35 miles per hour. So I'd have to leave early and just make sure I figured in enough time. My husband works at home so if his flight gets in around rush hour he might deal with some traffic.

Do you ever worry about crime?

I feel pretty safe, but yes, I worry about crime. It has been absolutely beautiful so I had all the windows open and I had the back door open the other day. I was upstairs working out and I stopped halfway through and almost lost my breath and realized, "I have my back door open." Anyone could come in. There's good reason to have precautions but I do feel safer knowing my neighbors. I left my garage door open the other day and one of my neighbors called me and said, "You left your garage door open, should I close it?" We didn't get that in Plano. Overall I feel very safe.

Does the area offer a lot culturally?

There are a lot of cultural events going on. Our community publishes a monthly newsletter. There's Earth Day events coming up this month, there's something like the cowboy extravaganza going on, celebrating downtown historic McKinney. At the end of the month, the second or third Saturday of each month, there's wine and music and art, just kind of a downtown event. Next weekend we're going to go to the Plano Symphony. There's a lot to offer. McKinney has the HEARD museum for natural science. Tomorrow I'm taking my kid to the zoo. There's a large variety of what you want to see and you can definitely find it.

Do you feel like you have a good quality of life?

We do. We are really happy up here, some of it might have to do with me quitting my job and staying home to take care of my family. We love it. Nothing beats loving your life in Texas. There's something about being in Texas. I can walk out my front door and I'm pretty sure one of my neighbors will be out there too and I can be sure they're just as happy as I am. It's refreshing.

CHAPTER 32

JAMIE WHITMAN

CARROLLTON

Tell me about how you came to live in Carrollton

Actually, we found it by mistake. My wife and I were on our way from Coppell to visit her uncle in Richardson and we just came upon it. We turned into a neighborhood and thought, "wow this looks kind of cool," and that's how we found the neighborhood where our first house was. That's not where we live now, but that was in 1990 when we came to the area. We moved and now we've lived in this neighborhood for a year and a half. We moved to be closer to school and church, which is now a 6-minute drive instead of a 15-minute drive

What are your neighbors like?

Many of our neighbors have been in Carrollton a while. It seems people who move here, stay because they love it. Quite a few people on my street are in their second neighborhood in Carrollton to live in. We happen to live in a newer development and we know many people from our church and from our children's school here, which is wonderful.

What don't you like about living in Carrollton? What would you change?

I don't think I'd really change anything. I'd like lower property taxes if I had to change anything. But we don't have to live and shop here. Being part of a large Metroplex means it's big and spread out and there's everything you need, even if it's not in your particular town. We're out in a little bit of country. One of the problems we've had is cattle getting out of pasture land and roaming the neighborhood, which is not much a problem. We are very fortunate to be where we live.

What makes Carrollton Special?

It's enough of a small town but not the glamorous and glitzy suburbs like Plano and Frisco. It's still got a down-to-earth feeling more than other suburbs around. One good part about the area we're in is it's convenient to several major highways and in just a few moments you can be going wherever you like. You can get to Frisco, you can get to Plano, where there are a lot of shopping features for the family. But the best part for us is it's close to church and school.

Where do you go if you want to go out to eat, or for a drink or for other entertainment?

There are plenty of movie theaters around. We're not going to go party. But within 10-12 miles there are literally hundreds of restaurants and some shopping areas 5 or 6 minutes away. There' two malls within 6 miles. There's a lot within a very short driving distance. But when you turn out the lights it gets real dark around here because there isn't a whole bunch around our neighborhood; it is a new neighborhood. In a way you feel like you're out from everything but you aren't.

Are there a lot of outdoors activities in Carrollton?

There are a lot of youth sports available. Our kids are teenagers but we're beyond some of that. You can go city leagues or church based leagues for youth sports. This is a neighborhood where there are hills and there aren't a tremendous number of areas with hills so we get more than our fair share of bikers. We're near the city of Plano and there's a nature preserve with trails and our neighborhood butts up against that nature preserve so we get wildlife and get to spend time outdoors where it isn't so developed.

Do you ever worry about crime?

Probably not. If my wife were here she'd say I need to be more worried about crime. She fusses when I leave doors unlocked. There is normal neighborhood stuff. You shouldn't leave your garage door open at night. But as long as you open your garage doors you don't feel that threatened. It's well patrolled here; I see 2-3 policemen a week here.

Do you ever think about relocating to somewhere else nearby? If you did where would you go?

When we first checked out the area, we have thought that Coppell would be there area we'd end up in. When we went there we could never find the amount of house we got for the money in Carrollton. That was kind of what attracted us to Carrollton is that we could seem to get quite a bit of house for the money.

Do you have any advice for people relocating to the North Dallas area?

What we really liked about Carrollton is it seemed like we could get a lot of house for the money. Get a good REALTOR make sure you get your home inspected. If you are looking to move quickly, looking to invest, the days of "I'm going to live in the house a few years and make a killing on the appreciation," that probably won't happen. If you want a place to stay a long time, North Dallas has plenty of great places, depending on whatever you want to spend. You couldn't go wrong being in Carrollton. If you want to live in Plano you probably want to live in East Plano. West Plano is inflated; Frisco is inflated for home prices.

Do you feel that you have a good quality of life?

Sure, absolutely. I live close to my wife's work, close to school, great wife great kids, those are a lot of things that are important. There are a lot of choices of churches around here and I think that's important. Wherever you are comfortable in your worship you have a lot of options in North Texas.

How are the local business opportunities?

I run a business called Crown Printwear, and I've found the North Dallas area to be a great place to do business. We produce T-shirts and embroidered corporate apparel and provide promotional products and there are plenty of great companies around here I work with.

I was recently at a presentation by the dean of the SMU business school. Texas is a great place to be. In the next 20 years Texas is predicted to have more population growth than the rest of the country. Texas has no state income tax; there are a lot of opportunities. A lot of people will be moving to flocking to the North part of the Metroplex and Carrollton is a gem. You get a lot of the amenities. The house we purchased here would be 10-15 percent more in Plano or Frisco and we are just as central as they are. We aren't far from a baseball park, we're near highways and we can get to any professional sport. There's a lot happening in Dallas. While Carrollton is not a marquee city, if you want to put your roots down someplace Carrollton is not a bad idea.

How often do you go to Dallas?

We do something entertainment-wise in Dallas often. My wife went with my daughter down to downtown Dallas about 3 weeks ago. Once or twice a quarter we are there. My son and I went in a concert in October then we won't go for months. I go for business maybe once or twice a month.

How's traffic?

Here's the thing. Most of rush hours are North-South and my wife's commute is opposite the flow of traffic and takes 6 minutes to get to her office. My office is in my home. I'm rarely stuck in traffic, but Carrollton to Dallas is a 45-60-minute drive in rush hour. The traffic inside my city isn't a big deal unless you are going with the traffic during rush hour. Fortunately because of our work situation, it's not much of a consideration.

CHAPTER 33

BRENDA HAROLD

CARROLLTON

Can you tell me what originally brought you to Carrollton?

I was there until just recently – until January – and I purchased my house about five years ago. Actually, that was the first home that I ever purchased on my own.

Why did you choose Carrollton?

Two reasons: They're known as a Blue Ribbon District – it's a good school district and I had two kids in school at the time. And also, it's a nice area. My sister lived there and a dear friend lived there too. It was a great area.

Is there a lot to do for entertainment right in town?

Oh yes, they've got great restaurants out there. About two blocks down from where I purchased my home was a nice park. There were tennis courts close by. There was a hospital at the end of my street. There were schools; there were so many things to do in my area. There were three shopping areas close by.

Did you have to deal with any bad traffic?

Sometimes I did, of course. I was close to Hugo. It's a very busy street but you just have to time things. You just time it, but other than that it's probably no worse than any other areas.

Were there opportunities for outdoors activities?

Yes. The park also had a barbecue area so people would go out there and barbecue with their families, and there was a volleyball net and a lot of young parents would stroll their kids in the paved areas. It was a great place to walk your dog, and I like to run so I could run there. It was very well maintained, a lot of flowers and well manicured. You know, there were times we saw people playing soccer out there, too. And we saw people with Frisbees and their dogs. One thing that was good is they had little stopping areas where they had little bags, and if your dog pooped you had to stop and pick it up and people were very good about that. There was something for everyone there. I often walked there from my house.

I had two dogs and I would walk my dogs up there, too.

Could you walk other places?

I could walk to the hospital because that was down the street but there were busy streets, so if you wanted to go to any restaurants it would probably be easier to drive. But there were Starbucks and other coffee places close enough by and a lot of restaurants and a library. And I could walk to the library. That was around the corner as well. And they often hold elections in that library, so that was very convenient. The other thing that was important was that about three or four blocks down was the post office. That was really nice if you needed to pick up packages or send letters.

PART IV: INTERVIEWS

Did you ever worry about crime?

There were some kids that, being normal teens, would stay out late at night and sometimes get little rowdy. But the police were out there and would stop and talk to them and call their parents. But there was never bad crime -- it was just kids being kids that needed to be home. Being that I had my daughter with me and I was single, it was particularly important to me.

Was there a grocery store nearby?

Oh yeah, there were several stores around. Kroger, Albertsons, there were several stores you had to choose from and then we had CVS and Walgreens that were close, too. It was a very convenient area.

Were there cultural and other activities?

One of the fun things that was close were salsa lessons that my husband and I took. Another thing is the Oak Creek Tennis Center. We got plugged into that and we played tennis about three to four times a week. We had two LA Fitness centers close by. The high school had plays so we would sometimes go to those. They had fliers that they would send out so you'd know what was going on in the community. There's a lot to do if you want to check it out. We went bowling once. There was always something to do.

What was your favorite thing about living there?

For somebody with young kids, it has great schools. They've got the park. It's a friendly area, people there are just really friendly. People walk in the neighborhood so you get to know your neighbors that way. I would also say it is a safe area. I lived somewhere else before this, and the move to Carrollton was like a breath of fresh air. You've got the mall close by, and the hospital is a big thing, too. It was Trinity Hospital and it's now Baylor hospital. And then of course with children needing to do homework and all, the library was so close by. They had computers, they had books, and they had videos you could check out.

What were your neighbors like in Carrollton?

There was totally a mix in the neighborhood I was in. There were people with young kids and then people like myself who were divorced. But culturally there was a mix. And people were watching out for you. My screen fell off once and people called to tell me. Or a couple times my dogs got out and people called me to tell me. Once when we had storms, one of the slats fell off my fence and people not only told me about it, they helped me put it back up.

Did you feel like you had a good quality of life?

Oh absolutely, yes, I really did. It just had a very good feel to it. People kept their yards up, they kept their houses up; all the homes were well kept there.

CHAPTER 34

RYAN JOHNSTON

LEWISVILLE

Tell me about how long you've lived in Lewisville and what brought you there originally?

My situation was that I retired from the Air Force and was living in Hawaii, and we relocated from Hawaii to the Dallas area in October of 2009. The purpose of the move was to get closer to some family that we have in the north Dallas/Fort Worth area.

What is Lewisville like?

What kind of drew us here, to our actual subdivision – called Castle Hill – was it was very close to some family. Lewisville does have a lake, lake Lewisville, and it's kind of north central to the whole Dallas/Fort Worth Metroplex, so that was another attractive feature in addition to being near the family and work.

Do you go into Dallas and Forth Worth a lot?

Yes, mostly Dallas. But we do go to Forth Worth about once a month, but mostly it's all in the Dallas area. In Dallas we definitely go for entertainment and shopping –that's what we do for the majority of our time there. For Fort Worth we have some family that we visit and there's a military base that I go to when I have some business there. But 99 percent of the time it's the Dallas area. All these cities out here are just suburbs that are intertwined and you don't really know when you've left one and gone into the other.

How is the traffic where you live?

That was another key feature to Castle Hill. It's probably five minutes from three major freeways. So being able to deal with the traffic made a big impact on our decision to relocate.

Are there opportunities for outdoors activities where you live?

In Lewisville, yeah, there is a lake, there are biking trails and hiking stuff within the vicinity and plenty of shopping and food to eat. There are sports and everything you want to do with your children; it's all close by. The pool system is pretty nice so we'll take advantage of that, also. We see a lot of joggers and walkers and stuff, and there's the big Lewisville Lake with lots of people walking around it.

Do you worry about crime?

No. And we did do a few quick searches for crime statistics for sex offenders and stuff like that, and we didn't have any concerns about crime or anything. The crime rate in the whole Lewisville area doesn't seem to be very high.

What would you tell someone who was considering moving to Lewisville?

The benefits would be the full proximity to three of the major freeways and tollways, and definitely all the shopping and entertainment all within probably 20 minutes of you. The housing communities –

there's several different ones out there but lots of good neighborhoods to choose from. School districts would be one of the positive things.

Is there anything you don't like about the area?

So far I haven't found anything that I don't like, not yet.

What are your neighbors like?

There's definitely a mix in our community. We have houses that range from the mid $200 thousands to $3 million, so you have a mix of all different income bases. I think it's pretty young as far as children are concerned. There are a lot of different parks and elementary schools and things like that so I think it's a pretty young family base. People are all very friendly who you come across.

Are you happy in Lewisville? Do you ever think about relocating to another town nearby?

I'm pretty happy where we are right now, and we had driven around a lot of the different neighborhoods and everyone talked about the city of Plano…but with the neighborhood we're in I'm very satisfied right now.

Are there a lot of business opportunities for people looking for jobs?

You know I have a friend that was looking to relocate down here and I think it's still going to be based on the individual skill set, but I definitely think there's a lot of opportunity here in terms of jobs. It depends on what they're looking for, but in the Dallas/Fort Worth area there's definitely a lot here. And I can't remember the numbers or specifics for the unemployment rate but I'm almost sure in Dallas the unemployment rate is pretty low for a city of this size.

Are there many cultural opportunities?

There are definitely lots of concerts, plays, any type of jazz and musical things in the parks. Entertainment-wise I think you have everything you could want. Definitely in the sports range you've got all the major sports here. They even have the leagues right underneath the professionals, like triple A baseball teams. Even on the high school level there's plenty of sports here. So if you're a sports fan you can't go wrong in this area. But the plays, the concerts, if that's what you like, there are plenty of them and they happen all the time.

Do you feel like you have a good quality of life?

Oh yeah, I definitely think, at least for me, the quality of life has increased with the cost of living going down from the high cost of living that I had in Hawaii. So I definitely think the Dallas area is an area where the cost of living is very reasonable

PART V

THE NEWCOMERS GUIDE TO THE PLANO AREA

CHAPTER 35

GETTING SETTLED

Welcome to Plano! You are now lucky enough to live in one of the best places in the country according CNN Money Magazine. Thousands before you have been drawn here by the region's climate, economy and attractions. Before you can establish roots in your new home, though, you'll need to take care of basics such as hooking up utilities, getting your car registered, and finding a doctor.

UTILITIES

Residents of Plano Texas and North Dallas have some choices to make when it comes to the basic utilities they use in their homes. While electricity and natural gas options are few, the number of companies offering local and long distance telephone service and Internet access has recently grown increasing the competition for customers and decreasing rates.

In Texas, the Public Utility Commission of Texas oversees telecommunications and electric utilities in the state. Contact the commission for general utility questions at 512-936-7000 or *www.puc.state.tx.us*. For complaints about utility services, you should first try to resolve the dispute with the company in question. If you are still not satisfied, contact the commission's Customer Protection Division at 888-

782-8477 or file a complaint online at *www.puc.state.tx.us/ocp/complaints/complain.cfm*.

The Texas Commission on Environmental Quality, 512-239-1000, *www.tceq.state.tx.us/index.html* oversees water utilities in Texas. The Railroad Commission of Texas, 877-228-5740, *www.rrc.state.tx.us/*, oversees natural gas utilities in the state.

Electricity

Unless you are renting a home where utilities are included, your first step will likely be to call the electric company.

Oncor Electric Delivery Group, 888.313.6862, *www.oncor.com* and CoServ Electric/Gas, 800-274-4014, *www.coserv.com* are the electric utility companies that operate in Plano. Your company is determined by your geographical location, so check with your Realtor to find out who to call.

Natural Gas

If your home uses natural gas for heating, cooling or to operate a gas range or other appliances, you will need to contact Atmos Energy, 888-286-6700, *www.atmosenergy.com* to set up service. CoServ Gas, 800-274-4014, *www.coserv.com* is another option for natural gas.

TELEPHONE

There are several companies that provide local telephone service to the City of Plano and other Northern Dallas homes and the three main telephone providers are listed below.

- AT&T, 800-422-0499, *www.att.com*
- Time Warner Cable, 972-742-5892, *www.yourtwc.com*
- Verizon Southwest, 800-837-4966, *www22.verizon.com*

PART V: THE NEWCOMERS GUIDE TO THE PLANO AREA

Area Code

The area code for Plano Texas is 972. Other area codes for the surrounding Northern Dallas cities and towns are 469 and 214.

Cell Phones

Both AT&T and Verizon, listed above under "telephone," offer cell phone service. In addition, here are some of the many companies that offer wireless service and phones.

- Verizon Wireless, 1-800-922-0204, *www.VerizonWireless.com*
- Sprint, 888-211-4727 , *www.sprint.com*
- T-Mobile, 800-T-MOBILE, *www.t-mobile.com*
- VirginMobile, 888-322-1122, *www.virginmobileusa.com*
- Boost Mobile, 866-402-7366, *www.boostmobile.com*
- Metro PCS, 888-8metro8, *www.metropcs.com*

Cell phone service will start at about $30 a month for a single phone and the prices will go up from there as you add services, phones and minutes. A family plan with two phones and 200 minutes will run about $60 a month with most companies. This is an increasingly popular option, as some families choose to give up their home phone in favor of using cell phones. Many companies offer free or low-price phones when you sign up for their service.

Another increasingly popular option for people who don't use their cell phones much is the pay-as-you-go plan. Under these plans, you pay about $20 for 200 minutes. Usually you have to add minutes to the phone every month in order for the minutes to roll over, or every three months to keep the same phone number. Virgin Mobile has a variety of pay-as-you-go options, as does AT&T and smaller companies such as Boost Mobile and Metro PCS.

INTERNET

There are a number of major and smaller internet service providers in the North Dallas area. Below is a list of businesses to choose from to meet your needs.

- Clear, 877-513-7921, *www.clearwirelessinternet.com*
- AT&T, 800-288-2020, *www.att.com*
- Texas Comcast Internet, 888-375-4888, *www.comcastspecial.com*
- Verizon, 888-625-8111, *www22.verizon.com*
- Earthlink, 800-EARTHLINK, *www.earthlink.net*

WATER AND SEWER

The City of Plano, 972-941-7105, purchases its water from the North Texas Municipal Water District (NTMWD), *www.ntmwd.com* which also serves Murphy, Sachse, Wylie, Fairview, Parker, Lucas, and Rowlett. The cities of Highland Village and Corinth operate their own water and sewer systems.

Water restrictions are common throughout North Dallas in times of drought, usually limiting outdoor watering to evenings and mornings on certain days of the week. In the summer of 2007, the North Texas Municipal Water District (NTMWD) lifted Stage three restrictions of their Water Conservation and Drought Contingency Plan to member cities. Late spring rains that continued into the summer brought relief from nearly two years of drought conditions across the area. Check with your town government to get a list of its water restrictions.

GARBAGE AND RECYCLING

The City of Plano picks up garbage one day each week and recyclable items every other week from homes throughout the city. The city's Environmental Services Division, 972-769-4150, *www.plano.gov*, issues either a 95 or 68 gallon roll-out cart for garbage and recycling. The department also offers a monthly bulky waste pick-up for larger items such as furniture, building materials and appliances that don't fit in the carts provided. Bulky waste pick up can also be arranged for a fee. Additionally, the city picks up yard waste, which is used to make Texas Pure compost, topdressing, soil blend or wood mulch that is for sale to the general public.

The towns of Murphy, Sachse, Wylie, Fairview, Parker, Lucas, Rowlett, Highland Village, Corinth run their own solid waste departments. A complete list of refuse collection services and convenience centers throughout North Dallas, as well as a listing of where various materials should be disposed of, is available from Collin County at *www.co.collin.tx.us/public_works/trash_collection.jsp*, Dallas County at *www.dallascounty.org/department/plandev/hhw_intro.htm* , and Denton County at *www.cityofdenton.com*.

DRIVING IN TEXAS

Getting a license and registering your car seems to require a new sheet of paper every few years, and has almost always required a bit of waiting in line. But you might want to make it a priority to get yourself and your car set up for Texas soon after you arrive. You can be ticketed for having an out-of-state license or registration after you've been in Texas more than three months. To drive legally, you will also need to buy insurance.

Driver's Licenses, State IDs, and Automobile Registration

Getting set up to drive will mean spending some quality time at the TX Department of Motor Vehicles, 888-DMVGOTX (368-4689), *www.txdmv.gov*. You can find a DMV office or see a full list of the types of identification that are accepted to get a driver's license or register a car at the DMV website. To save some time, you can also download the forms you will need so that you can fill them out before you get to the office.

Driver's Licenses and State IDs

To get a Texas license, you will have to prove your residency, age, identity and U.S. citizenship or legal residency through a combination of documents. Most commonly, applicants bring a license from another state, a social security card and a utility bill showing a Texas address. If you don't have another license yet, a birth certificate may serve as your identification.

The same documents are required to obtain a state ID card, which works only for identification purposes and does not make you eligible to drive a car. A social security card or other proof of legal residency in the United States is now required to get a driver's license or state ID. You will also have to prove that your car is insured.

Drivers as young as 15 who have taken a driver's education course are eligible for a learner's permit, though anyone younger than 18 is considered a provisional driver and is subject to certain restrictions. Young drivers go through tiered rules that become less strict the longer they drive without any violations.

Original licenses are issued for a period of two to six years, and cost $24. Learner's permits are issued to new drivers at a cost of $5 and expire a year after your next birthday. ID cards cost $5 for people 60 years old and over and $15 for everyone under sixty. All applicants for driver's licenses will have to pass a vision screening and a written test covering road signs and driving knowledge. First-time applicants will also have to pass a road test. A driver's handbook is available in English and Spanish at the DMV website and all offices.

Automobile Registration

New residents need to register their vehicle(s) in person at a county tax office or approved substation. The registration fee is due at this time. To register your car, you will need to have proof of current liability insurance, a Texas driver's license or ID card. Active duty members of the U.S. Armed Forces and non-resident, full-time students attending a Texas college or university are not required to register their vehicles in Texas. To use an out-of-state license, you'll need documentation showing that you are in the military, a student or one of a few other exceptions that can be found on the website or by calling the DMV. For more information and county tax office locations please visit *www.co.collin.tx.us/tax_assessor/vehicles/vehicles.jsp* or *www.txdmv.gov/vehicles/registration/register.htm*.

Automobile Insurance

All cars registered in Texas must carry liability insurance in the amount of $20,000 for medical expenses incurred by a single individual, $40,000 for the combined medical expenses of all of the occupants of the vehicle at the time of an accident as well as $15,000 in property damage coverage.

Violations, Towing and Theft

Tickets for parking violations are given out by the Dallas Parking Management/ Enforcement office, 214-670-5946, *www.dallascityhall.com/pwt/parking_faq.html*. You can find information on reporting parking violations, getting no parking signs for your neighborhood or even pay or contest your ticket online.

If your car is towed and you have outstanding tickets, call the auto pound at 214-670-5116.

If you suspect your car has been stolen or broken into, call 911 immediately.

BROADCAST AND PRINT MEDIA

Television

Most households can expect to get all the major networks without an antenna. With the purchase of an antenna from an electronics store, a household can receive up to 20 stations. For access to the hundreds of stations available these days, you'll have to purchase cable or satellite service.

Cable access:
- AT&T U-verse, 800-288-2020, *www.uverse1.att.com/launchAMSS.do*
- Time Warner Cable, 972-742-5892, *www.timewarnercable.com*
- Verizon FIOS, 888-591-6076, *www22.verizon.com/*

Satellite service is the other way to buy access to more channels. Those companies include:
- Direct TV, 919-233-0675, *www.directv.com*
- Dish Network, 919-341-1161, *www.dishnetwork.com*

North Dallas Television Stations
- KDFW (FOX Affiliate) Channel 4; *www.myfoxdfw.com*
- KTVT (CBS affiliate) Channel 11; *www.cbstv.com*
- KXAS-TV (NBC affiliate) Channel 5; *www.nbcdfw.com*
- WFAA-TV (ABC affiliate) Channel 8; *www.wfaa.com*

Radio

North Dallas radio listeners can access a wide variety of local and national programming through stations based in Plano and beyond.
- KATH 910 AM, Frisco, 888-764-3476, Religious

- KMKI 620 AM, Plano, 877-870-5678, Children's
- KESS 107.9 FM, Lewisville, 214-787-1079, Spanish
- KESN 1037.3 FM, Allen, 888-549-9116, Sports
- KHKS 106.1 FM, Denton, 214-866-8000, Top-40
- KPMZ 96.7 FM, Flower Mound, 817-695-3500 ,Oldies
- KFZO, 99.1 FM Denton, 214-525-0400, Spanish
- KWRD 100.7 FM Highland Village, 214-561-9673, Religious
- KBFB 97.9 FM, Dallas, Hip Hop
- KNON 89.3 FM, Dallas, 214-828-9500, Variety
- KERA 90.1 FM, Dallas, 972-263-3151, Public Radio

Newspapers and Magazines

The city of Plano and the surrounding North Dallas area has several newspapers and magazines for anyone seeking local and statewide information. In addition to print, Plano has an informational site at *www.planochamber.org.* Some Newspapers and Magazines in North Dallas are:

- The Plano Star Courier, 972-398-4200, *www.planostar.com*
- Inside Collin County Business, 972-612-2425, *www.ccbusinesspress.com*
- The Denton Record-Chronicle, 940-387-3811, *www.dentonrc.com*
- Dallas Morning News, 214-977-8222, *www.dallasnews.com*

Spanish Language Newspapers

- Al Dia, 866-933-1313, *www.aldiatx.com/*
- El Extra, 214-309-0990, *www.elextranewspaper.com*
- El Heraldo News, 214-827-8200, *www.elheraldonews.com*
- El Hispano News, 214- 357-2186, *www.elhispanonews.com*
- La Semana, 817-704-3270, *www.lasemanatx.com*

Local Magazines

- Plano Profile, 972-769-7272, *www.planoprofile.com/planoprofile/*
- D Magazine, 214-939-3636, *www.dmagazine.com*
- ON Magazine, 972-596-8686, *www.onmagazine.net*
- Addison Magazine, 214-696-9525, *www.addisonmagazine.com*
- North Texas Kids, 972-516-9070, *www.northtexaskids.com/php/index.php*
- Living Magazine, 972-882-1300, *www.livingmagazine.net*
- Texas Monthly, 800-759-2000, *www.texasmonthly.com*
- Brides of North Texas, 214.347.9470, *www.bridesofnorthtexas.com*

Blogs

A number of blogs (that's Web logs to the uninitiated) are cropping up where people discuss all kinds of local issues. These tend to come and go pretty quickly, but here is a sampling of what's available at the moment:

- Dallas News, *www.planoblog.dallasnews.com*
- Plano Homes and Land, *www.planohomesandland.com/west-plano-blog*
- A Capitol Blog, *www.acapitolblog.com/*
- Texas Monthly Blogs, *www.texasmonthly.com/blogs/*

OFFICIAL DOCUMENTS

Voter Registration

To vote in Texas, you must be registered. To do so, simply pick up a Voter Registration application, fill it out and mail it at least 30 days before the election date. You don't even need a stamp. Texas enables residents to vote in days and weeks before an election to make the voting process more convenient and accessible. There are two ways to vote early: by showing up in person during the prescribed early voting period or by voting by mail.

The Texas Board of Elections, 1-800-252-8683, *www.sos.state.tx.us/elections/index.shtml*, is the place to find all the information you need about elections, including polling and one-stop voting places, upcoming election dates and sample ballots.

Library Cards

Plano operates 6 libraries throughout the county. Most offer computer access, children's activities such as weekly story times, classes for adults, and other activities. A full list of libraries and the activities they offer are available at 972-769-4208, *www.plano.gov/Departments/Libraries/Pages/GeneralInformation.aspx*.

You can apply for a library card at any library, and the card is good for all Plano library locations. There are several different types of cards available. Any resident is eligible to register for a library card providing he/she can verify a current local address. If children are under 18 years of age, a parent or legal guardian must sign their application and agree to take responsibility for all materials borrowed on the card. Visitor cards will be issued for library privileges requested by patrons age 18 and over who reside outside the library's service area and who are temporarily living and working in Plano. Visitor's cards are valid for six months only. Temporary internet cards will be issued to people who only want internet access and are only valid for one business day.

Interlibrary loan is a service provided to obtain materials which are not owned by Plano Public Library System (PPLS). The system also offers other special services which include ask a librarian, books by mail, computer printouts, copy machines, equipment for visually impaired, holds, income tax forms, microfilm/fiche readers and printers, microsoft office suite, online database services, reference and used magazine and book sales.

Passports

"Think ahead" should perhaps be your mantra these days when you're preparing for international travel. With the process for obtaining a U.S. passport getting ever stricter, you will need to allow at least 6 weeks to get a passport, and at least three weeks if you pay an extra $60, plus shipping, to expedite service.

The U.S. State Department, 877-4-USA-PASSPORT, *www.travel. state.gov/passport*, issues passports from its 15 regional offices. The closest office to Plano is in Dallas, TX but you can also apply in person at some area post offices. Forms are available at these locations and at the passport Website:

- Collin County District Clerk, 900 E. Park Plano, 972-881-3090
- Plano Coit Station 3400 Coit Road, Plano, 972-599-9631
- Plano Northwest Station, 3905 Hedgecoxe Road, Plano, 972-377-3166
- Plano Wildcat Station, 2901 W. Parker Road, Plano, 972-769-8804
- Rowlett Post Office, 3416 Enterprise Drive, 972-475-4473
- Dallas County (East) District Clerk, 3443 St Francis,214-321-3183
- Dallas County (North) District Clerk, 10056 Marsh Lane Ste 137, 214-904-3030
- Dallas County District Clerk, 600 Commerce, 214-653-7691
- Dallas Main Post Office, Finance Unit 401 Tom Landry Hwy, 214-760-4555
- DFW Airport Mail Center, 2300 W 32nd St., 972-453-3372
- Joe Pool Station, 5521 S. Hampton Rd, Dallas, 214-467-1004
- Northwest Station, 2341 W Northwest Hwy., Dallas, 214-357-8649
- Oaklawn Station, 2825 Oak Lawn Avenue, Dallas, 214-521-9648

- Richland Postal Station, 9130 Markville Drive, Dallas, 972-690-0216
- Spring Valley Post Office, 13770 Noel Road, Dallas, 972-386-3440

You must apply in person if you are applying for the first time, are under 16 (or were when your current passport was issued), lost your passport or suspect it was stolen, or your name has changed. Otherwise, you may send the forms and documents by mail. Generally you will need to provide a birth certificate and picture ID for a new passport, as well as two passport photos. Contact the passport office for alternative forms of ID if you don't have these handy.

PETS

Your dog, cat, or more exotic pet will likely find North Dallas as hospitable a home as you do, as long as your landlord or neighbors are welcoming. You'll also want to know the ropes to keep your pet legal or safe in its new home. Keep in mind that for truly unusual pets, you might want to check with the local animal control to see if any specific laws pertain to your out-of-the-ordinary friend.

Licensing and Pet Laws

Dogs, cats and ferrets must be registered with the City of Plano Animal Services Division as required by City Ordinance. The cost is $10 each for spayed or neutered animals and $30 for non-spayed/neutered animals. Call 972-769-4360 or visit *www.plano.gov/Animal/Services/Pages/registration.aspx* for more information on the tags.

The city's leash law prohibits dogs and cats from roaming unattended within the city limits, though this law is rarely enforced unless there is a specific complaint.

Local laws mandate that pets receive adequate food, water and shelter. Pet owners are also required by "pooper scooper' laws to clean up after their dogs and cats.

Spay/Neuter and Rabies

Low-cost spay/neuter services are available through the Denton Low Cost Pet Sterilization and Vaccination Program, 940-566-5551, *www.texasforthem.org*. Low cost rabies and vaccination are offered at the Plano Animal Shelter, 972-769-4360, *www.planotx.org/animal*.

Acquiring a Pet

There are no shortage of rescue groups and shelters where cats, dogs, or even rabbits and birds await new owners. Even pure-bred dogs are available, largely through rescue groups who focus on particular breeds. Most will charge an adoption fee that also covers vaccinations and spaying or neutering. A good place to start any pet search is with these local shelters, where knowledgeable staff can find your pet of choice or point you to another source:

- Second Chance SPCA of Plano, Texas, 972-424-0077, *www.scspca.org*
- Collin County Animal Services, 972-547-7292, *www.co.collin.tx.us/animal_services/index.jsp*
- The Humane Society of Dallas County, 214-350-7387, *www.petfinder.com/shelters/TX72.html*

Pet Recreation

Plano only has one area where pets can legally be off leash. The Plano Dog Park is a fenced two acre area in Jack Carter Park. All owners must have proof of a current rabies vaccination and residents must have a City License.

Plano and the surrounding towns run several parks where dogs can roam free for a spell without running afoul of local leash laws.

- Dog Park at Jack Carter Park, 6199 Pleasant Valley Dr, Plano, 972-941-BARK
- Unleashed Indoor Dog Park, 5151 Samuell Blvd., Dallas, 214-388-0701, *www.unleashedindoordogpark.com*
- White Rock Lake Dog Park, 8000 Mockingbird Lane, Dallas, 214-670-5656, *www.whiterockdogpark.com*
- Wagging Tail Dog Park, 5841 Keller Springs Road, Dallas, 214-670-1589, *www.waggingtaildogpark.org/home.html*

CRIME AND SAFETY

Plano consistently has one of the lowest crime rates in Texas for cities of its size. Serving more than 260,200 citizens, the Plano Police Department is nationally known for its highly trained officers and is the largest law enforcement agency in the northern Dallas metropolitan area.

The Plano Police Department classifies and reports crime statistics according to the FBI Uniform Crime Report. Each month a report is prepared and submitted to the FBI, through the Texas Department of Public Safety, that reports offenses known to the Plano Police Department.

Information regarding crime in Texas can be found at the Texas Department of Public Safety website at: *www.txdps.state.tx.us/*.

Should you need to contact law enforcement, the Plano Police department uses only one number: 911. For non-emergencies here is contact information for the Plano Police department:

- Plano Police Department, 909 East 14th Street, 972-424-5678, *www.plano.gov/Departments/Police/Pages/default.aspx*
- Murphy Police, 972-468-4200, *www.murphytx.org/policedepartment/policeindex.asp*
- Sachse Police, 972-495-2271, *www.cityofsachse.com/police/default.asp*

- Wylie Police, 972-442-8170, *www.ci.wylie.tx.us*
- Fairview Police, 972-547-5350, *www.fairviewtexas.org*
- Parker Police, 972-442-6999
- Collin County Sheriff, 972-547-5100, *www.co.collin.tx.us/sheriff/*
- Rowlett Police, 972-412-6200, *www.ci.rowlett.tx.us*
- Highland Village Police, 972-317-6551, *www.highlandvillage.org*
- Corinth Police, 940-498-2017, *www.cityofcorinth.com*

CHAPTER 36

THE JOB MARKET

Plano and the Dallas-Fort Worth area have consistently ranked as one of the best places to move and build personal wealth. When it comes to the "work" aspect of that equation, Plano is the biggest and one of the oldest "Relovilles" in the country, according to Forbes. Once a booming site for young transferring workers, the city has slowed down in that respect and now also appeals more to those who may be ready to retire instead of the younger set who might be looking for land and new housing. Still, in terms of the economic recession, Relovilles such as Plano have fared better than other parts of the United States.

Plano's economic base is substantial; the city is home to multiple Fortune 500 companies, offices of global corporations, and more than 10,000 other businesses. An affordable housing market and top-notch schools have drawn some of the country's most talented, educated workers to the area, and businesses have followed to be near a strong employee base. In fact, in Plano there are more than 300,000 workers in a 30-mile radius.

But Plano isn't just a place for the biggest business giants. Several other business professionals have started turning their vision into reality in Plano. In 2008, five of them were recognized by The CEO Institute and the Southern Methodist University Cox School of Business Caruth

Institute. Some of the up-and-comers include Genband, Aspire HR, and Texas Advanced Opteoelectronic Solutions.

While Plano's diverse corporations and economic conditions make for an overall stable and strong job market, that's not to say it's a job seeker's paradise either. No region is truly recession proof, and though Plano has fared better than many comparable metropolitan areas, it's best for each potential job seeker to get the lay of the land and evaluate opportunities relative to their strengths, experience, and professional aspirations. Below is a collection of statistics and figures to help you become familiar with the opportunities that Plano may offer.

WHAT JOBS ARE OUT THERE

In July 2009, Forbes.com named Plano No. 25 on its list of "America's 25 Best Places To Move." Certain amenities, including a major airport nearby in Dallas-Fort Worth, and a large number of global employers helped Plano secure its place on this list.

Plano has the benefit of being located in a state that's quite conducive to promoting businesses. In 2009, the state topped the list of Fortune 500 and 1000 companies, reporting that 64 Fortune 500 businesses headquartered their operations in the state, along with 118 Fortune 1000 businesses. Additionally, the Small Business and Entrepreneurial Council ranked Texas in the top three states for small business and entrepreneurship on its Small Business Survival Index 2009: Ranking the Policy Environment for Entrepreneurship Across the Nation. Factors considered in the index include regulatory costs, property rights, and health care and energy costs.

Depending on your skill set, a wide range of career opportunities exist in Plano, including positions in health care, technology and several other professional services. What follows are a series of graphs highlighting the most popular industries and occupations in Plano.

As you look through the data, don't forget the occupations and industries included are only a small representation of Plano's overall job market. If you prefer to evaluate job opportunities by employer, data showing what percentage of the workforce is employed by a particular industry follows.

Employment by Occupation in Plano, 2000 Census Data

- Management, professional, technical occupations (55.5%)
- Service occupations (8.0%)
- Sales and office occupations (27.3%)
- Farming, fishing, forestry occupations (0.0%)
- Construction, maintenance, production, transportation occupations (9.1%)

Employment by Occupation in Plano, 2005 American Community Survey

- Management, professional, technical occupations (51.9%)
- Service occupations (8.1%)
- Sales and office occupations (30.4%)
- Farming, fishing, forestry occupations (0.0%)
- Construction, maintenance, production, transportation occupations (9.6%)

Top Industry Clusters

- Headquarters Regional Offices
- Financial Services
- Electronics
- Telecommunications
- Software/IT

- Health, Medical, and Bio Science
- Digital Media
- Energy
- Professional and Business Service
- International
- Manufacturing

WHERE TO FIND JOBS

Plano has plentiful opportunity for professionals in an array of fields. Helping the city live up to its "best place" rankings is Legacy business park. Created by Ross Perot, this 2,665-acre campus serves as the home to such companies as JCPenny, Frito-Lay, Rent-A-Center, AT&T Wireless and others. Nearly 50,000 people live and work here, and there's still space for more businesses to establish themselves. Legacy's location in the "Platinum Corridor" and proximity to the Dallas-Fort Worth International and Love Field airports and downtown Dallas make the space an ideal place to do business.

Large companies aren't the only ones who have found a home in Legacy. The new Legacy Town Center has become a nationally recognized urban town center within the park. Apartments and town homes offer people places to live and the Center sports a range of shops, restaurants and even a hotel.

PLANO'S LARGEST EMPLOYERS

A number of corporate powerhouses have established roots in Plano. Thanks in part to its proximity to other major areas such as Dallas/Fort Worth and Plano's lower cost of living compared to other metropolitan areas, a considerable list of worldwide business giants have set up shop in Plano, and they've brought jobs with them. Below is a selection of the area's largest employers.

- **J.C. Penny, Inc.**, 6501 Legacy Drive, Plano, (972) 431-1000, *www.jcpenny.net*, is a leading retailer in the country which has chosen to headquarter its operations in Plano. The corporate office occupies a 125-acre space equipped with many amenities, including childcare and a medical facility. To learn more about potential career opportunities, visit *www.jcpenney.net/careers/ n3_home_office/default.aspx.*
- **Electronic Data Systems**, 5400 Legacy Drive, Plano, (800) 566-9337, *h10134.www1.hp.com*, is now known as HP Enterprise Services. Headquartered in Plano, HP employs more than 50,000 workers around the country. The company focuses on IT, applications and business process services and IT transformation services. For more information on potential employment opportunities, visit *h10055.www1.hp.com/jobsathp/.*
- **Perot Systems Corporation**, 2300 West Plano Parkway, Plano, (888) 317-3768, *www.perotsystems.com*, announced that it would be acquired by Dell in 2009. Founded by Ross Perot, the company employs workers around the globe. As of the writing of this book, the two companies maintained separate recruiting websites. For more information on potential employment opportunities, *visit www.perotsystems.com/Careers/.*
- **Frito-Lay**, P.O. Box 660634, Dallas, (800) 352-4477, *www.fritolay.com*, is another large source of work for Plano. The popular snack food company has hired more than 45,000 workers in the United States and Canada. For more information on potential employment opportunities, visit *www.fritolay.com/about-us/careers.html.*
- **Medical Center of Plano**, 3901 West 15th Street, Plano, (972) 596-6800, *www.themedicalcenterofplano.com*, first opened in 1975. Over the years, the facility has grown to provide work for more than 900 physicians and more than 1,300 employees. For more information on potential employment opportunities and

online application procedures, visit
www.themedicalcenterofplano.com/eRecruit.asp.

- **Texas Health Presbyterian Hospital**, 6200 West Parker Road, Plano, (972) 981-8000, *www.texashealth.org*, is one of the largest health care systems in Texas. Named as one of the Best Employers for Healthy Lifestyles in 2009, Presbyterian Hospital has almost 1,300 physicians and 1,200 employees. For more information on potential employment opportunities, visit *www.texashealth.org/body_subsite.cfm?id=2288*.

FURTHER JOB OPPORTUNITIES

Although the employee statistics for Plano's largest employers are indeed impressive, it's important not to forget other not-so-little companies with operations in the city as well. Those entities include:

- **Dr Pepper Snapple Group, Inc.**, 5301 Legacy Drive, Plano, 972-673-7000, *www.drpeppersnapplegroup.com*; markets, bottles and distributes beverages; employs approximately 20,000 people in the United States, Mexico and Canada
- **CIGNA Healthcare of Texas**, 1640 Dallas Parkway, Plano, 972-863-4300, *www.cigna.com*; provides health insurance; employs more than 1,000 workers
- **Ericsson Components Inc.**, 6300 Legacy Drive, Plano, 972-583-0000, *www.ericsson.com*; provides telecommunications services; employs 82,500 people worldwide
- **Texas Instruments**, 12500 TI Boulevard, Dallas, 972-995-2011, *www.ti.com*; develops digital signal processing, analog, and semiconductor technologies; employed 26,300 workers, including 10,000 in Texas, as of 2009
- **Baylor Regional Medical Center at Plano**, 4700 Alliance Blvd., Plano, 469-814-2000, *www.baylorhealth.com*; health care provider; Baylor Health Care System employs more than 15,000 workers

- **Dallas Morning News**, 508 Young St., Dallas, 214-977-8222, *www.dallasnews.com*; area newspaper; employs 515 workers
- **Safety-Kleen**, 5360 Legacy Drive, Building 2 Suite 100, Plano, 800-669-5740, *www.safety-kleen.com*; offers green waste management solutions for businesses; employs 400 workers

PLANO BY THE NUMBERS

When Forbes.com ranks its "Best Places To Move," several indicators are factored into the rankings: the number of people born outside the state who moved a "considerable distance" to a town within one to five years, and who moved for work. This information was considered more heavily than other data, including population growth, family incomes, cost of housing, and the nearness of "multinational companies."

Setting all accolades like "Best Place to Move" aside, it's only reasonable for potential job seekers to ask: How does Plano fare in terms of these indicators? And the answer is: Quite well.

MEDIAN HOUSEHOLD INCOME

In 2008, Collin County had one of the highest median household incomes in the entire state, "out earning" the state average by more than $31,000 dollars. Moreover, the median household income for Collin County also outpaced the U.S. average by nearly $30,000. Plano topped a recent Census survey of wealthiest U.S. cities with populations of at least 250,000, and ranked in the top 10 for Texas cities with a population of at least 65,000.

But what do stats like the median household income mean when it comes to things like the "Best Cities for Jobs" ranking? Median household incomes are calculated by adding the income received during a calendar year by all of a household's members (15 years old and over) and then finding the average of that figure across a particular region. This figure is considered to be a general indicator of economic well being of households in that particular region. As a result, through an expert's eye, Plano's households as a whole are likely faring much better than some of their state counterparts.

Region Median Household Income, 2008

United States $52,029
Texas $50,049
Collin County $81,875

Dallas County

(Dallas, TX) $47,155

Denton County

(Denton, TX) $73,678

Source: www.ers.usda.gov/Data/Unemployment/

Wealthiest Cities in 2008, population of at least 250,000

Plano, TX $84,492
San Jose, CA $76,963
Anchorage, AK $68,726
San Francisco, CA $68,023
San Diego, CA $61,863

Wealthiest Texas Cities in 2008, population of at least 65,000

Flower Mound $105,812
The Woodlands $94,626
Frisco $93,478
Allen $93,392
Sugar Land $92,719
Plano $84,492

* High-dollar communities that fell below population requirements were not included.

Source: www.dallasnews.com/sharedcontent/dws/dn/latestnews/stories/ 090908dnmetplanowealth.19e52ac.html

UNEMPLOYMENT RATE

Since the economic fallout in 2008, Plano's job market has weathered the storm fairly well. In the face of a volatile economy, Collin County's employment growth measured 1% in the third quarter of 2008, and dropped to -1.4% by the third quarter of 2009. In 2007 and 2008 unemployment for Collin County stood at 3.9% and 4.6%, respectively, while the national unemployment rate was 5.8% in 2008.

Even with this seemingly inevitable downturn, Plano's unemployment rates still fall below the national average (9.4% in May 2009 and 9.5% in June 2009), demonstrating Plano's economic resilience.

COST OF LIVING

The low cost of living in Plano is one of the city's best attributes. The proximity to the Dallas area offers the city many wonderful lifestyle perks, with the additional benefits of reasonably priced housing and a homestead exemption that contributes to lower property taxes.

According to statistics from the Plano Economic Development Board/Money Magazine's Best Places to Live 2008, housing costs in Plano are below average for many other cities compared in that year. The Center for Housing Policy ranked the Dallas area 110th in terms of the country's most expensive housing markets for that year. The region finished 71st with regard to the most expensive home rentals. When comparing Plano to many other parts of the country, however, it's easier to see the cost-of-living advantages Plano offers.

Median Home Price 2008
City Compared to National Average

- Plano, TX $232,750
- Phoenix, AZ $235,000
- Chandler, AZ $270,000
- Atlanta, GA $170,000
- Denver, CO $213,500
- Seattle, WA $410,000
- Orlando, FL $230,000
- Boston, MA $365,000
- St. Louis, MO $93,000
- Wayne, NJ $470,000

Source: www.planotexas.org/media/docs/City%20Comparisons-Housing.xls

A number of other organizations have produced similar cost-of-living figures. The ACCRA Cost of Living Index takes into account the variances in the cost of consumer goods and services for each region and is considered one of the dependable stats on cost of living in U.S.

metropolitan areas. According to the ACCRA, the Plano's composite cost-of-living index is 94.1 (National cost of living = 100), which is considered relatively low for the U.S.

City Cost of Living Index

- Plano, TX 94.1
- Dallas, TX 92.1
- Fort Worth, TX 89.2
- Houston, TX 90.7
- Denver, CO 105.0
- St. Louis, MO 90.7
- Chicago, IL 112.5
- San Diego, CA 136.4
- Miami, FL 116.6

*Source: www.planotexas.org/media/docs/
ACCRA%20Cost%20of%20Living%20Index.xls*

Regardless of which data is used, the bottom-line is the same: When compared to other large metropolitan areas in the United States, Plano's cost-of-living advantage is fairly competitive.

Combine this cost of living with the other advantages Plano has to offer, and it creates an area that bodes well for a wide range of people and lifestyles. This combination of factors helps explain why the city was listed by *Money Magazine* on its "Best Places to Live," and as a "Best Place to Build Wealth" at Salary.com.

Affordability also plays a key role in where businesses decide to set up headquarters and satellite offices, and Plano's affordability makes it an appealing city in which to do business.

HOW TO LOOK FOR JOBS

Now that you've read about what kind of jobs are out there and what companies are likely to offer those jobs, a more important question remains: How do you find those jobs? With the pervasiveness of the Internet, "hitting the pavement" has been replaced by "hitting the search engines."

Nearly every major corporation these days posts job openings on their corporate Websites. Others may choose to use online job-posting sites such as CareerBuilder.com or Monster.com to get the word out about open positions. A lot of job-hunting footwork can actually be done by your fingers. Here are some of the best resources for sniffing out job openings in and around Plano:

- **Corporate Websites** are some of the best resources for job posting, especially if you have a particular company in mind for which you would like to work. Employment opportunities are usually posted under the human resources sections of companies Websites. Some companies only advertise job openings on their Website so it's a good idea to regularly check company sites to see if anything has opened up.
- **CareerBuilder**, *www.careerbuilder.com*, is one of the largest online job-posting sites available today. According to CareerBuilder, more than 300,000 employers post more than 1 million jobs on the Website. Job seekers can browse job openings for free and can even post their resumes for recruiters to review.
- **Monster**, *www.monster.com*, is another popular online job-posting site. Since its launch in 1994, Monster has become well known as a go-to place for potential job opportunities. Like CareerBuilder, job seekers can search the site for free and post their resumes for potential employers to review.
- **Simply Hired**, *www.simplyhired.com*, makes job search easy by dividing work opportunities by categories like "Teaching," "Biotech/Science," or "Architecture/Engineering." Job seekers

can also perform searches by skill level or company. The website has been widely recognized as a valuable search tool in the job market.

- **Indeed.com**, *www.indeed.com*, is a great resource if you're not too keen on searching through dozens of job postings on CareerBuilder or Monster. Indeed.com is essentially a search engine that pulls information down from job-posting sites and puts them into one free, searchable database. Indeed.com doesn't always catch every post, but it can be a great time saver if you're in a time crunch.
- **WorkInTexas.com**, *www.twc.state.tx.us/jobs/job.html*, is a more localized approach to searching for work in Texas. The Texas Workforce Commission, supported by 28 local workforce boards, can aid Texas job seekers in their search for employment and also provide career development information.
- **Plano Star-Courier**, *www.planostar.com/plano_star-courier/news/*, an area paper, also provides a link to a job network aimed at helping job seekers secure work in this region of the state.

CHAPTER 37

CHILDCARE AND EDUCATION

For families with children, one of the highest priorities when moving to a new city is finding quality childcare and quality schools. The task can be a daunting one when moving to the North Dallas area, which is one of the most highly populated regions in Texas. Like many other quickly growing areas, there are hundreds of childcare options and a large number of public schools and private schools from which to choose.

Childcare and education options can significantly influence where you and your family purchase your home, especially if you're choosing to enroll your children in a public school, where location determines which school your child will attend. As such, it's advisable to begin researching childcare and education options as early as possible. Below is a collection of resources that can be valuable in your research. They include a number of local and national agencies and other Websites that provide tips and suggestions, maintain comprehensive directories, and/or operate helpful hotlines in addition to other services.

Please note that the inclusion and/or mention of businesses, schools, agencies, and other service providers in this chapter are not an endorsement of any kind. To ensure your child receives the best care and/or education, never underestimate the value of thoroughly researching childcare centers, agencies, and schools.

CHILDCARE

When it comes to childcare in Plano and the surrounding areas, families are not without their options, and more often than not, it's not finding quality childcare that's the issue, but rather it's narrowing down the options and then picking the "right" option that can be tricky and overwhelming.

Luckily, there are some great resources available to families new to the area that can help bring the daunting task down to a more manageable level. Many Plano-area childcare centers have a considerable Web presence, which can be a great help in comparing providers. The Texas Department of Family and Protective Services (DFPS), 701 W. 51st Street Austin, Texas, 78751, 512-438-4800, *www.dfps.state.tx.us,* also provides a searchable database of childcare centers in the state (*www.txchildcaresearch.org*) as well as advice on researching and selecting a provider for your family.

DAYCARE

Whether you're considering a family daycare home, a childcare center, or a church-organized daycare, there are numerous options in and around Plano and the North Dallas area in general. For a comprehensive list of businesses offering childcare services, look under "Child Care Services" and "Day Care Centers & Nurseries" in the Yellow Pages.

The Child Care Source, *www.thechildcaresource.com,* a commercially owned publication and website, provides a comprehensive look at childcare options in Texas, including in the Plano area. In addition to general advice on selecting the best childcare provider for your family, the site includes a Zip code-based search option that allows users to look up licensed daycares, nannies and babysitters as well as other local resources and activities. I have also utilitized the services of a great group *www.seekingsitters.com* which offers babysitting services across the Metroplex at affordable rates.

WHAT'S HERE

The North Dallas area offers a number of different types of daycare options ranging from small-group environments to preschools to more typical childcare centers. The DFPS classifies these childcare options in the following ways:

- **Home-based care** consists of a licensed center in a family's home. There are two types of these centers: Listed Family Homes, which are able to accept 1-3 children and Registered Child Care Homes, which can accept six children under age 14 as well as six more school-aged children. No more than 12 children can be in the daycare at any time, including the children of the caregiver.

- **Center-based care** includes licensed daycare centers. These centers provide care for seven or more children under 14-years-old for less than 24 hours per day at a location that is not the caregiver's home. The North Dallas region is home to numerous privately owned childcare centers La Petite Academy, *www.lapetite.com*, Kiddie Academy, *www.kiddieacademy.com*, Bright Horizons, *www.brighthorizons.com*, and Kindercare, *www.kindercare.com*.

- **24 hour residential care** is another designation listed by the state, and includes foster family homes, foster group homes, child care institutions, which provides 24-hour care for 13 or more children under 18-years-old (such as maternity homes and halfway houses) and child placement agencies.

QUESTIONS TO ASK

Regardless of what type of daycare center you're considering, there are basic questions you'll want to ask to evaluate the quality of care your children will receive and whether it's the right fit for your child and your family.

- **Childcare provider and/or the childcare center manager:** The DFPS provides information (*www.dfps.state.tx.us/Child_Care/dontbeinthedark/5steps.asp*) about what kinds of questions to ask potential childcare providers, as well as what to look out for when visiting daycares. First of all, the DFPS urges parents to use the searchable database to locate centers that meet their specifications. The database also provides information on each provider's licensing history and compliance with health and safety requirements. Other suggestions include visiting daycare centers before making your decision, interviewing childcare providers and watching interactions at the center between the staff and the children. DFPS also urges parents to stay involved, even when your child is already enrolled, and continue to communicate with providers and ask questions.

- **Other parents:** Don't be afraid to ask other parents what their experiences have been like. Ask questions about what they like and dislike about the center's program and procedures, the dependability of the childcare provider, and whether they and their children feel comfortable at the center or home.

- **Yourself:** You are first and foremost looking for a childcare option that fits what your family and your child need. Make sure you carefully consider how your family's schedules and, more importantly, values fit into the structure of the childcare center's programs.

NANNIES

Families who choose nannies as their primary childcare providers often point to the one-on-one attention and flexibility that's commonly associated with having a nanny (as compared to daycare centers or other group settings) as some of the most important reasons behind their choice. But this one-on-one attention does come at a price.

According to a 2009 survey released by the International Nanny Association, a private non-profit organization, full-time live-out nannies in Texas earned an average of $12.54 an hour. Actual salaries vary widely based on the region in which the family lives and the nanny's experience. In addition, families who directly employ nannies are required by federal law to pay Social Security tax and sometimes state unemployment taxes on the nanny's salary.

Nanny Placement Services

If you're a first-time nanny seeker or prefer services that help you prescreen nanny candidates, placement agencies can help with the logistics of finding a nanny for your family. These agencies screen candidates and perform background checks. Even so, always verify the status of these checks with the agency before hiring any nanny. Agencies do require placement fees, deposits, and sometimes other fees for their services. Contact each agency directly for detailed information on their fees and requirements.

- **Domestically Yours, Inc.**, P.O. Box 702131, Dallas, 972-669-5059, *www.domesticallyyours.com*
- **The Nanny Agency, Inc.**, 972-713-7773, *www.thenannyagencyinc.com*
- **Premier Family Staffers.**, 6009 West Parker Road, Plano, 469-442-7693, *www.premierfamilystaffers.com*
- **Nannies and More**, 4514 Cole Avenue, Suite 600, Dallas, 888-466-4525, *www.nanniesandmore.com*

Finding a nanny on your own

If you prefer to find a nanny on your own, there are a number of resources at your disposal:

- **4EverythingNanny.com**, *www.4nanny.com*; provides helpful how-to articles and a classified ads section
- **International Nanny Association**, 888-878-1477, *www.nanny.org*; provides helpful tools for your nanny search and hiring process
- **NannyAnswers.com**, *www.nannyanswers.com*; a catch-all Website for frequently asked questions about nannies
- **GoNannies.com**, *www.gonannies.com*, is a searchable website by zip code, helping families find nannies and nannies find jobs

Nanny taxes

As mentioned above, families who do not use placement agencies but rather directly employ nannies are expected to pay taxes on the salaries paid to their nannies. The "Nanny Tax", as it's called, includes Social Security and Medicare taxes and federal unemployment tax. You may also be required to pay state unemployment taxes and/or state disability taxes.

There are several Website and agencies that can guide you through the particulars of the Nanny Tax and help you determine how much Nanny Tax you owe. Some such resources include:

- **Internal Revenue Service**, *www.irs.gov/taxtopics/tc756.html*
- **The Nanny Tax Company**, 800-747-9826, *www.nannytaxprep.com*; provides tax-filing services
- **NannyTax Inc.**, 888-NANNYTAX, *www.nannytax.com*; provides tax-filing services

AU PAIRS

The terms "au pair" and "nanny" are often used interchangeably, but there are notable differences between the two. As such, while a nanny may be a good fit for one family, an au pair may be a better fit for another.

Au pairs are typically between the ages of 18 and 26 and usually remain with a family for one year. Unlike nannies, au pairs aren't necessarily seeking professional careers in childcare; their yearlong commitment provides work experience but also functions as a cultural exchange program. Families with au pairs act as "host families"; the au pair provides childcare, and in return, the host family provides room, board, use of a vehicle, and a small stipend. Host families are also encouraged to facilitate continued education of the au pair while he/she is working in the U.S. Compensation for au pairs can be considerably less than nannies, ranging from $176.85 to $250 per week (approximately $9,000 to $13,000 per year, respectively).

Agencies that can assist with au pair screening and placement include:

- **Au Pair in America**, 800-928-7247, *www.aupairinamerica.com*
- **AuPairCare Live-In Child Care**, 800-428-7247, *www.aupaircare.com*
- **Cultural Care Au Pair**, 800-333-6056, *www.culturalcare.com*
- **GreatAupair**, 775-215-5770, *www.greataupair.com*
- **InterExchange AuPair USA**, 1-800-AUPAIRS, *www.aupairusa.org*

BABYSITTERS

Babysitting is no longer just a neighborhood business; babysitting is now big business, which can be both good and bad for the newcomer families.

The best babysitters are usually ones suggested by close friends of coworkers, but if you're new to the area, those solid referrals may be hard to come by—at least at the beginning. The growth of babysitting as a fortified business segment, however, has given rise to a slew of babysitting agencies that will gladly screen potential babysitters and narrow the field for your family. This can be a great way to find a babysitter if you're new to the area.

These agencies can be helpful resources, but know that they all charge fees for their services, whether it's a one-time "finders" fee or a membership fee to browse their pool of potential babysitters. Contact each agency for specific details on fees and memberships. Some local and national babysitter-finder agencies include:

- 4Sitters, 651-756-8085, *www.4sitters.com*
- Babysitters of Dallas, 214-692-1354, *www.babysittersofdallas.com*
- Babysitters DFW and Babysitters Tarrant, 1220 G Airport Freeway #467, Bedford, 817-689-4217, *www.babysittersdfw.com*; provides babysitting options in the Dallas-Fort Worth Metroplex
- Sittercity, 888-748-2489, *www.sittercity.com*; provides large database of local babysitters
- Seeking Sitters *www.seekingsitters.com-provides* babysitters who have been background checked and at affordable rates on an as needed basis or repeat needs

If you prefer to avoid the added fees for these services, there are several local resources that may be able to help you find the right babysitter. Community centers such as the local YMCA or the Plano Public Library usually have community boards that teens often use to advertise their babysitting services or that parents can use to advertise a babysitter opening. Churches, synagogues, or other places of worship might also be helpful resources.

And if all else fails, tapping into the North Dallas's (as well as the Dallas area in general) large populations of college students may prove to be helpful. University of North Texas, Collin County Community College and Dallas Baptist University, are all four-year universities located in the region, and they more than likely have a number of students looking for small side jobs. Checking in with the student employment service, posting fliers around campus, or running an ad in the college paper are all ways to find potential babysitters. Remember to request references for each candidate and to conduct your own thorough interview before hiring any babysitter.

Once you've found a babysitter, now comes the all-important question of how much to pay them. **Sittercity.com** provides a simple Rate Calculator (*babysitters.sittercity.com/rate_calculator.html*), which calculates an approximate rate based on geographic location, age of the babysitter, number of children that will be cared for, and the babysitter's experience. For example, according the calculator, an 18-21-year-old babysitter with two to four years' experience should be paid approximately $12 per hour to care for two children in Plano (zip code 75023).

PARENTING PUBLICATIONS

Dallas Child magazine, *www.dallaschild.com*, 972-447-9188, is the area's leading parenting publication. Its Website can provide a wealth of resources for parents new to the area, such as a calendar of family-friendly events, children's movie reviews, a list of playgrounds and getaways for the whole family. The magazine is available at bookstores, childcare facilities, local restaurants, schools and parents support groups, as well as other locations. The magazine is published in other Texas locations under different names, including *Fort Worth Child* and *North Texas Child,* and the magazine's website features a regularly updated blog (*www.dallaschild.blogspot.com*) with a list of fun activities for the family on a day-to-day basis.

SCHOOLS

Parent resources

Here are some resources with which to begin your school research:

- **Plano Independent School District**, 469-752-8100, *www.pisd.edu*; the Plano "ISD" serves the residents of 100 square miles in southwest Collin County. The website provides information on the district, including school, student and teacher statistics.
- **National Association of Independent Schools**, 202-973-970, *www.nais.org*; an organization dedicated to non-public schools. The NAIS maintains a searchable database of independent private schools in the U.S.
- **Texas Education Agency**, 1701 N. Congress Avenue, Austin, 512-463-9734, *www.tea.state.tx.us*; the agency provides educational resources to Texas residents, including information on testing, curriculum, funding and many other subjects.
- **Texas PTA**, 408 West 11th Street, Austin, 512-476-6769, *www.txpta.org*; includes information on organizing a local parent-teacher association as well as other resources for parent in Texas

Public schools

The North Dallas region, including Plano, is served by a number of independent school districts. The **Plano Independent School District (ISD)** 2700 W. 15th Street, Plano, (469) 752-8100, *www.pisd.edu*, includes 68 schools, serving over 53,000 students and employing over 7,000 people. There are five education "phases" in the school district: early childhood (Pre-K), elementary (grades K-5), middle (grades 6-8), high (grades 9 and 10) and senior (grades 11 and 12). The school district's Website features information on all its individual schools and educational programs.

Cities and towns surrounding Plano are also served by independent school districts, including the Frisco ISD (*www.friscoisd.org*), the Allen ISD (*www.allenisd.org*), the McKinney ISD (*www.mckinneyisd.net*), the Richardson ISD (*www.risd.org*), the Carrollton-Farmers Branch ISD (*www.cfbisd.edu*), the Coppell ISD (*www.coppellisd.com*), the Irving ISD (*www.irvingisd.net*), the Lewisville ISD (*www.lisd.net*) and the Garland ISD (*www.garlandisd.net*).

Growth

Texas is highly populated – and growing. A census bureau report released in 2008 showed that more people moved to the Dallas-Fort Worth area than to any other metropolitan area in the country the year prior.

Plano itself is known as a wealthy suburb, and has been praised throughout the years for its schools. Once a rural town, Plano grew exponentially in the 1980s and 1990s, including the building of bigger houses in gated communities, as well as new offices drawing a strong workforce. Eventually the Plano Independent School District was created. Soon the top-notch school district attracted a diversified population to the area, and Plano has continued to grow in leaps and bounds. The school district has been in the news in recent years, due to rezoning decisions and the angry reactions from parents.

As Plano and the surrounding areas grow, the school system will no doubt change, as well, but disputes aside, the area is still known for its excellent education system and resources.

Registering your children

The first step to registering your child or children for a school in the North Dallas region is to determine your independent school district, which will almost always match with the town or city in which you reside.

- When registering your child, the following documents will be requested:
    - A certified copy of the student's birth certificate or a passport
    - Proof of residency (such as an electricity bill or lease agreement)
    - An updated immunization record
    - Most Recent Report Card/Withdrawal Slip from Previous School
    - Social Security card, if available (if not, the child will be assigned a state ID number)
    - High school transcript (if applicable)
    - Parent's Driver's License or Texas Department of Transportation ID card or Guardian Information Form and Guardian's Driver's License or Texas Department of Transportation

Additional newcomer information

Most ISDs located in the North Dallas area provide ample information for newcomers on their websites. On the Plano ISD site, for example, parents are able to view information about dress codes, bus transportation, special education and school menus and nutrition.

The site also provides a long list of additional community resources (*www.pisd.edu/parents/community.resources*) that parents may want to take advantage of once they have relocated to Plano or surrounding areas.

Evaluating schools

Public schools play a critical role in many families' home-buying decisions. All parents want their children to excel in school, and to be comfortable in their learning environments. The ultimate question is: how do you determine which school is best for your child?

One of the most straightforward ways to evaluate the quality of schools in your area is to look at their **Texas Education Agency's** Academic Excellence Indicator System (AEIS), *www.ritter.tea.state.tx.us/perfreport/aeis/*, which provides information for each public school, district or region in Texas, including school report cards. The AEIS includes yearly results of the Texas Assessment of Knowledge and Skills (TAKS) test, but also school dropout rates, college readiness indicators and other information.

The Texas Education Agency, which is run by the state, is an excellent resource for parents anxious to evaluate all aspects of schools in the state before choosing their home. In addition to the AEIS and other reports, the agency's website provides press releases and other news about the school system, news and events and information about alternative schooling.

Other factors that should be considered when choosing a school are:

- School philosophy as outlined in the school's statement of philosophy or mission statement
- Instructional approaches
- School facilities/personnel resources
- School policies
- School reputation
- School safety
- Curriculum
- Family and community involvement issues

Many of these factors can be evaluated by looking at the school's Website and by personally visiting the school you and your family are considering. Contact each individual school to discuss the options for a possible on-campus visit. Moreover, don't underestimate the value of asking neighbors, friends, family, and coworkers about their experiences in their school district.

Charter schools

For parents looking for a public-education alternative to traditional public schools, charter schools are a good option to consider. Charter schools are public schools with limited enrollment, and they often incorporate characteristics associated with private-school education such as smaller class sizes or rigorous curriculum for college- and university-bound students.

Funded with public money, charters are not required to meet all the rules and regulations of traditional public schools but are subject to accountability for producing certain academic results among its students. Because charter schools receive public money, they do not charge tuition. However, each school does have an admissions process. The particulars of the process vary from charter school to charter school, but the basic process is the same: Students and their families submit an application to the school(s) of their choice. Students meeting the admission requirements for the school are then entered into a lottery, and numbers are picked at random to determine which students will be granted available openings. For admission requirements and for particulars on each school's admission process, it's best to check each school's Website for details.

The Resource Center for Charter Schools, 700 Lavaca Street, Suite 930, Austin, 512-584-8272, *www.charterstexas.org*, a non-profit organization, provides a list of all charter schools in Texas. There are no charter schools in Plano itself, but there are several in surrounding cities and towns:

- **Life School McKinney**, 4045 Eldorado Pkwy., McKinney, 972-529-8125, *www.lifeschools.net*, K-grade 3
- **Evolution Academy Charter School**, 1101 South Sherman Street, Richardson, 972-907-3755, *www.evolutionaryacademy.org*, grades 9-12

- **Winfree Academy Charter School**, 1661 Gateway Blvd, Richardson, 972-234-9855, *www.winfreeacademy.com*; grades 9-12
- **Vista Academy of Carrollton**, 2400 North Josey Lane, Carollton, 972-242-9864, *www.vista-academies.com*; grades K-5
- **Universal Academy**, 1001 East Sandy Lake Road, Coppell, 972-393-5834, *www.universalacademy.com*; grades K-11
- **Honors Academy – University School**, 1404 West Walnut Hill Ln., Irving, 972-753-6165, *www.honorsacademy.org*; grades 7-12
- **North Hills Preparatory**, 606 E Royal Lane, Irving, 972-501-0645, grades K-12, *www.northhillsprep.org*; grades K-12
- **Winfree Academy Charter School**, 3110 Skyway Circle S., Irving, 972-251-2010, *www.winfreeacademy.com*; grades 9-12
- **iSchool High**, 1800 Lakeway Drive, Lewisville, 972-317-2470, *www.ischoolhigh.com*; grades 9-12
- **Alpha Charter Secondary School**, 701 West State Street, Garland, 972-272-2173; grades 8-12
- **Education Center International Academy**, 2422 North Jupiter Road, Garland, 972-530-6157, *www.eciacharter.com*; grades 2-12
- **Vista Academy of Garland**, 3024 Anita Drive, Garland, 972-840-1100, *www.vista-academies.com*; grades K-5

Private and parochial schools

After much consideration, some parents decide a private or parochial school is the best option for their child. There are a wide range of private and parochial school offerings in Plano and the North Dallas region. They include both large and small school settings and both religiously affiliated schools and those without religious ties. Below is a small selection of private schools located in Plano. There are several ways to research and compare private and parochial schools on the Web, including the site Education Bug, *www.texas.educationbug.org*, which includes a list of private schools searchable by school name and by county.

- **St. Mark Catholic School,** 1201 Alma Drive, Plano, 972-578-0610, *www.stmarkcatholicschool.com*; Catholic affiliation
- **Willow Bend Academy,** 2220 Coit Road, Plano, 972-599-788, *www.willowbendacademy.com*
- **West Plano Montessori School,** 3425 Ashington Lane, Plano, 972-618-8844, *www.montessorischool.com*
- **Faith Lutheran School,** 1701 East Park Boulevard, Plano, 972-423-7448, *www.flsplano.org;* Lutheran affiliation
- **Bethany Christian School,** 3300 West Parker Road, Plano, 972-596-5811, *www.bethanybible.com;* Christian
- **Great Lakes Academy,** 6000 Custer Road, Plano, 972-517-7498, *www.greatlakesacademy.com*
- **Prestonwood Christian Academy,** 6801 W Park Blvd Plano 75093 972-930-4001
- **Prince of Peace Catholic School,** 5100 W Plano Pkwy Plano 75093 972-380-5505

Homeschooling

As per Texas law, families are permitted to homeschool their children. According to a Web page dedicated to the subject (*www.ritter.tea.state.tx.us/home.school/homeltr.html*), the Texas Education Agency does not regulate, monitor or approve homeschooling programs, but does offer the state-mandated curriculum to those interested in using it in their homeschooling efforts.

The Texas Home School Coalition, 806-744-4441, *www.thsc.org*, is a good resource for those families interested in homeschooling their children. According to the Coalition, the required homeschool curriculum in Texas must teach, "reading, spelling, grammar, mathematics and a study of good citizenship, and you must pursue that curriculum in a bona fide (not a sham) manner."

Home schools in Texas are considered "private" schools and therefore there is not a stringent set of rules that these schools must adhere to. There are not a set number of days or hours that a child must attend his or her homeschool, and the school district does not have to approve a homeschool curriculum.

Once parents decide to homeschool their children, they must first withdraw the children from the public or private school in which they are enrolled, and then develop a curriculum. If the child is not yet enrolled in school, parents may simply begin the homeschooling process.

The Texas Home School Coalition Website includes much more information on the subject of homeschooling, including support groups, events and news.

CHAPTER 38

HEALTH CARE

With its prime location in the Dallas-Fort Worth metropolitan area, it's no wonder that there are an abundance of health care resources in greater Plano. With such world-class medical institutions as the University of Texas Southwestern Medical School, Baylor College of Medicine, and The Texas A&M Health Science Center College of Medicine within the state of Texas, Plano offers its residents easy proximity to world-class medical care. In this chapter you'll find all the major health organizations and the hospitals that comprise them.

Baylor Regional Medical Center at Carrollton

Established in 1985, Baylor Medical Center at Carrollton is a 237-bed acute care facility that provides a broad spectrum of medical and health care services. The hospital offers a full continuum of care for inpatients and outpatients with services including surgery, emergency care, women's services, therapy and sports medicine, diagnostic imaging and more.

4343 N. Josey Lane
Carrollton, TX 75010
972.492.1010
www.baylorhealth.com/PhysiciansLocations/Carrollton

Baylor Regional Medical Center at Frisco

Baylor Medical Center at Frisco strives to provide the highest standard of health care services, designed with excellence, delivered with dignity, and demonstrated with respect. With a focus on service and hospitality, the hospital is committed to providing every patient with a comfortable, friendly environment.

5601 Warren Parkway
Frisco, TX 75034
214.407.5000
www.baylorhealth.com/PhysiciansLocations/Frisco

Baylor Regional Medical Center at Garland

For more than 40 years, Baylor Medical Center at Garland has been striving to make a positive difference for their patients every day. From family medicine to cardiovascular surgery, Baylor Garland provides patients with advanced medical care in a healing, supportive environment.

2300 Marie Curie Blvd.
Garland, TX 75042
972.487.5000
www.baylorhealth.com/PhysiciansLocations/Garland

Baylor Regional Medical Center at Irving

Baylor Medical Center at Irving is a not-for-profit, full-service, accredited hospital that offers advanced health care services in cardiovascular care, diagnostic imaging, digestive disorders, physical medicine and rehabilitation, oncology treatment, orthopedic surgery, and emergency medicine. The 298-bed hospital is an accredited Chest Pain Center by the Society of Chest Pain Centers.

1901 N. MacArthur Blvd.
Irving, TX 75061
972.579.8100
www.baylorhealth.com/PhysiciansLocations/Irving

Baylor Regional Medical Center at Plano

A 128-bed hospital, Baylor Plano has received several awards including the Texas Health Care Quality Improvement Award of Excellence and the VHA Leadership Award for Clinical Excellence. Backed by 100 years of experience, the hospital is part of the Baylor Health Care System, which expanded in Collin County in 2004. All physicians on the medical staff are board certified or board eligible. In 2007, the hospital was awarded the Pathway to Excellence™ designation of American Nurses Credentialing Center.

4700 Alliance Blvd.
Plano, TX 75093
469.814.2000
www.baylorhealth.com/PhysiciansLocations/Plano

Centennial Medical Center

As a full-service hospital, Centennial Medical Center is committed to the total health of each patient. The hospital's commitment to quality is to deliver safe, cost-effective care to the community and patients that they serve. Medical specialties include: Cardiology, Open Heart and Vascular Surgery, a Neonatal Intensive Care, General Surgery, Orthopedics and more.

12505 Lebanon Road
Frisco, TX 75035
972.963.3333
www.centennialmedicalcenter.com

Irving Coppell Surgical Hospital

Providing a broad range of outpatient surgical procedures, Irving Coppell Surgical Hospital strives to provide first-class surgical services in a safe, welcoming environment. With seven operating rooms, the hospital offers state-of-the-art equipment to perform procedures in the specialty areas of: Ear Nose and Throat, General Surgery, Gynecology, Ophthalmology, Pain Management, Plastic/Reconstructive Surgery, Spine and Podiatry.

400 West I-635, Suite 101
Irving, TX 75063
972.868.4000
www.ic-sh.com

Las Colinas Medical Center

Built in 1997, Las Colinas Medical Center is a 100 bed full service, acute-care facility offering a wide range of services to the community and families they serve. The hospital takes pride in offering state-of-the-art technology in an aesthetically pleasing environment. Amenities include: private rooms, concierge service, cable television, wireless Internet access and an executive chef.

6800 N. MacArthur Blvd.
Irving, TX 75039
972.969.2000
www.lascolinasmedical.com

LifeCare Hospital of Plano

LifeCare Hospital provides critical care services to patients that are considered medically complex and require extended hospitalization. The hospital strives to shorten the recovery process and improve the outcomes for their patients. Their treatment team includes physicians, nurses, pharmacists, nutritionists and therapists across a range of disciplines. In recognition of their highly qualified respiratory therapists and industry best practices in providing respiratory care, the hospital has been awarded the Quality Respiratory Care Recognition (QRCR) for 2008 and 2009 by the American Association for Respiratory Care (AARC).

6800 Preston Road
Plano, TX 75024
214.473.8822
www.lifecare-hospitals.com

Medical Center of Lewisville

The Medical Center of Lewisville strives to be recognized regionally as the premier Medical Center for health services, information and education. Services include a breast imaging center, cardiac rehabilitation, day surgery, diabetes self-management center, women's and children's services and much more.

500 West Main Street
Lewisville, TX 75057
972.420.1000
www.lewisvillemedical.com

Medical Center of McKinney

Medical Center of McKinney provides a wide range of health services, including: cardiology, cardiovascular surgery, joint replacement, obstetrics and gynecology and occupational health. In 2010, the hospital was named a Blue Distinction Center for Knee and Hip Replacement by Blue Cross and Blue Shield of Texas. The hospital has expanded their facilities, remodeled existing patient care areas, recruited top-notch physicians and added sophisticated medical and surgical services to meet the evolving needs of McKinney residents.

4500 Medical Center Drive
McKinney, TX 75069
972.547.8000
www.medicalcenterofmckinney.com

Methodist McKinney Hospital

Opened in 2010, Methodist McKinney Hospital strives to provide quality and compassionate care for their patients. Boasting some of the latest medical technology, the hospital provides patient- and wellness-focused inpatient, outpatient and emergency care to the residents of McKinney and surrounding communities. The hospital offers 6 operating rooms, 2 procedure rooms, a 15-bed inpatient nursing unit and a 24-hour emergency room.

8000 W. Eldorado Parkway Drive
McKinney, TX 75070
972.569.4500
www.methodistmckinneyhospital.com

Methodist Richardson Medical Center

As the first health care facility to receive the Texas Award for Performance Excellence, Methodist Richardson Medical Center offers medical, surgical and behavioral health services and is committed to delivering advanced technology and quality health care to the community. With 205 beds, the hospital boasts more than 700 staff physicians—each meeting their high credentialing standards.

401 W. Campbell Road
Richardson, TX 75080
972.498.4000
www.richardsonregional.com

Texas Health Center for Diagnostics & Surgery

A unique hospital dedicated to excellence in surgical care and imaging services, Texas Health Center for Diagnostics & Surgery (THCDS) boasts board certified surgeons with expertise in specialties including: spine, orthopedics, gynecology, urology, general surgery, podiatry and ear, nose and throat. Its surgeons are known to perform some of the most advanced treatment options available today.

6020 West Parker Road
Plano, TX 75093
972.403.2700
www.ppcds.com

Texas Health Presbyterian Hospital Allen

Since 2000, Texas Health Allen has been serving the needs of the area's growing number of families. A full-service, 62-bed community hospital, the hospital offers medical staff physicians, caring and trained staff members, advanced technology, and an inviting environment to meet the needs of every patient. In 2008, the hospital was designated a "Baby-Friendly Hospital" by the World Health Organization, recognizing its comprehensive approach to supporting breastfeeding of newborns.

1105 Central Expressway
Allen, TX 75013
972.747.1000
www.texashealth.org

Texas Health Presbyterian Hospital Plano

Opened in 1991, Texas Health Plano, a member of Texas Health Resources, is a not-for-profit, faith-based health care facility with nearly 1,300 physicians on its staff in 67 specialties. The hospital has won the

2008 Texas Award for Performance Excellence (T.A.P.E), which is the state's highest honor for quality and performance.

6200 West Parker Road
Plano, TX 75093
972.981.8000
www.texashealth.org

The Heart Hospital Baylor Plano

The Heart Hospital Baylor Plano offers safe, quality compassionate care to improve their patients' heart conditions or prevent future cardiovascular disease. The hospital's advanced cardiovascular services combine medical excellence and a patient-centered experience.

1100 Allied Drive
Plano, TX 75093
800.4BAYLOR
www.thehearthospitalbaylor.com

The Medical Center of Plano

A world-class medical facility offering a comprehensive range of healthcare services and the latest in technologies, The Medical Center of Plano has provided Plano and Collin County with superior healthcare since 1975. It is a full-service, 427-bed acute-care facility with over 900 physicians on staff, representing more than 70 specialties and subspecialties. The hospital continues its growth as a leader in Texas healthcare.

3901 West 15th Street
Plano, TX 75075
972.596.6800
www.themedicalcenterofplano.com

REHABILITATION HOSPITALS

HealthSouth Rehabilitation Hospital of Plano

As a 65-bed rehabilitation hospital, HealthSouth Rehabilitation Hospital of Plano offers comprehensive inpatient and outpatient rehabilitation services. Accredited by The Joint Commission, the hospital offers the latest rehabilitation technology for patients throughout the greater Dallas and Fort Worth area.

2800 West 15th Street
Plano, TX 75075
972.612.9000
www.healthsouth.com

Integra Hospital Plano

A unique comprehensive physical rehabilitation center for the Dallas Fort Worth Metroplex, Integra Hospital Plano strives to change the way that rehabilitation care is delivered. The hospital offers rehabilitation therapy for a wide range of diagnosis and conditions, including: arthritis, back and neck injury, cancer and brain injury.

2301 Marsh Lane
Plano, TX 75093
972.428.1600
www.integrahospitalplano.com

Plano Specialty Hospital

As the first and only hospital of its kind in the area, Plano Specialty Hospital provides comprehensive medical management of medically complex patients needing an extended stay. The hospital's dedicated and highly trained staff provides specialized care for patients with acute or chronic respiratory disorders who may have tracheotomies, ventilators, or require extensive respiratory treatments.

1621 Coit Road
Plano, TX 75075
972.758.5200
www.specialtyhospital-plano.com

Regency Hospital of North Dallas

Regency Hospital of North Dallas offers a team of highly trained medical professionals in a caring, yet highly technical environment. The hospital provides services to medically complex patients who have suffered recent catastrophic illnesses or injuries and require an extended length of stay in an acute care environment.

2225 Parker Road
Carrollton, TX 75010
972.236.6800
www.regencyhospital.com

Reliant Rehabilitation Hospital

Designed to provide the highest quality of rehabilitative care, Reliant Rehabilitation Hospital is a state-of-the art facility featuring 50 private patient rooms with flat-screen televisions, oversized shower and bathroom, personal desk and wood floors. With an experienced and compassionate team dedicated to each patient's recovery, the hospital strives to restore quality of life and inspire hope.

3351 Waterview Parkway
Richardson, Texas 75080
972.398.5700
www.relianthcp.com

Twin Creeks Hospital

As a 42,000-square foot, 40-bed all-private suite physical rehabilitation hospital, Twin Creeks Hospital provides state-of-the-art amenities and rehabilitation facilities for patients requiring a specialized level of acute rehabilitative care. They offer an individualized, multidisciplinary approach to in-patient care based on the latest methods and are committed to providing their patients with optimal care in an intimate, state-of-the-art facility.

1001 Raintree Circle
Allen, TX 75013
972.908.2000
www.twincreekshosp.com

URGENT CARE

There are dozens of urgent care clinics in the Plano area, operated both by the health systems listed above and by other private organizations. Listed below are just some of the urgent care clinics according to location.

Acute Kids Urgent Care – Allen
109 Central Expressway, Suite 509
Allen, Texas 75013
972.359.6900
www.acutekidscare.com

Acute Kids Urgent Care – Flower Mound
2701 Cross Timbers, Suite 232
Flower Mound, Texas 75028
469.549.0300
www.acutekidscare.com

Acute Kids Urgent Care – Frisco
3401 Preston Road, Suite 11
Frisco, Texas 75034
214.618.3920
www.acutekidscare.com

Acute Kids Urgent Care – McKinney
8080 Highway 121, Suite 110
McKinney, Texas 75070
972.727.3800
www.acutekidscare.com

Acute Kids Urgent Care – Plano
3305 Dallas Parkway, Suite 345
Plano, Texas 75093
972.300.4200
www.acutekidscare.com

CareNow Urgent Care
3821 W Spring Creek Pkwy.
Plano, TX 75023
972.599.0077
www.carenow.com

Concentra Urgent Care
701 E Plano Pkwy, Ste 103
Plano, TX 75074
972.578.2212
www.concentraurgentcare.com

E-Care Emergency Centers - Frisco
8837 Lebanon Rd., Suite 800
Frisco, TX 75034
972.731.5151
www.e-carecenters.com

E-Care Emergency Centers - McKinney
2810 S. Hardin, Suite 100
McKinney, TX 75070
972.548.7277
www.e-carecenters.com

ERCA Urgent Care and Minor Emergency Center
6501 Preston Road
Plano, Texas 75024
972.403.1300
www.ercenters.com

First Choice Emergency Room – Flower Mound
2628 Long Prairie Rd., Suite 107
Flower Mound, TX 75022
972. 899.6660
www.firstchoiceer.com/flowermound

First Choice Emergency Room – Plano
2401 Preston Road, Suite D
Plano, TX 75093
972.384.4600
www.firstchoiceer.com/plano

Frisco Urgent Care

550 Parkwood Boulevard, Suite A-205
Frisco, TX 75034
972.668.3990
www.friscourgentcare.com

NR Urgent Care

7920 Preston Rd., Suite 500
Plano Texas 75024
972. 334.9610
www.nrurgentcare.com

Pediatrics After Hours

7212 Independence Parkway
Plano, TX 75025
972.618.2493
www.pediafterhours.com

Primary Care Clinic of North Texas

1200 Medical Avenue
Plano, TX 75075
972.596.6005
www.primarycareclinic.org

Town Center Emergency Room

820 S. MacArthur Blvd. Ste. 100
Coppell, TX 75019
972.462.0911
www.towncenterer.com

CHAPTER 39

SHOPPING GUIDE

The Plano, TX region has shopping a-plenty. The town is home to JC Penney corporate headquarters; not to mention that the greater Dallas area is renowned for being home to the flagship of luxury department store chain Neiman Marcus. Yet the area is filled with shopping delights of all varieties and to fit all budgets and needs. Whether you are an avid chef, fashionista or outdoor enthusiast, this suburban area north of Dallas will keep you well supplied and feeling at home.

SHOPPING MALLS

Air-conditioning and ample parking are certainly top draws to shopping malls in and around Plano, TX. Listed below is but a handful of the dozens of shopping centers in the area. You'll find more than 160 shops at Collin Creek Mall, including mall standbys such as Gap and Ann Taylor. The **Shops at Willow Bend** offer free strollers to families and a bit further afield, two miles north of Dallas-Fort Worth International Airport is the 1.6 million-square-foot outlet mall **Grapevine Mills**, dubbed by TourTexas.com "the first super-regional value-oriented mega-mall in Texas and the Southwest." If you're looking to give your credit cards a workout, the nationally known **Galleria Mall**, home to Gucci, Tiffany and Co., an ice skating rink and a Westin hotel, will fit the bill. But if you are looking for the mecca of shopping malls look no further than Frisco where Stonebriar Mall is the huge magnet for the shoppers. You can find amazing deals at Sam Moon, or furniture and housewares at Ikea. The over 4 million square feet of retail shopping are second to none!

- **Collin Creek Mall**, 811 North Central Expressway, Plano, 972-422-1070, *www.collincreekmall.com*
- **El Dorado Shopping Plaza,** 2750 South Central Expressway, McKinney
- **Firewheel Town Center,** 301 Horseshoe Drive, Garland, 972-496-4070, *www.simon.com/mall/default.aspx?ID=1074*
- **Galleria Mall**, 13350 Dallas Parkway, Dallas, 972-702-7100, *www.galleriadallas.com/*
- **Golden Triangle Mall**, 2201 South I-35E, Denton, 940-566-6024, *www.shopgoldentriangle.com/*
- **Mockingbird Station**, 5321 East Mockingbird Lane, Dallas, 866-381-6267, *www.mockingbirdstation.com*
- **NorthPark Center**, 8687 N. Central Expressway, Dallas, 214-361-6345 *www.northparkcenter.com*
- **Preston Park Village**, 1900 Preston Road, Plano, 214-706-2500, *www.shopprestonpark.com*
- **Richardson Square**, 501 S. Plano Road, Richardson, 972-675-1041, *www.simon.com/mall/?id=221*
- **Robertson's Creek Shopping Center**, 5801 Long Prairie Road, Flower Mound, *www.shoprobertsonscreek.com*
- **The Shops at Legacy,** 200 Bishop Road, Suite 250, Plano, 214-473-9700, *www.shopsatlegacy.com*
- **The Shops at Willow Bend**, 6121 W. Park Boulevard, Plano, 972-202-4900, *www.shopwillowbend.com*
- **Stonebriar Centre**, 2601 Preston Road, Frisco, 972-668-6255, *www.shopstonebriar.com*

- **Town East Mall**, 2063 Town East Mall, Mesquite, 972-270-4431, *www.towneastmall.com/*
- **Valley View Center**, 13331 Preston Road, Dallas, 972-661-2424, *www.shopvalleyviewcenter.com*
- **Village at Fairview/Village at Allen**, 329 Town Place, Fairview, 972-678-4939, *www.villageatfairview.com/*
- **Vista Ridge Mall**, 2401 S. Stemmons Parkway, Lewisville, 972-315-0015, *www.vistaridgemall.com*
- **West Village,** 3699 McKinney Avenue, Dallas, 214-219-1144, *www.westvil.com*

OUTLET MALLS

- **Allen Premium Outlets**, 820 W. Stacy Road, Allen, 972-678-7000, *www.premiumoutlets.com/allen*, is in the heart of Collin County, just off Highway 75. Its 90 stores offer shoppers panoply of discounts on name brands and department store labels such as Banana Republic, Barneys New York, Kenneth Cole, Mikasa, Tommy Hilfiger, Crate and Barrel, Ralph Lauren Polo and WestPoint Stevens.
- **Grapevine Mills**, 3000 Grapevine Mills Parkway, Grapevine, 972-724-4900, *www.grapevinemills.com,* located two miles north of Dallas-Fort Worth International Airport, encompasses some 1.6 million square feet of outlet shopping space.
- **Plano Market Square**, 750 East Spring Creek Parkway, Plano, 972-578-1591, *www.planosqmall.com,* has 40 stores conveniently located in Plano off of Highway 75.
- **Tanger Outlet Center,** 301 Tanger Drive, Suite 113, Terrell, 972-524-6034, *www.tangeroutlet.com*, is the Dallas-area branch of the nationally known outlet mall chain. Located in Kaufman County, two counties south of Plano, this outlet mall has 37

stores including Casual Corner Annex, Old Navy, Levi's and Bass Company Store.

DEPARTMENT STORES

- **Barneys New York**, *www.barneys.com*, NorthPark Center, 8687 N. Central Expressway, Dallas, 469-221-4700, offers the latest in high-end urban chic style and beauty, with looks from newer designers such as Alexander Wang and Phillip Lim to the time-honored such as Givenchy and Yves Saint Laurent.
- **Belk,** 866-235-5443, *www.belk.com*; locations at Robertson's Creek, El Dorado Shopping Plaza.
- **Dillard's**, 800-345-5273, *www.dillards.com*; locations at NorthPark, Golden Triangle, Stonebriar, Firewheel Town Center, Town East, Collin Creek, Willowbend, and at the Village at Fairview/Village at Allen.
- **JC Penney**, *www.jcpenney.com*; the mid-range department store, with corporate headquarters right here in Plano, offers traditional department store fare, including men's and women's apparel, shoes, jewelry, and home goods. Local retail locations include Village at Fairview/Village at Allen, Collin Creek, Stonebriar, Valley View, Robertson's Creek and Town East.
- **Macy's**, *www.macys.com*; locations in Collin Creek, Firewheel Town Center, Shops at Willow Bend, Village at Fairview, Stonebriar, Galleria, NorthPark and Town East. Macy's is a mid-range department store that offers a wide variety of women's, men's and children's clothing, home goods, perfume, and furniture.
- **Neiman Marcus**, *www.neimanmarcus.com*, is synonymous with extravagance. The luxury fashion and beauty department store, besides its flagship in downtown Dallas' Main Street District, has local branches at NorthPark and the Shops at Willow Bend.

Neiman's home décor outlet Horchow Finale has stores in Plano and at Grapevine Mills; the latter is also home to a Neiman Marcus Last Call discount outlet.

- **Nordstrom,** *www.nordstrom.com*, is known for higher-end fashion, most notably its shoe department. The department store has local locations at Stonebriar, Galleria and NorthPark.

- **Saks Fifth Avenue,** *www.saksfifthavenue.com*, locations at Galleria and Shops at Willow Bend; this upscale department store is the destination for everything luxurious and chic. Saks Fifth Avenue is a must-stop for the high-end shopper looking to scoop up the latest in high-end looks and beauty trends.

- **Sears,** 800-349-4358, *www.sears.com*; locations in Collin Creek Mall, Richardson Square, Valley View and Stonebriar; Sears is one of the oldest names in the department store business and is likely most well known for its offerings outside the realm of apparel and home goods. Sears offers a wide variety of home appliances, lawn and garden equipment, and home electronics.

DISCOUNT RETAILERS

- **Target,** *www.target.com*; 13 locations in and around Plano, nine of which are Super Targets

- **Wal-Mart,** *www.walmart.com*; 20 locations in the Plano area, 13 of which are Wal-Mart Supercenters

- **Kohls** *www.kohls.com*

HOUSEHOLD SHOPPING

With every new home comes the need–or maybe more accurately, the desire–for new appliances, furniture, lamps, rugs, and/or a new coat of paint. Below is a list of stores that can help you get your home improvement projects started and help you make your new house a home.

The list includes just a handful of the options available; don't forget **Target** and **Wal-Mart** (especially their "Super" locations) can also be great places to save a couple bucks on household basics. Though quick Google searches will definitely give you several names of stores to check out, the good 'ol Yellow Pages is the best resource to compile a comprehensive list of stores available in the Plano area.

Appliances/electronics/cameras/computers

- **Apple,** *www.apple.com,* 6121 W Park Boulevard, Suite C120, Plano, 972-202-5651
- **Appliance Bargain City,** 1201 N Central Expressway, Plano, 214-473-8061
- **Best Buy,** 888-237-8289, *www.bestbuy.com;* five locations in and around Plano
- **Conn's,** 866-765-1513, *www.conns.com;* locations in Plano, Richardson, Lewisville, Dallas
- **Home Depot,** 800-553-3199, *www.homedepot.com;* 20 locations in and around Plano
- **Lowe's,** 800-445-6937, *www.lowes.com;* locations in Plano, Frisco, Carrollton
- **Office Max,** 800-283-7674, *www.officemax.com;* three locations in Plano, one in Richardson, one in north Dallas; offers home office electronics
- **Rodenbaugh Appliance Outlet,** *www.rodenbaughs.com,* 1104 14th Street, Plano, 972-423-3340; 103 North Austin Street, Allen, 972-727-3454
- **Sears,** 800-349-4358, *www.sears.com;* locations in Collin Creek Mall, Richardson Square, Valley View and Stonebriar; in the Plano area, Sears has an appliance outlet store in Carrollton at 1215 Marsh Lane, Suite 180, 972-418-2293, as well as two auto

service drop-off centers in Garland (3845 Grader Street, 214-553-6789) and Dallas (13131 Preston Road, 972-458-3528).

- **Staples**, 800-STAPLES, *www.staples.com*; multiple locations in the area including Plano, Lewisville, Frisco, Richardson; offers home office electronics

Beds, bedding, and bath

- **Bed Bath & Beyond**, 800-462-3966, *www.bedbathandbeyond.com*; two locations in Plano, one in Richardson, one in Dallas
- **Horchow**, 972-629-1700, *www.horchow.com*; Neiman Marcus-Shops at Willow Bend, Plano,
- **Horchow Finale**, 3400 Preston Road, Plano, 972-519-5406; Grapevine Mills, 3000 Grapevine Mills Pkwy #233, Grapevine, 214-513-1527
- **IKEA**, *www.ikea.com* 7171 Ikea Dr Frisco 75034 972-712-4532 Stonebriar Mall
- **Mattress 101**, *www.mattress-101.com/*; 204 Central Expressway South, Suite 18, Allen, 866-713-0467
- **Mattress Firm**, *www.mattressfirm.com*, 800-628-3476; several locations, including five in Plano
- **Mattress Land Outlet**, *www.mattresslandoutlet.net,* 6000 North Central Expressway, Plano, 972-423-5656; 4109 Preston Road, Frisco, 972-334-9299
- **Nationwide Mattress Forever Bed Gallery**, *www.nationwidemattress.biz/*, 866-968-7233, 101 West Spring Creek Parkway, Plano; 1514 South Tennessee Street, McKinney
- **Room Store**, *www.roomstore.com*; 866-287-3203, two Plano locations
- **Rooms to Go**, *www.roomstogo.com*, 800-766-6786, locations in Plano and Frisco

- **Sleep Experts,** *www.sleepexperts.com*, 888-557-5337; two Plano locations, one Flower Mound location, two Frisco locations, one Garland location, one Lewisville location, two McKinney locations

Carpets and rugs

- **Builders Carpet and Design Center,** *www.builderscarpet.net/*; 3100 Alma Road, McKinney, 972-540-6600
- **Carpet One Floor & Home,** *www.carpetoneplano.com*, 2001 Coit Road, Suite 301, Plano, 972-535-8072
- **Coker Floor Company,** *www.cokerfloor.com/*; 866-462-6537; showrooms in Frisco, McKinney, Lewisville and Plano.
- **Nadine Floor Company,** *www.nadinefloors.com*; 972-424-2525; two Plano locations, one Frisco location.
- **Nationwide Floor and Window Coverings** *www.FloorsandWindows.com* 972-966-2200-Jennifer and Jeff Teller-they will bring the samples to your home
- **North Texas Flooring and Design,** *www.northdallasflooring.com*; 701 East Plano Parkway, Suite 406, Plano, 469-443-3187

Furniture

Texans are known for their hospitality and appreciation for luxury; home furnishings are no exception. For these reasons, furniture stores are aplenty across the Dallas-Fort Worth Metroplex, with many locations in and around Plano.

- **Ashley Furniture Home Store,** *www.ashleyfurniturehomestore.com*, 1201 N Central Expressway, Plano, 972-509-2560
- **Cantoni,** *www.cantoni.com*, 4800 Alpha Road, Dallas, 972-934-9191

- **DFW Furniture Direct**, *www.dfwfurnituredirect.com*, 1401 Jupiter Road, Suite 107, Plano, 972-881-7503
- **D'Hierro**, *www.dhierro.com*, The Shops at Legacy, 7200 Bishop Road, Suite D9, Plano, 972-943-9934
- **Far Fetched Imported Furniture**, *www.farfetchedplano.com*, 5813 Preston Road, Suite 558, LakeSide Market, Plano, 972-378-9922
- **Fusion Home Fashion**, *www.fusionhomefashion.com*, The Shops at Legacy, 5760 Legacy Drive, Suite B8, Plano, 972-378-3874
- **Garden Ridge**, *www.gardenridge.com*, 1717 E. Spring Creek Parkway, Plano, 972-509-8001; 2512 South Stemmons Freeway, Lewisville, 972-316-0392
- **Havertys**, *www.havertys.com*; 601 Accent Drive Collin Creek Village, Plano, 972-424-8880; 8049 Gaylord Parkway, Frisco, 972-668-5820; Vista Ridge Village 598 East Fm 3040, Lewisville, 972-315-2800
- **Ikea**, *www.ikea.com/us/en/store/frisco*, 7171 Ikea Drive, Frisco, 972-712-4532
- **My Favorite Room**, *www.kbmdesigns.com/favoritroom.html*, 1029 East 16th Street, Plano, 972-801-4901
- **Robb and Stucky Furniture**, *www.robbstucky.com*; 7240 North Dallas Parkway, Plano, 972-403-3000
- **Room Store**, *www.roomstore.com*; 866-287-3203, two Plano locations
- **Rooms to Go**, *www.roomstogo.com*, 800-766-6786, locations in Plano and Frisco
- **Weir's Furniture Village**, *www.weirsfurniture.com*; 5801 Preston Road, Plano, 972-403-7878

Housewares

- **Bed Bath & Beyond**, 800-462-3966, *www.bedbathandbeyond.com*; two locations in Plano, one in Richardson, one in Dallas
- **Cost Plus World Market**, 877-WORLD MARKET, *www.worldmarket.com*; locations in Plano and Garland
- **Crate & Barrel**, *www.crateandbarrel.com*, 5221 Alpha Road, Dallas, 972-934-1800
- **The Iron Bed/Bliss Linens**, *www.theironbed.com*, The Shops at Legacy, 5760 Legacy Drive, Suite B2, Plano, 972-403-3000
- **Pier 1 Imports**, 800-245-4595, *www.pier1.com*; several locations, including two in Plano, two in Garland and one in Lewisville
- **Pottery Barn**, *www.potterybarn.com*, Stonebriar Center, 2601 Preston Road, Frisco, 919-881-0188
- **Williams-Sonoma**, *www.wshome.com*, The Shops at Legacy, 7300 North Dallas Parkway, Plano, 972-673-0229

Lamps and lighting

- **Bright Memories Lamps and Gifts**, 3400 Greenbriar Lane, Plano, 972-423-5877
- **Lamps Plus**, *www.lampsplus.com*; 1705 Preston Road, Plano, 972-447-0019; 800 Fulgham Road, Plano, 469-229-0071
- **LifeStyles Stores**, *www.lifestylesstores.com*, 3500 Preston Road, Plano, 972-985-0096
- **Light Motif**, 4709 W Parker Road, Suite 440, Plano, 972-964-0630
- **The Market@Home**, 4017 Preston Road, Suite 546, Plano, 972-596-2699
- **Restoration Hardware**, *www.restorationhardware.com*, 5217 Alpha Road, Dallas, 972-404-8707

Hardware/paint/home improvement

- **Ace Hardware**, 866-290-5334, *www.acehardware.com*; multiple locations, including in Coppell and McKinney
- **Avanti Specialty Hardware**, 1101 Ohio Drive, Plano, 469-467-8730
- **Elliott's Hardware**, *www.elliottshardware.com*, 2049 Coit Road, Suite 300, Plano, 972-312-0700
- **Home Depot**, 800-553-3199, *www.homedepot.com*; 20 locations in and around Plano
- **Lumber Liquidators**, 1717 North Central Expressway, Plano, 972-422-0727
- **Lowe's**, 800-445-6937, *www.lowes.com*; locations in Plano, Frisco, Carrollton
- **Sears Home Services**, *www.sears.com*; 851 N Central Expressway, Plano, 972-422-8484
- **Stone Appliance Gallery**, *www.kivahome.com/default-stone.shtml* 111 Central Expressway North, Allen, 469-519-2828
- **Skanadario by Goodman Supply**, 9750 John W. Elliott Drive, Frisco, 972-668-4663

ANTIQUE STORES/VINTAGE

Given the Texan predilection toward finery, the area around Plano is a veritable treasure trove of the best examples of design history. The downtowns of Plano and McKinney have an array of stores selling antique home goods and vintage clothing. Indulge a bit and go for that wrought iron pillar once part of a cattle ranch fence or those white vintage ostrich pumps. You're a Texan now, so live it up in style.

- **A Rare Find**, 4001 Preston Road, Plano, 972-781-2121
- **Accetera Antiques**, *www.accetera.com*, 3301 Preston Road, Suite 6, Frisco, 972-668-6400

- **Antique Company Mall,** *www.antiquecompanymall.com,* 213 East Virginia, McKinney, 972-548-2929
- **Antique House,** *www.jeanwilliams.brinkster.net,* 212 East Louisiana Street, McKinney, 972-562-0642
- **Antique Stop,** *www.antiquestop.com,* 3400 Preston Road, Suite 205, Plano, 972-312-1501
- **Clydes Antique Mall,** 102 East Louisiana Street, McKinney, 972-562-1945
- **Cobwebs Antique and Consignment,** 1400 J Avenue, Plano, 972-423-8697
- **History House Antiques Emporium,** 1004 E 15th Street, Plano, 972-424-9764
- **Inessa Stewart's Antiques and Interiors,** 5800 Legacy Drive at Bishop, Suite C-4, Plano, 972-378-5100
- **Market Square,** *www.artloftmarketsquare.com,* 101 W. Louisiana, McKinney, 972-548-2250
- **Nanny Granny's Antiques,** 1408 J Avenue, Plano, 972-423-3552
- **One of a Kind,** *www.oneofakindmckinney.com,* 214 N. Kentucky Street, McKinney, 972-542-7977
- **Plano Antique Mall,** *www.planoantiquemall.com,* 1717 East Spring Creek Parkway, #192, Plano, 972-424-2995
- **Plano Antiqueland Antique Mall and Interior Market,** *www.planoantiqueland.com,* 800 North Central Expressway, Plano, 972-509-7878
- **Red Awning Antiques and Collectibles,** 1006 E 15th Street, Plano, 972-424-3003

FLEA MARKETS

Year-round warm weather and the surrounding bucolic landscape help to make the Plano area's flea markets hopping and full of merchandise and customers, as well as sampling of the finest in Tex-Mex

266

cuisine. Among the one of the bigger shopping draws in the greater Dallas-Fort Worth Metroplex is Traders Village in Grand Prairie, located a short drive away from Dallas' northern suburbs. Below is but a sampling of local open-air shopping.

- **Harry Hines Mercado**, *www.harryhinesmercado.com*, 10778 Harry Hines Boulevard, Dallas
- **Mexico Linda Bazaar**, 10724 Garland Road, Dallas, 214-321-1599
- **Moroccan Bazaar**, 1121 South Jupiter Road, Garland, 972-485-4488
- **Third Monday Trade Days**, *www.tmtd.com*, 4550 West University Drive, McKinney, 972-562-5466
- **Traders Village**, *www.tradersvillage.com*, 2602 Mayfield Road, Grand Prairie, 972-647-2331
- **Vikon Village Flea Market**, 2918 S Jupiter Road, Garland, 972-278-7414

THRIFT AND VINTAGE SHOPS

Trying to find the diamond in the rough at thrift and vintage shops can be quite a task, but if you're up to the challenge, the payoff can be big.

The Plano area has a number of thrift and vintage stores that can offer a lot of bang for the buck. To increase your chances of finding that "diamond," ask the stores' managers or sales associates when they typically put new items out. With a little bit of planning, you can take advantage of new stock before the crowds pick through them.

In addition, if you decide to do your thrift shopping at the **Salvation Army Thrift Store**, at a **Goodwill** store, or at one of the stores sponsored by Plano-area charities, you're not only getting great deals but you're also helping great causes.

- **Allen Community Outreach Resale Shop,** *www.acocares.org*, 801 East Main Street, Allen, 972-727-4751; ACO is a local affiliate of the United Way
- **Animal Rescue Klub,** *www.animalrescueklub.org*, 1806 Avenue K, Plano, 972-509-1404
- **Crissa's Closet,** 3131 Custer Road, 972-769-0610, benefits Hope's Door, a charity supporting domestic abuse victims
- **Dallas Vintage Shop,** *www.dallasvintageshop.com*, 901 West Parker Road #117, Plano, 972-422-7256
- **Garland Road Thrift Stores,**10030 Garland Road, Dallas, 214-324-1010
- **Genesis Women's Shelter Thrift Store,** *www.genesisshelter.org*, 3419 Knight Street, Dallas, 214-520-6644
- **Goodwill Industries,** *www.goodwilldallas.org*, 2116 E. Belt Line Road, Carrollton, 972-416-6051; 3106 N. Shiloh Road, Garland, 972-530-4542; 451 West IH 30, Suite 100, Garland, 972-240-8010; 919 West Main Street, Lewisville, 972-436-3181; 6104 Alma Drive, Plano, 972-517-2940
- **Habitat for Humanity Restore,** 1400 Summit Ave Plano 75074 972-424-0791
- **Ladies of Charity Thrift Store,** *www.ladiesofcharity.com*, 2710 Samuell Boulevard, Dallas, 214-821-5775
- **Once Upon a Child,** *www.onceuponachild.com*, 7200 Independence Parkway, Plano, 972-618-5800
- **Plano Community Charity,** *www.planocharity.org*, 2436 Avenue K, Plano, 972-578-0399
- **Plato's Closet,** *www.platoscloset.com*, 832 West Spring Creek Parkway, Plano, 972-633-0567
- **Revente-Ladies Thrift Store,** *www.reventeresale.org*, 5400 East Mockingbird Lane, Dallas, 214-823-2800

- **Salvation Army Thrift Store,** *www.salvationarmydfw.org*, 5900 Avenue K, Plano, 972-423-8254; 451 West Avenue D, Garland, 972-272-4531; 207 Elm Street, Lewisville, 972-353-9400; 600 Wilson Creek Parkway, McKinney, 972-542-6694
- **Thrift Plus Store,** 1405 Jupiter Road, Plano, 972-509-9365

FOOD

A number of national supermarket chains serve the Plano area. No matter where you live in Dallas County, Collin County or Denton County, you'll more than likely only be a short drive away from at least one of the area's major grocery store chains, Tom Thumb/ Kroger or Albertsons, plus Whole Foods and Central Market, the upscale brand of San Antonio-based grocery chain H-E-B.

For those looking to stretch their dollars a bit, there are a number of Super Targets and Wal-Mart Supercenters that offer formidable selections of produce, meat, bakery, and other grocery items that can help budget-conscious shoppers trim their grocery bills.

In addition to the more traditional grocery stores, Plano-area residents also have access to a variety of stores and shops that can help them fill their kitchens and pantries with more than just the traditional fare. From traditionally Mexican grocery store chains such as **El Rancho Supermercado** to health food stores to seafood markets, even the most discerning home cooks will find what they need in the northern Dallas suburbs.

Supermarkets

Four main supermarket chains serve the Plano area:
- **Albertsons**, 877-932-7948, *www.albertsonsmarket.com*; more than 20 locations within a 20-mile radius of Plano. Many Albertsons locations have in-store

- **ALDI**, the discount grocery store chain has more than 20 locations in the Metroplex including a East Plano location *www.aldi.com*
- **Kroger**, 866-221-4141, *www.kroger.com*; 43 locations within a 20-mile radius of Plano. At some of its locations, Kroger offers additional services including 24-hour service, film developing and pharmacy services. Moreover, at select locations, shoppers can even fill up their gas tanks at Kroger's gas stations. Kroger is also known as the home of the "double and triple coupons"
- **Tom Thumb,** 877-723-3929, *www.randalls.com,* 31 locations around Plano. Both owned by Safeway, supermarket chain has at some locations sushi bars, olive bars, digital photos, Redbox DVD rental kiosks, Coinmasters, Jamba Juices,Starbucks, adult immunizations, travel immunizations, wi-fi access and Wells Fargo Bank services. Tom Thumb, gas station services.

Natural food grocers and specialty market chains

As the market for organic food and other "green" products grows, the number of national chains specializing in organic produce and health-food products continues to increase. In addition, a number of specialty market chains have popped up, providing not only premium produce but also a wide variety of gourmet foodstuffs. These stores make up a small segment of the food-shopping market in the Plano area, but they're nonetheless worth a mention, especially for shoppers with an eye for organic or the home cook in search of some not-so-common ingredients.

- **Central Market**, 320 Coit Road, Plano; 469-241-8300; *www.centralmarket.com*; Central Market Plano, run by San Antonio-based grocery chain H-E-B, also has an on-site coffee and café, as well as a bagel/breakfast bar on the weekends, complete with all-you-can-eat pancakes.

- **Market Street**, 1929 Preston Road, Plano, 972-713-5500, *www.marketstreetplano.com*; Owned by north and west Texas supermarket chain United, Market Street offers top-quality meat, produce, grocery and bakery goods, as well as on-site cooking, medical and nutritionist staff.
- **New Flower Farmers Market**, *www.sfmarkets.com*, 3312 Preston Rd., Suite 100, Plano, 972-599-2942, offers organic produce, a full deli, meat counter, seafood, bulk nutritional items, coffee and beer and wine.
- **Sprouts Farmers Market**, 888-5SPROUT,*www.sprouts.com*, locations in Plano, Flower Mound, Coppell, Richardson, Frisco; provides shoppers with a boutique shopping experience complete with organic grocery and bulk nutritional goods.
- **Whole Foods**, *www.wholefoods.com*; one location in Plano and one location in Richardson. Whole Foods is the mega store of natural and organic products and produce. If you're looking for a one-stop shop for organic produce, organic meats, and health food supplements and products, Whole Foods will likely meet your shopping needs.

Warehouse shopping

Buying in bulk can be one of the most effective ways to trim a grocery budget, especially if you're feeding a crowd. **Costco Wholesale** and **Sam's Club** both serve the area—but don't forget: These stores don't just open their doors to anyone. Each chain requires customers to have memberships in order to shop in their warehouses. Check each chain's Website for details on the cost and terms of their memberships.

- **Costco Wholesale**, two locations in Plano, one in Lewisville, 800-774-2678, *www.costco.com*

- **Sam's Club**, *www.samsclub.com*; 888-746-7726, locations in Plano, McKinney, Addison, Garland, Irving, Lewisville, and one in Morrisville

Seafood markets

Dallas may be well inland from the Gulf Coast, yet area residents still have access to top notch, fresh seafood. The city's supermarkets often run specials on fish and seafood, but nothing beats what you can find in local seafood markets. The markets below offer better, fresher seafood than traditional supermarkets and at much lower prices. They may be one more shopping stop to make, but the drive is certainly worth it.

- **Capt'n Dave's Seafood Market**, 700 Alma Drive, #104, Plano, 972-424-3474
- **Rex's Seafood Market**, 5200 West Lovers Lane, Dallas, 214-351-6363, *www.rexsseafood.com*

Butcher's shops

Now that you found your home not too far from the range, why not take advantage? Dallas earned its economic stripes from cattle ranching, and certainly the local selection of meat is tough to beat. Below is but a few of the dedicated butcher's shops in and around Plano.

- **Burgundy Pasture Beef**, 800 McDuff Grandview, 817-866-2247, *www.burgundypasturebeef.com*
- **Hirsch's Meats**, 1301 West Parker Road, #100, Plano, 972-633-5593, *www.hirschsmeats.com*
- **La Michoacana Meat Market,** *www.lamichoacanameatmarket.com*, 972-276-5082; locations in Garland, Irving, Plano, Carrollton
- **Ye Ole Butcher Shop**, 811 East 15th Street, Dallas, 972-423-1848, *www.yeolebutchershop.com*; offers lunch order call-in

Ethnic districts

The Plano area's stable job market and attractive real estate market is attracting professionals, couples, and families from all across the country. With this slow but steady migration has come an influx of people from all backgrounds, with the ethnic markets to cater to these groups. Of course, Texas has a longstanding Mexican community; the area around Plano is no exception. Whether you seek to dabble with the finest ingredients in your forays into Tex-Mex cuisine or roll some sushi, you can fulfill your culinary exploration with local ethnic shops.

- **Asia World Market,** *www.asiaworldmarket.com*, 240 Legacy Drive, Plano, 972-517-8858
- **Assi Plaza Plano**, 2060 W Spring Creek Parkway, Plano, 919-232-2288; specializes in Korean grocery items, also carries Chinese and Japanese items
- **Bollywood Video,** 520 Lockwood Drive, Richardson, 972-671-1717, Indian grocery items
- **Café Izmir Market & Deli,** *www.cafeizmir.com*, 3607 Greenville Avenue, Dallas, 214-826-7788, Turkish/Mediterranean deli
- **Carnival Food Stores,** 2440 West Illinois Avenue, Dallas, 214-331-1044, Mexican grocery
- **El Rancho,** 14211 Coit Road, Dallas, 972-284-0900, Mexican grocery
- **El Rio Grande Supermercado,** *www.elriogrande.net*, 3460 West Walnut Street, Garland, 972-487-3512, Mexican grocery
- **Fiesta Mart,** 2940 South 1st Street, Garland, 972-271-9060, Mexican grocery
- **Hiep Thai Market,** 3530 West Walnut Street, Garland, 972-272-1993
- **Hong Phat Supermarket,** 3212 North Jupiter Road, Garland, 817-861-5188, Vietnamese shop

- **La Michoacana Meat Market,** *www.lamichoacanameatmarket.com*, 972-276-5082; Mexican-style butcher and grocery with locations in Garland, Irving, Plano, Carrollton
- **May Hua Supermarket,** 2220 Coit Road, Plano, 972-398-6987, Asian supermarket
- **Oriental Foods Supermarket,** 1927 East Belt Line Road, Suite 113, Carrollton, 972-417-0784
- **Royal Sweets,** *www.royalsweets.net*, 524 West Belt Line Road, Richardson, 972-669-4973, Indo-Pak bakery shop
- **Shop Minoya 99 Cent Plus,** 3115 W. Parker Road, Plano, 972-769-8346, carries Japanese items
- **Spice Rack,** 2865 Mcdermott Road, Suite 105, Plano, 972-727-7225, Indian items
- **Super H Mart,** *www.hmart.com*, 2625 Old Denton Road, Carrollton, 972-323-9700, full-service Korean grocery store with meat, seafood, produce and food court
- **Terry's El Mariachi Supermarkets,** *www.terrysupermarkets.com*, 1804 K Avenue, Plano, 972-633-1500; 1706 W. Irving Blvd. Irving, 214-441-0377; 1019 Fox Avenue, Lewisville; 214-222-4426; Mexican-style grocery store with meat, seafood and tortilla counters
- **Tian Tian Supermarket,** 400 North Greenville Avenue, Richardson, 972-907-8898, Asian supermarket

CHAPTER 40

CULTURAL LIFE

Plano and the surrounding North Dallas area offers something for everyone: professional Broadway productions, community theatre, museums, art galleries, lecture series, and the list goes on and on. So, if you're just moving to Plano, welcome! We can guarantee there is a lot for you (and your family) to experience.

The Plano Convention and Visitors Bureau (Plano CVB), 2000 E. Spring Creek Pkwy, Plano, 800-81-PLANO, *www.planocvb.com/main/index.php*, is a great source for tips and tools to explore Plano's cultural scene. Though the Plano Convention and Visitors Bureau do cater, of course, to tourists, it's a great place to start if you're a new resident. Another helpful resource is the Plano Economic Development Board, 5601 Granite Parkway, #310, Plano, 972-208-8300, *www.planotexas.org*.

Plano's proximity to Dallas allows you to experience all of its rich amenities including culture and recreation. Living in Plano provides you all the rewards of a big city without the hassles. Dallas has biggest urban Arts District, 214-744-6642, *www.thedallasartsdistrict.org*, in the country. The District was founded in 1983 includes the Dallas Museum of Art, 1717 North Harwood Street, 214-922-1200, *www.dallasmuseumofart.org*, the Morton H Meyerson Symphony Center, the major performing arts venue in Dallas, 2301 Flora Street, 214-670-3600, *www.meyersonsymphonycenter.com*, and the Dallas Theater Center, 3636 Turtle Creek Boulevard 214-522-8499, *www.dallastheatercenter.org*.

To obtain tickets to cultural events in Dallas, residents and visitors should contact the individual venues. Other places to get information about cultural life include the weekly Dallas Observer, *www.dallasobserver.com*, and the City of Dallas Office of Cultural Affairs, *www.dallasculture.org*.

TICKETS

Tickets for most major concerts, theatre productions, and other cultural events are available through the venues' box offices. If you're keen on avoiding service charges, purchasing tickets directly from the venue's box office will be your best option.

Most event tickets are also available through **Ticketmaster**. You can purchase tickets through Ticketmaster over the phone by calling 800-745-3000 or by visiting *www.ticketmaster.com*. If you prefer to buy the tickets in person, Ticketmaster has a number of retail locations throughout North Dallas. Visit *www.ticketmaster.com* to find the most convenient location.

Concerts and performances can sell out quickly, and if you find yourself looking for tickets to a sold-out show, **StubHub** may be a good solution. Fans and concerts goers often use StubHub to sell their extra or unneeded tickets. To search for available tickets for events in and around Plano, visit *www.stubhub.com*.

But buyers beware: Purchasing tickets through Ticketmaster and StubHub often come with significant service charges and processing fees. Ticketmaster's fees can vary from state to state and event to event; make sure to check what (and how much) these fees will be to avoid unexpected costs. StubHub charges a service fee equal to 10% of the full ticket price in addition to a delivery fee.

CONCERT HALLS, STADIUMS, AND ARENAS

North Dallas has a number of performance venues, ranging from the new 2009 Dallas Cowboys stadium that can accommodate 80,000 fans to the Amphitheater at Oak Point Park that can hold nearly 1500 patrons for concerts and other outdoor events. From rock concerts to Broadway shows to live operas, North Dallas offers performance facilities that rival many other metropolitan areas. These venues play host to some of biggest names in the performing arts. For the most up-to-date information about upcoming shows, available tickets, ticket prices, and seating, contact each venue or visit the venue's Website.

- **Dallas Cowboys Stadium**, 1104 E Randol Mill Rd, Arlington, 817-892-4400, *www.dallascowboys.com*
- **Gerald J. Ford Stadium at Southern Methodist University**, 5801 Airline Road, Dallas, 214-768-3388, *www.smumustangs.cstv.com/facilities/ford-stadium.html*
- **Cotton Bowl Stadium**, 1300 Robert B. Cullum Boulevard, Dallas, 214-670-8400, *www.cottonbowlstadium.com*
- **Dr. Pepper Ballpark**, 7300 Rough Riders Trail, Frisco, 972-731-9200, *www.web.minorleaguebaseball.com/index.jsp?sid=t540*
- **Verizon Theater in Grandprairie**, 1001 Performance Place Grand Prairie 75050 972-854-5111 *www.verizontheater.com*
- **Pizza Hut Park**, 9200 World Cup Way, Frisco, 214-705-6700, *www.pizzahutpark.com*
- **Amphitheater at Oak Point Park Concerts**, 2801 W Spring Creek Pkwy., 972-941-5202, Plano, *www.plano.gov/Departments/Arts/Planos%20Stages/Pages/default.aspx*,
- **American Airlines Center**, 2500 Victory Avenue, Dallas, 214-222-3687, *www.americanairlinescenter.com*
- **Smirnoff Music Center,** 1818 First Ave Dallas 75210 214-421-1111

PERFORMING ARTS

Music – Symphonic, Choral, Opera, Chamber

Plano and the surrounding North Dallas area bring together the best in both professional and community music. From symphony orchestras to choral performances, the organizations listed below provide extensive programs through which musicians and vocal performers share their talents with North Dallas:

- **Plano Symphony Orchestra**, 972-473-7262, *www.planos ymphony.org*, performances are held at three main locations including the Courtyard Theatre, 1509 Avenue H, St. Andrew United Methodist Church, 5801 West Plano Parkway both in Plano and the Eisemann Center, 2351 Performance Drive in Richardson.

- **Plano Community Band**, some performances held at Haggard Park, 901 East 15th Street, Plano, 972-941-2117, *www.newsite. planoband.com,* consist of 95 musicians who are best known for their summer concerts in Haggard Park. They also play indoor concerts and perform at various city functions including the Memorial Day Ceremonies and the Tree Lighting in Haggard Park each year. **Plano Civic Chorus**, P.O. Box 864411, 972-606-5220, *www.planocivicchorus.org,* includes more than 100 voices that perform several concerts a year throughout the Dallas-Fort Worth area, frequently with local symphony orchestras. The Chorus that was chartered in 1972 also sings in community events throughout the year with a musical repertoire ranging from the great works of the choral masters to contemporary favorites.

- **Repertory Company Theatre**, 650 N Coit, Richardson, 972-690-5029, *www.rcttheatre.com/Home_Page.html,* has year round training in theatre arts for all age groups with an emphasis on performance. The theatre's school was selected best summer theatre camp by the Dallas Morning News and the best children's theatre program by the Dallas Observer.

- **Shakespeare in the Park**, 3630 Harry Hines Blvd., 3rd Floor, Dallas, 214-559-2778, *www.shakespearedallas.org*, began in 1971 and offers North Texas residents a unique opportunity to experience Shakespeare in an informal park setting. It also provides cultural and educational programs to audiences of all ages.

- **Dallas Symphony Orchestra**, Morton H. Meyerson Symphony Center, 2301 Flora Street, Dallas, 214-692-0203, *www.dallassymphony.com*, began in the spring of 1900 with a 40 member ensemble performing under the direction of German-born conductor Hans Kreissig. Jaap van Zweden is the current director and he will begin his third year in the position in September 2010.

- **University of North Texas Opera**, 415 Avenue C, Denton 940-369-7802, *www.music.unt.edu/opera/*

- **Frisco Chorale**, P.O. Box 711, 972-335-4380, ext. 104 *www.friscochorale.org*, comprised of volunteer vocalists from Frisco and the surrounding North Texas area. Concerts are held seasonally and the choir performs choral music that spans the Renaissance era through modern composition. The Chorale also offers performances in private, business, and civic venues throughout the year.

- **The Dallas Opera**, 2403 Flora Street, 214-443-1000, *www.dallasopera.org*

Dance – Ballet and Modern

- **Plano Metropolitan Ballet**, 3131 Custer Road, Suite #195, 972-769-0017, *www.planometballet.org*, is a non-profit ballet company that was founded in 1987. It provides affordable, high-quality dance performances to the local community while instilling a love of dance in its dedicated young dancers. Each year the group performs an original fairy-tale ballet and hosts the Plano Dance Festival in addition to participating in other performances and outreach initiatives.

- **Collin County Ballet Theatre**, 972-747-0600, *www.ccballet.com,* began in the Fall of 2001 by Artistic Directors, Kirt & Linda Hathaway.

- **Charles W. Eisemann Center for Performing Arts and Corporate Presentations**, 2351 Performance Drive, Richardson, 972-744-4650, *www.eisemanncenter.org/tickets/,* opened in September 2002, to serve the entertainment and special events needs of both the cultural and business clients of the entire North Texas region.

- **McKinney Performing Arts Center**, 111 N. Tennessee St., McKinney, 972-547-2650, *www.mckinneyperformingartscenter.org,* located at the Historic Collin County Courthouse in Downtown McKinney's Commercial Historic District. It is dedicated to providing the community with a unique and professional venue to nurture and support cultural, artistic and educational opportunities.

- **Texas Ballet Theater**, two administrative offices in Dallas, 214-369-5200, and Fort Worth, 817-763-0207 and two school locations in Fort Worth, 817-763-0207, and Richardson, 214-369-5200, *www.texasballettheater.org,* employs 38 professional dancers and operates two ballet academies for 300 students. It is the largest, critically acclaimed, fully professional, resident classical ballet company of North Texas. The Ballet Theater was originally incorporated in 1961 as Fort Worth Ballet and transitioned to full-time professional status in 1984.

Theatre – Professional and Community

If you're looking for high-caliber Broadway performances, **Dallas Summer Musicals**, *www.dallassummermusicals.org* should be at the top of your list. Dallas Summer Musicals has brought some of the biggest and most well-known stage productions to Texas for 70 years now, including Phantom of the Opera, Shrek the Musical, and Dreamgirls. You can order tickets to individual shows or purchase season tickets at the box office at 542 Preston Royal Shopping Center in Dallas or call 214-691-7200. Tickets can also be purchased online at *www.dallassummermusicals.org* or at Northpark Mall, 8687 N Central Expressway, Dallas, 214-363-2955.

If your wallet is tight or if local, smaller productions are more up your alley; North Dallas has a number of well-established professional and community theatre groups:

- **Collin Theatre Center,** performs in three theaters on the Spring Creek campus of Collin College in Plano including the John Anthony Theatre, Black Box Theatre and the ALT Lab Theatre. 2800 E. Spring Creek Pkwy, 972-881-5679, *www.collintheatrecenter.com/home.htm*
- **Frisco Community Theatre,** PO Box 1221, 972-370-2266, *www.friscocommunitytheatre.com*
- **Courtyard Theatre**, 1509 H Avenue, Plano, 972-422-7460, *www.plano.gov/Departments/Arts/Planos%20Stages/Courtyard/Pages /default.aspx*
- **Greater Lewisville Community Theater**, 160 W. main Street, 972-221-SHOW, *www.glct.org*

FILM

Plano may not be a destination for small, independent films, but that's not to say there aren't theatres in and around Plano featuring not-so-mainstream flicks. You may be far from the Hollywood glitz and glamour in Plano, but there are certainly theaters and local film festivals that can win over even the most movie-lover. Below are some great theatres and local film festivals for catching some of the latest "indy" and foreign films.

If you're in the mood for a Hollywood blockbuster, there are a number of national theatre chains in North Dallas including, Cinemark, Studio Movie Grill, AMC Theaters and Regal Entertainment Group theaters. For theatre location and ticket information, visit the movie-ticket Website Fandango at *www.fandango.com*.

- **The Majestic Theatre**, 1925 Elm Street Dallas, 214-880-0137, *www.liveatthemajestic.com,* opened on April 11, 1921 during the Vaudeville era. Today the theater offers plays, musicals, concerts and a variety of other entertainment and artistic events including acting workshops for children and adults.

Film Festivals

- **USA Film Festival**, 6116 North Central Expressway, Dallas, 214-821-3456, *www.usafilmfestival.com,* began in 1970 and is a year round film and video arts organization that offers 20-30 free screenings per year to its members. Additionally, it hosts the official Dallas Oscar party each year, the festival also offers an outdoor film series in the summer, a children's film festival each year and you might even get to meet filmmakers at different premieres.

- **Dallas International Film Festival**, 3625 N Hall St, 214-720-0555, *www.dallasfilm.org,* created in 2006 and is one of the fastest growing film festivals in the world. Has been named by Movie Maker Magazine as one of the "25 Festivals Worth the Entry Fee." In the first three years, there were over 110,000 people in attendance from all over the world for over 600 screenings and special events during the Festival. Some film screenings have been award nominees and winners.

MUSIC (CONTEMPORARY) AND NIGHT LIFE

When most people think of "cultural life," they associate the phrase with Broadway theatre or symphony orchestras. Yet for many, live contemporary music is just as much a part of their cultural life as art museums or literature. Below is a list of clubs and bars that offer nightly or weekly live music.

Alternative, Rock and Hip Hop

- **Club DMX**, 10733 Spangler Road, Dallas, 972-501-9335
- **Fat Daddy's Sound Shack**, 11345 Emerald Street, Dallas, 972-891-2263, *www.fatdaddyssoundshack.com*

Blues

- **Hat Tricks**, 101 E Corporate Dr. # 300, Lewisville, 972 315-8406, *www.hattricksdallas.com*
- **Bent Tree Grill**, 18100 Midway Rd., Carrollton, 972 248-3559, *www.benttreegrill.com*
- **AllGood Cafe'**, 2934 Main St., Dallas, 214 742-5362, *www.allgoodcafe.com*
- **Down Under Pub**, 3231 Preston Rd., Frisco, 972 668-0062, *www.downunderpub.com*
- **Ernie's of North Dallas Restaurant**, 5100 Belt Line Rd # 502, Dallas, 972 233-8855, *www.erniesofnorthdallas.com*

Country

- **Last Chance Saloon,** 1410 K Ave, Plano, 469-252-0456, *www.lastchancesaloontx.com/*

- **Wylie Opry**, 111 North Ballard Avenue, Wylie,972-442-3047, *www.wylieopry.com*
- **Gilley's Dallas,** 1135 S Lamar St, Dallas, 214-421-2021, *www.gilleysdallas.com*
- **Poor David's Pub**, 1313 South Lamar Street, Dallas, 214-565-1295, *www.poordavidspub.com*
- **Adair's Saloon**, 2624 Commerce Street, Dallas, 214-939-9900, *www.adairssaloon.com*
- **Cowboys Red River,** 10310 Technology Boulevard East, Dallas, 214-352-1796, *www.cowboysdancehall.com/*
- **Sons of Hermann Home,** 3414 Elm Street, Dallas, 214-747-4422, *www.sonsofhermann.com*

Jazz

- **The Balcony Club**, 1825 Abrams Rd, Ste B, Dallas, 214-826-8104
- **Brooklyn Jazz Cafe**, 1701 S Lamar St., Dallas, 214 428-0025, *www.brooklynjazzcafe.com*

Irish

- **Fillmore Pub**, 1004 East 15th Street, Plano, 972-423-2400, *www.thefillmorepub.com.dnnmax.com*
- **De Laney's Irish Pub**, 6150 West Eldorado Parkway, Mckinney, 972-529-6777, *www.delaneysirishpub.com*
- **Trinity Hall Irish Pub & Restaurant**, 305 Central Expressway North, Allen, 469-854-6810, *www.trinityhall.tv/*
- **Irish Rover Pub & Restaurant**, 8250 Gaylord Parkway, Frisco, 214-618-6222, *www.irishroverpub.com*
- **Lochranns Eatery & Irish Pub**, 6195 Main Street, Frisco, 214-423-2600, *www.lochranns.com*

- **Black Finn Inc**, 4440 Belt Line Road, Addison, 469-374-7667, *www.blackfinndallas.com/Addison/*
- **Idle Rich Pub**, 2614 McKinney Avenue, Dallas, 214-965-9926, *www.idlerichpub.com*

Nightclubs

- **W w Fairfields,** 147 North Plano Road, Richardson, 972-231-3844, *www.wwfairfields.com*
- **ORb Night Club**, 807 South Central Expressway, Richardson, 972-234-4672, *www.orbdallas.com*
- **Karma**, 15203 Knoll Trail Drive, Dallas, 972-980-9199, *www.karmadallas.com*
- **Ranch House**, 7610 Highway 78, Sachse, 972-442-2820, *www.ranchhousetexas.com/web/Home.html*
- **Deep Ellum**, *www.ondaweb.com/deep_ellum/*, so named because of its location on Elm Street has been a part of Dallas's cultural roots since the 1800's. It remains a popular location for restaurants and nightlife, including clubs like Club Clearview, Curtain Club, Liquid Lounge, Galaxy Club, Club Dada, Trees, and Indigo, all within walking distance of each other.

Reggae

- **Taste of the Islands Caribbean Restaurant and Nightlife**, 909 W Spring Creek Pkwy, Plano, 972-517-5900, *www.tasteoftheislands.net*

ART MUSEUMS

- **Dallas Museum of Art**, 1717 N. Harwood Street, Dallas, 214-922-1200, *www.dm-art.org*, features art from all over the world including ancient America, Africa, Indonesia, contemporary art, and decorative art. There are also two restaurants and a Museum Store on site for your convenience.

ART GALLERIES

- **The ArtCentre of Plano**, 1039 E 15th St., 972-423-7809, *www.artcentreofplano.org*, began in 1981 as a private non-profit organization to promote the growth and development of emerging community arts groups.
- **The Arts Gallery at Collin County Community College**, Spring Creek Campus, 2800 E. Spring Creek Parkway, Room A175, Plano, 972-516-5008, *www.ccccd.edu/theartsgallery/*, offers arts programming for the community including visual arts exhibits, performing arts rehearsals, classes, lectures, local arts organizations' meetings, and other cultural events.
- **Arts of Collin County**, 305 Century Parkway, Third Floor, Allen, 214-495-5810, *www.artsofcollincounty.org*, is being developed through a public-private collaboration between the three cities of Allen, Frisco and Plano, Texas. It will be a place where all visitors can enjoy the diversity and vitality of the arts.

HISTORICAL AND CULTURAL MUSEUMS

- **Interurban Railway Museum**, 901 E.15th Street, Plano, 972-941-2117, *www.plano.gov/Departments/ParksandRecreation/Parks_ Facilities/Pages/interurban.aspx*, transportation history is brought back to life with this interesting exhibit. The interurban is one of the original electric cars that ran through Plano between Denison and Waco. It was an important part of the Texas Electric Railway System. You can also find Car 360 at this museum which carried mail and passengers.
- **Cavanaugh Flight Museum**, 4572 Claire Chennault, Addison, 972-248-0907, *www.cavanaughflightmuseum.com*, displays

50,000 square feet of warbirds that have been restored to their original condition. This museum is on the grounds of Addison Airport and includes an aviation gift shop, aviation art and memorabilia gallery as well as a snack shop.

- **North Texas Automotive Museum**, 677 W. Cambell Road, Richardson, 972-918-0084, *www.ntxautomuseum.com,* has a large assortment of automobiles on display throughout the year including consignment vehicles available for purchase. The cars rotate as new automobiles come in and others go on to the next showcase. You will find the best quality classic, antique, muscle, movie-related or race cars.

- **Frisco Heritage Museum**, 6455 Page Street, Frisco, 972-292-5665, *www.friscomuseum.com,* consists of a living village that represents the rich history of Frisco. Visitors may even participate in recreating historical events in some of the interactive exhibits throughout the museum.

- **The Collin County Farm Museum**, 7117 County Road 166, McKinney, 972-548-4729, *www.co.collin.tx.us/parks/myers/farm_ museum.jsp*, created to educate and inform people about the history of farming in Collin County and its impact in North Texas. The museum includes farming equipment from different periods of farming history in the 8,528 square feet Wells Building, the blacksmith shop, the granary and the confinement house.

- **The Sixth Floor Museum at Dealey Plaza**, 411 Elm Street, Dallas, 214-747-6660, *www.jfk.org*, presents the history of the assassination and legacy of President John F. Kennedy. The museum opened in 1989 and has welcomed almost 4,000,000 visitors.

- **The African American Museum**, 3536 Grand Avenue, Fair Park, Dallas, 214 565-9026, *www.aamdallas.org*, began in 1974 as a part of the Bishop College Special Collection. The Museum has operated independently since 1979. It is the only museum in the Southwestern U.S. dedicated to the preservation and display of African American artistic, cultural and historical materials. It houses one of the largest African American folk art collections in the country. The Museum incorporates a wide variety of visual art forms and historical documents that portray the African American experience in the U.S. Southwest, and Dallas.

- **Nasher Sculpture Center**, 2001 Flora St., Dallas, 214-242-5100, *www.nashersculpturecenter.org*, The Center was designed by architect Renzo Piano. It features the art collection of philanthropist and collector Ray Nasher and his late wife, Patsy, and a two-acre sculpture garden created by landscape architect Peter Walker. There are more than 300 pieces, featuring works by Calder, Matisse, Picasso, and Serra, just to name a few. The garden features outdoor works with stone walls and walkways, ponds, trees and meadow areas.

SCIENCE MUSEUMS

- **Heard Natural Science Museum & Wildlife Sanctuary**, 1 Nature Place, McKinney, 972-509-5253, *www.heardmuseum.org*, is a 289-acre outdoor preserve and nature museum that features the Living Lab, an interactive science laboratory, venomous snakes of Texas exhibit, a rotating nature art exhibit and other seasonal exhibits.

CULTURE FOR KIDS

The days when your children say, "I'm bored!" are now a thing of the past – at least for the time being! Plano and the surrounding North Dallas area has a broad range of attractions and programs specifically designed with kids in mind. Below are just a few of the top picks for indoor and outdoor kid fun, learning, and entertainment.

Most of the museums and many of the area's annual festivals and events offer children's programs and/or family friendly activities. For more information, check venue or event Website.

Museums

- **Heritage Farmstead Museum**, 1900 West 15th Street, Plano, 972-881-0140, *www.heritagefarmstead.org*, has programs for children including summer camp, birthday parties, tours and fun on the farm activities.
- **The Children's Museum at the Museum of Nature and Science**, has several buildings all located in Dallas including the Nature Building at 3535 Grand Avenue, the Science Building at 1318 South Second Avenue and the Planetarium Building at 1620 First Avenue, 214-428-5555, *www.natureandscience.org/dcm/default.asp*

Arts and Theatre

- **Plano Children's Theatre**, 1301 Custer Road, #706, Plano, 972-422-2575, *www.planochildrenstheatre.org*
- **Morrow's Performing Arts Center**, 4101 E. Park, Suite 121, Plano, 972-516-1653, *www.mpacplano.com,* focuses on training in dance and drama education for all ages ranging from toddlers to adults.
- **Frisco Area Children's Theatre**, classes held at the Frisco Association of Arts, 6827 Main Street, *www.friscoacts.com*
- **Frisco Arts Youth Council, 6827 Main Street,** 972-668-5180, *www.friscoarts.org/html/fayc.html,* is a community-based organization formed by citizens of Frisco whose long term goals are to provide a facility to give the citizens access to full participation in the arts and to satisfy the requirements of the varied artists and art groups in the area.

- **Music Conservatory of Texas**, has two locations including 700 Parker Square #105, Flower Mound, 972-899-9330 and 9255 Preston Rd, Frisco, 972-377-5977, *www.mcot.com,* provides private and adult lessons in various areas including voice, piano, guitar, violin, flute, percussion and more from university trained teachers.

- **Dallas Children's Theatre**, Rosewood Center for Family Arts, 5938 Skillman, Dallas, *www.dct.org,* was ranked one of the top five youth theaters in the country by TIME Magazine. It is a professional theater that serves more than 270,000 young people and their families through its 11 main stage productions, national touring company, and education and outreach programs.

INDOOR/ OUTDOOR FUN

- **Soccer Spectrum**, 1251 Digital Drive, Richardson, 972-644-8845, *www.soccerspectrum.com,* is an indoor soccer field to help keep your child active all year long or even have a birthday party here.

- **Fieldhouse USA**, 6155 Sports Village Rd., Frisco, 972-668-6207, *www.fieldhouseusa.com,* offers incredible basketball, soccer, football, volleyball and other sports experience to everyone that enters the state of the art facility. It is easily accessible to anyone living in Plano or North Dallas.

- **Dallas Arboretum and Botanical Garden**, 8525 Garland Road, 214-515-6500, *www.dallasarboretum.org,* offers guided tours, self-instructing materials and educational programs with hands-on experiences that make learning fun. Additionally, these programs incorporate language arts, math, social studies and fine art components.

LITERARY LIFE AND HIGHER EDUCATION

Bookstores

Plano and the surrounding North Dallas area have quite a lot to offer when it comes to satisfying your inner bookworm. From the familiar national book retailers to independent booksellers to the not-so-familiar (and often eccentric) used bookstores, the wide array of booksellers in the area are sure to offer something for everyone's literary tastes.

Chain Book Retailers

- **Barnes & Noble**, 800-843-2665, *www.barnesandnoble.com*, multiple locations throughout Plano and North Dallas
- **Books-A-Million**, 800-201-3550, *www.booksamillion.com*, multiple locations throughout Texas
- **Borders**, 800-770-7811, *www.borders.com*, multiple location throughout North Dallas
- **Half Price Books, Records, Magazines**, 214-360-0833, *www.halfpricebooks.com*, multiple location throughout North Dallas
- **Mardel Christian & Educational**, 888-2MARDEL, *www.mardel.com*, multiple location throughout North Dallas
- **Family Christian Store**, *www.familychristian.com*, three locations in North Dallas: 601 W Plano Pkwy #153, Plano, 972-423-9568, Garden Park Shop Center, 1565 W Main St Ste 102, Lewisville, 972-420-1322, Frisco Village, , 2930 Preston Rd Ste 300, Frisco, 972-731-8394; Christian book and gift retailer

Independent And Used Booksellers

- **75 Percent Off Books**, 1717 East Spring Creek Parkway, Plano, 972-423-8120, *www.75offbookstores.com*

- **Lone Star Comics Games and Gifts**, 3100 Independence Parkway, Plano, 972- 985-1593, *www.mycomicshop.com/ourstores/plano*
- **PJ's Campus Books**, 1210 East Parker Road, Plano, 972-881-8733
- **Madness Games & Comics**, 3131 Custer Road Suite # 125, Plano, 972-943-8135, *www.madnessgames.com/Madness.html*
- **Agape Christian Bookstore**, 4201 Stanton Boulevard, Plano, 972-964-7113
- **Bright Minds Critical Thinking**, P.O. Box 260287, Plano, 866-710-7027, *www.brainbuildingfun.com*
- **Kids Write On**, 6508 Hillswick Drive, Plano, 972-862-7257
- **Dicho's Books & More**, The Shops at Willow Bend, 6121 West Park Boulevard, D208, Plano, 972-202-8581, *www.dichosbooks.com*
- **Cokesbury Book & Church Supply**, 19200 Preston Road, Dallas, 972-964-5777, *www.cokesbury.com/forms/home.aspx*
- **Magic Storyland Bookstore**, 3231 Preston Road, Frisco, 214-618-4141
- **SBD Spanish Book Distribution**, 6706 Sawmill Road, Dallas, 214-369-1345, *www.sbdbooks.com/*
- **Atomic Age Collectibles**, 4043 Trinity Mills Road, Dallas, 972-735-8333
- **Varsity Books,** 300 N Coit Rd, Richardson, 972-231-2903
- **Richland Bookstore Discount Textbooks**, 445 Walnut St, Richardson, 972-231-6986
- **Medbooks**, 101 W Buckingham Rd, Richardson, 972-643-1809
- **Nerdbooks.Com**, 1681 Firman Dr, Ste 101, Richardson, 972-470-9600
- **Off Campus Books,** 561 W Campbell Rd, Richardson, 972-907-8398

- **World Bookstore**, 400 N Greenville Ave, Richardson, 972-690-0163
- **Herald Book Store,** 110 N Mckinney St, Richardson, 972-680-2999
- **Christian Science Reading Room**, 1930 N Coit Rd, Richardson, 972-231-0114

Literary Workshops And Groups

Whether you're an aspiring writer looking for constructive criticism or a book lover hoping to share your literary passion with others, there are likely a number of literary groups and book clubs that can match your needs and interests.

Libraries and many national book retailers as well as independent booksellers host book clubs or other literary groups. Check with your local library branch and booksellers for more information.

Another great resource to find local writers' workshops or book clubs is a website called Meetup, *www.meetup.com*. The Website provides a great directory of local social groups, and groups use the site to keep their members up-to-date on information about upcoming events. Literary groups and book clubs in and around Plano are plentiful on Meetup.

Other literary groups and book clubs include:

- **Farris Literary Agency, Inc.,** P.O. Box 570069, Dallas, 972-203-8804, *www.farrisliterary.com/index.html,* provides a list of upcoming literary groups and conferences in the area. Additionally, this agency will help new and established authors publish their works.
- **DFW Writer's Workshop,** meetings held every Wednesday at 7:00pm at the Ruth Millican Center, 201 Cullum Drive, Euless, 817–714–6573, *www.dfwwritersworkshop.org*

Libraries

Seventeen public libraries and branches make up the Collin County Public Library system including six in Plano. Collin County library cardholders are welcome to use computers and to check out books and materials from any of the Collin County libraries.

Each library hosts a variety of literary events, book clubs for various age groups, and family-friendly activities. For more information on events, contact each branch directly or visit the Collin County Public Libraries Website at *www.co.collin.tx.us/education/libraries.jsp.*

There are also seventeen public libraries in the neighboring Denton County Public Library system and 27 public libraries in Dallas. A few are mentioned below and to get a complete list of these libraries visit *www.co.denton.tx.us/other/libraries.asp and www.dallaslibrary.org.*

North Dallas colleges and universities also offer additional resources, including extensive collections of academic texts and journals. While college and university libraries are generally open to the public, their hours and services for non-students and non-faculty patrons may vary. Check directly with each library for more details on services available to the public.

Public

- **Maribelle M. Davis Library**, 7501-B Independence Pkwy., Plano, 972-208-8000
- **W. O. Haggard, Jr. Library**, 2501 Coit Road, Plano, 972-769-4250
- **Gladys Harrington Library**, 1501 18th St., Plano, 972-941-7175
- **Christopher A. Parr Library**, 6200 Windhaven Parkway, Plano, 972-769-4300
- **L. E. R. Schimelpfenig Public Library**, 5024 Custer Road, Plano, 972-941-7175

- **McKinney Memorial Public Library**, 101 E. Hunt Street, McKinney, 972-547-7323
- **Rita and Truett Smith Public Library**, 800 Thomas Street, Wylie, 972-442-7566
- **Frisco Public Library**, 6101 Frisco Square Blvd., Frisco, 972-292-KNOW
- **Allen Public Library**, 300 N. Allen Drive, Allen, 214-509-4900
- **Alla Hubbard Library**, 3455 N. Preston Road, Celina, 469-742-9131
- **Charles J. Rike Memorial Library**, 203 Orange Street, Farmersville, 972-782-6681
- **Melissa Public Library**, 1713 Cooper Street, Melissa, 972-837-4540
- **Princeton Community Library**, 319 McKinney Street, Princeton, 972-736-3741
- **Prosper Community Library**, 300 Eagle Lane, Prosper, 972-346-2455 ext. 516
- **Carrolton Public Library at Hebron & Josey**, 4220 North Josey Lane, Carrollton, 972- 466-4800
- **Flower Mound Public Library**, 3030 Broadmoor Lane, Flower Mound, 972- 874-6200
- **J. Erik Jonsson Central Library**, 1515 Young Street, Dallas, 214-670-1400, *www.dallaslibrary.org/central/index.php*

Historical Libraries

- **North Texas Masonic Historical Museum and Library**, 1414 J Avenue Plano, *www.northtexashistory.org*; organized to preserve the history of Plano, Collin County, and North Texas. This includes the history of the first Masonic Lodge and the current Masonic Lodge in Plano as well as other Lodges in Collin County and the North Texas. Information on their founders, officers, members and their correlation and influence on the communities' history can also be found here.

College And University Libraries

- **Spring Creek Campus Library (Collin College)**, 2800 E. Spring Creek Parkway, Plano, 972-881-5860, *www.ccccd.edu/library/*
- **Central Park Campus Library (Collin College)**, 2200 W. University, McKinney, 972-548-6860, *www.ccccd.edu/library/*
- **Preston Ridge Campus Library (Collin College)**, 9700 Wade Blvd., Frisco, 972-377-1560, *www.ccccd.edu/library/*
- **Brookhaven College Library**, 3939 Valley View Lane, Bldg. L, Room L200, Dallas, 972-860-4863, *www.brookhavencollege.edu/library/*
- **Cedar Valley College Library**, 972-860-8140, 3030 North Dallas Ave., Lancaster, *www.cedarvalleycollege.edu/CurrentStudents/Library/default.aspx*
- **Dallas County Community College Libraries**, list all libraries in and around Dallas County, *www.dcccd.edu/Current+Students/Libraries/Area+Libraries/*

Lectures

Regular lecture series are abundant in Plano and the surrounding areas. A number of organizations in the area including colleges, universities, museums, public libraries, and local churches sponsor and organize regular lecture series.

On one hand, lecture series can be great resources for those doing professional research or considering the next step in their career paths. On the other hand, lecture series can simply provide a fun outlet for intellectual curiosity.

Organizations and institutions that regularly host lecture series include:

- **Collin County Community College**, Distinguished Speaker Series, 2800 East Spring Creek Parkway, Plano, *www.collin.edu/*
- **Southern Methodist University**, Tate Lecture Series, 6116 N Central Expy, Dallas, 214-768-8283, *www.smu.edu/tateseries/*
- **Dallas Philosophers Forum**, *www.philosophersforum.org/index.html*, visit the website to join the group, find out what lectures are available and where they will be held
- **Dallas Museum of Art**, Saturday Lecture Series, 1717 N. Harwood, Dallas, 214-922-1200, *www.dm-art.org/index.htm*

Higher Education

Those looking for intellectual stimulation will find plenty of options in Texas. North Dallas and its surrounding areas are home to some of the country's top universities and leading research institutions.

- **Southern Methodist University**, 6425 Boaz Lane, Dallas, 214-768-2000 *www.smu.edu/*, founded in 1911 by The United Methodist Church, the university opened in 1915 with support from Dallas leaders. SMU is a private university of 11,000 students near the center of Dallas that offers strong undergraduate, graduate, and professional programs through seven schools.
- **Texas Christian University**, 2800 S. University Dr., Fort Worth, 817-257-7000, *www.tcu.edu/*, founded in 1873 by brothers Addison and Randolph Clark in Thorp Spring, Texas, as AddRan Male and Female College. The school moved to Waco in 1895 and the name was changed to AddRan Christian University in 1889 and Texas Christian University in 1902. In 1910 the university relocated to downtown Fort Worth after the

Waco facility burned. Three new buildings were opened on the present campus in 1911.

- **Texas A&M University**, 979-845-3211, *www.tamu.edu/*, began in 1876 as the first public institution of higher learning in Texas. Now it is a bustling 5,000-acre campus with a nationally recognized faculty and is one of a select few universities with land-grant, sea-grant and space-grant designations. The 38,000-plus undergraduates and more than 9,000 graduate students have access to first-rate research programs and award-winning faculty. The University has two branch campuses, one in Galveston, Texas and one in the Middle Eastern country of Qatar.

- **Texas Tech University**, 2500 Broadway, Lubbock, 806-742-2011, *www.ttu.edu/*, was established in 1923 and carries the distinction of being the largest comprehensive higher education institution in the western two-thirds of the state.

- **Texas Wesleyan University**, 1201 Wesleyan Street, Fort Worth, 817-531-4444, *www.txwesleyan.edu/*, founded in 1890 by the Methodist Episcopal Church, South. Originally called Polytechnic College, the school held its first classes in September 1891, with a handful of faculty members and just 111 students.

- **Texas Woman's University**, 304 Administration Drive, Denton, 940-TWU-2000, *www.twu.edu/*, established in 1901 as the Girls Industrial College later became Texas Woman's University in 1957. The university offers a comprehensive catalog of academic studies, including baccalaureate, master's and doctoral degrees and men have been admitted since 1972. Now in its tenth decade, the University has grown from a small college to a major university and is the largest university primarily for women in the country. The main campus is in Denton with health science centers in Dallas and Houston.

- **University of Dallas**, 1845 East Northgate Drive, Irving, 972-721-5000, *www.udallas.edu/*, established in 1956, the university has been consistently ranked as one of the top liberal arts universities in the country. It is one of only eight in the state of Texas to receive Phi Beta Kappa status, and is one of 124 schools in the nation recognized for stressing character development among students.

- **University of North Texas**, 1155 Union Circle #311277, Denton, 940-565-2000, *www.unt.edu/*, founded in 1890 and is one of the state's largest universities. The university offers 97 bachelor's, 101 master's and 49 doctoral degree programs.

- **University of Texas Arlington**, 701 S. Nedderman Drive, Arlington, 817-272-2011, *www.uta.edu/uta/*, promotes an active learning environment for more than 28,000 students, who pursue nearly 190 bachelor's, master's and doctoral degrees within 10 colleges and schools.

- **University of Texas at Austin**, Freshman Admissions Center, southeast corner of Martin Luther King Blvd. and Red River St., Austin 512-475-7348, *www.utexas.edu/*, was founded in 1883. The university has grown from a single building, eight teachers, two departments and 221 students to a 350-acre main campus with 17 colleges, more than 50,000 students, 2,900 faculty and 21,000 staff members.

- **University of Texas at Dallas**, 800 West Campbell Road, Richardson, 972-883-2111, *www.utdallas.edu/*, owes its existence to three men who also founded Texas Instruments, Eugene McDermott, J. Erik Jonsson and Cecil Green.

CHAPTER 41

CLIMATE AND ENVIRONMENT

The weather in Plano, Texas is considerably warmer than most of the rest of the country. There's rarely any snow in the Dallas suburb, but then again, there's rarely any snow anywhere in Texas. But that should come as welcome news to all of you who desire a welcome respite from all the suffering that comes with sub-freezing temperatures. There's seldom a month where you can't enjoy your favorite outdoor activities. So break out the grill and go play football in the park with your family while your friends up north are snowed into their houses and enjoy all the environmental benefits of living in Plano, Texas.

WEATHER IN PLANO, TEXAS

Plano is less than twenty miles from Dallas and shares its humid subtropical climate. Warm, dry winds blow across Plano's landscape during most of the year. Plano maintains a four season weather pattern with January being the coldest month and July and August the hottest. The average temperature range in January is 31-53 degrees Fahrenheit and is 72-93 degrees Fahrenheit in July. Rainfall can be expected year round with an annual average of over 38 inches.

AVERAGE TEMPERATURE (F) COMPARED TO OTHER CITIES
SOURCE: U.S. N.O.A.A.

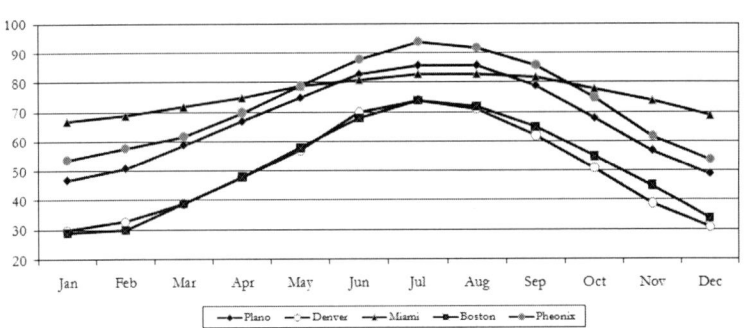

PLANO AVERAGE HIGH/LOW TEMPERATURES (F)
SOURCE: MSN.COM

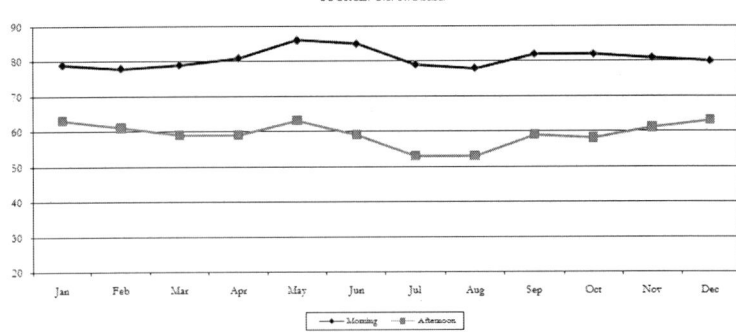

PLANO RELATIVE HUMIDITY (%)
SOURCE: U.S. N.O.A.A.

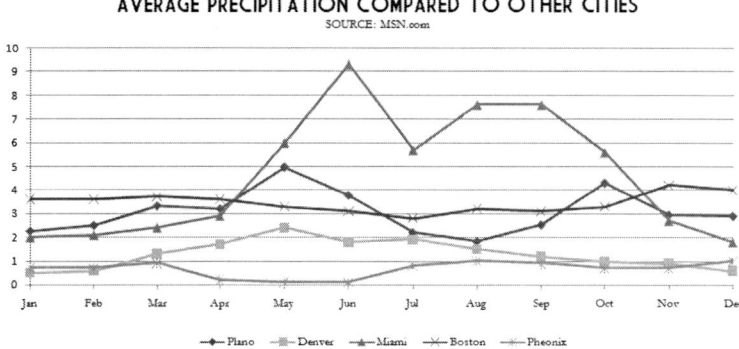

AVERAGE PRECIPITATION COMPARED TO OTHER CITIES
SOURCE: MSN.com

WHAT ARE THE FOUR SEASONS LIKE?

The seasons in Plano are more dynamic than one might think at first glance.

North Texas' climate is humid and sub-tropical. Springtime weather can be unpredictable as each spring, cool fronts moving south from Canada and collide with warm, humid air streaming in from the Gulf Coast, leading to severe thunderstorms with lightning, heavy rain, hail, and occasionally, tornadoes. Temperatures however are mostly mild.

In the summer, temperatures generally plateau out in the high-90's, but the all-time high was 114 degrees Fahrenheit, so don't be surprised by temperatures in the low 100's.

The weather in Plano is also generally enjoyable from late September to early December and on many winter days, but unlike in the springtime, major storms rarely form in the area. Try doing strenuous outdoor activities, such as mowing the lawn or jogging, in the morning or late evening during the hot summer months. And monitor local news outlets for advisories when ozone levels get high on hot days. Authorities will often recommend that vulnerable people – children and those with respiratory problems, for instance – stay inside on these days.

Though winters and summers are generally pleasant, the real treat of living in Plano might be spring and fall, when most days are neither too hot nor too cold for comfort. At night, try opening the windows and letting the cool breeze blow through your bedroom as you experience the best night's sleep you've ever had. Beautiful wildflowers also grow all over the region including bluebonnets and Indian paintbrushes.

SEVERE WEATHER

As a result of the city's proximity to the Gulf of Mexico, severe weather does occasionally visit the area in the form of thunderstorms, tornadoes, hail and hurricanes. While few of these events cause widespread damage, it's good to be prepared for all types of severe weather.

To keep tabs on the weather on your own, try these websites and contacts:

Forecasts

- Online weather at Weather Underground for various cities in Plano, *www.wunderground.com/US/TX/Plano.html*
- Forecasts from the Plano office of NOAA, *www.forecast.weather.gov/MapClick.php?CityName=Plano&state=TX&site=FWD&textField1=33.0462&textField2=-96.7467&e=0*

Severe Weather

- Find Local Weather, *www.findlocalweather.com/stormwarnings/tx/plano.html*, offers weather warning advisories for all regions of the country.
- NOAA's current watches for warnings and advisories in Plano area, *www.nws.noaa.gov/alerts/tx.html*, offers flood, tornado and hurricane watch information and preparation info.

- Collin County Emergency Management and Department of Homeland Security, 972-548-5537, *www.co.collin.tx.us/homeland_security/index.jsp*, provides weather preparedness information and current state of affairs statistics.
- Find out how to get a weather radio for the Plano, Texas region, *www.crh.noaa.gov/lot/?n=KXI58*
- Hurricane meet-up info for the Plano, Texas area, *www.hurricane.meetup.com/cities/us/tx/plano/*

WHAT ABOUT TORNADOES IN PLANO?

The north Texas region is at the heart of what is known as Tornado Alley, or the area of the country for which tornadoes are most prevalent. This includes between the Rocky Mountains and the Appalachian Mountains. Nearly 90 percent of all tornadoes in the United States hit this area. According to the storm events database of the National Climatic Data Center, Texas reports more tornadoes than any other state. As a result, building codes are stricter in Texas, requiring stronger roofs and more durable foundations.

To be prepared for a tornado, plan in advance where you will go in the event of a tornado warning. The best location is generally on the lowest level of your house and away from windows. If you live in a mobile home, you should plan to evacuate to a safer structure. (Often local schools or churches will serve as shelters. Check with local authorities to see where you can go during severe weather.) Pay close attention to weather reports during hurricanes and thunderstorms.

Also, be familiar with your tornado terms. A tornado watch simply means that weather conditions are ripe for tornadoes to form. A tornado warning means that at least one has been spotted, and residents in the area should take cover. People who have lived through tornadoes say they are extremely loud as they approach, making a sound often compared to a train approaching. If you suspect a tornado is approaching, take precautions even if you are not sure. Also keep your weather radio on if there is a power outage in your area.

Because of the frequency for which tornadoes hit The Lonestar State, the Texas Department of Emergency Management offers the following precautionary tips:

- Make sure to get to shelter in an interior room without windows on the lowest floor of your home, such as a bathroom, closet or room. Cover yourself with a mattress or cushions.
- In an office building, go to an interior room or hallway on the lowest floor.
- Never stay inside a car. Get out and lie flat in a ditch or a ravine. If a building is nearby, take shelter inside. Never try to outrun a tornado in your car.
- In open country, take cover in a low spot away from trees.
- Learn the difference between a Tornado Watch and a Tornado Warning. A Tornado Watch means watch the sky. A Tornado Warning means a tornado is on the ground and you must seek shelter immediately.

When tornadoes have been spotted in your area, state authorities suggest a three step plan: get in, get down and cover up. Stay inside in a safe place, and don't drive. If you suspect a tornado will hit your house or shelter, crouch down in the lowest part of the structure possible, cover yourself with pillows and try to move under a desk or other heavy furniture.

Here are some websites with information on tornadoes:

- NOAA's Tornado Guide, *www.nssl.noaa.gov/edu/safety/tornadoguide.html*, has information on how tornadoes form, the types and frequency of tornadoes, and tips for preparing for them.
- The Texas Department of Emergency Management, *www.txdps.state.tx.us/dem/pages/index.htm*, provides detailed

information on where to go, what to do as well as how to participate in the next statewide tornado drill and more.

WHAT SHOULD I KNOW ABOUT HURRICANES?

While many Texans know a thing or two about hurricanes, those living in Plano see hurricanes dissolve into thunderstorms by the time they reach the northern region of the state, since it is positioned inland from the coast. The storm surge produced by hurricanes can cause torrential rain, tornados, flooding and even mudslides.

It is rare for Plano and the rest of the north Texas region to be hit full force by a hurricane, but knowing what to do in case one ever makes it that far inland is always valuable. Besides, these tips can be used for when heavy thunderstorms hit the area and that most certainly will happen in Plano. When hurricanes arise on the coast, residents of Plano will typically face tropical storms or heavy thunderstorms. In any case, residents should prepare for heavy winds, lots of rain and the possibility of storm damage and electrical outages.

To be prepared for a hurricane or tropical storm, it is a good idea to make an emergency plan and kit using items listed by the Texas Department of Emergency Management, *www.txdps.state.tx.us/dem/pages/index.htm*. They outline several guidelines for riding out the worst hurricane:

- Secure your property. Permanent storm shutters offer the best protection for windows. A second option is to board up windows with plywood, cut to fit and ready to install. Tape does not prevent windows from breaking. Install storm shutters.
- Clear loose and clogged rain gutters and downspouts.
- Determine how and where to secure your boat.
- Bring in all outside objects that could potentially cause damage to property and people.

During a hurricane or tropical storm warning, stay indoors and monitor the weather on TV, radio or online. If a serious storm is approaching, some areas may be evacuated. Follow the directions of local authorities and stay inside, even if the weather seems to clear. An abrupt clearing of storm conditions may signify that the eye of the storm is passing, which means the storm will return just as abruptly as it stopped. Also, take the advice below on tornadoes, which often come along with hurricanes or other tropical weather.

WHY DO THUNDERSTORMS MATTER?

Hurricanes may lose a lot of their strength as they make their way inland from the Gulf of Mexico to the north Texas region but that doesn't mean they can't be just as deadly. Thunderstorms bring deadly lightning, hail, and falling branches or trees loosened by wind in rain that can knock out electricity, and cause injury or damage.

Most thunderstorms occur throughout the summer months and during the warmest part of the day typically the late afternoon and early evening hours.

During thunderstorms, stay indoors and monitor weather reports. Stay in the lowest floor of your house, particularly if nearby trees or limbs could hit your house. Be prepared to lose electricity. The Texas' Governor's Division of Emergency Management suggests taking the following precautionary measures when faced with a severe thunderstorm:

- The best place to be during a thunderstorm is inside a shelter fully enclosed by a roof, walls and floor. Small open shelters offer no protection from thunderstorms. Only shelters that contain plumbing or wiring throughout, or some other mechanism, for grounding from the roof to the ground, are safe during thunderstorms.
- Phone use during a thunderstorm is the leading cause of indoor lightning injuries in Texas.
- Do not lie on a concrete floor in the garage as it likely contains a wire mesh.

WHAT ABOUT DROUGHTS?

Texas has always had a history of droughts with irregular rain patterns and dry spells. Droughts have been a problem for those living in Texas ever since the Spaniards dwelled there. Every decade since the middle of the 19th century has had at least one drought period, so if you're going to live in north Texas. Luckily, modern technology and conservation methods have limited the problems associated with droughts.

To prepare, the best way to ease the pinch of water restrictions during drought is to landscape using drought-tolerant plants. Planting plants and laying sod during the rainy spring months will also help you avoid the pain of dry summers. Inside, make sure your toilets and other appliances use as little water as possible.

When dry weather hits, use a rain barrel to capture water for outside use. Reuse water from inside on your plants outside. Put off planting sensitive plants or sodding a new lawn.

Here are some useful websites about dry weather and droughts, including the rules and regulations governing droughts for the state of Texas:

- U.S. Drought Monitor, *www.drought.unl.edu/dm/monitor.html*
- Texas Climatic Bulletin, *www.met.tamu.edu/osc/*
- National Weather Service Climate Prediction Center, *www.cpc.ncep.noaa.gov*
- Texas Drought & Public Water Systems, *www.tceq.state.tx.us/nav/util_water/drought.html*
- Drought Contingency Planning, *www.tceq.state.tx.us/permitting/water_supply/water_rights/contingency.html*
- Water Department for Plano, Texas, *www.plano.gov/Water/Pages/default.aspx.*
- Helpful Tips for Water Conservation in Plano, *www.plano.gov/Departments/Water/Water%20Conservation%20and%20Education/Pages/default.aspx*

PLANTS AND ANIMALS

What kinds of plants and animals live in Northern Texas?

There is a variety of wildlife indigenous to the great state of Texas, ranging from majestic birds, exotic reptiles and a number of different types of fish.

Bird watching is a frequent activity in the Plano area as there are several endangered species all over the state. The "Eastern" Brown Pelican and the Whooping Crane are two of the more famous and predominant in the state, but the Red-cockaded Woodpecker and the Golden-cheeked Warbler also make their home in Texas. To find some bird watching pals, make sure to visit *www.birdingpal.org/tx.htm* for a list of active bird watchers and the regions they like to visit.

The American Fish and Game Club, the largest organization in the region offering ranges for fishing, hunting and camping, offers access to the most expansive collection of private, well-managed lakes and ranches to fish and hunt. AFGC properties expand throughout Texas and into southern Oklahoma. Visit *www.gtbc.com* for more information.

Among the least desirable of our animal and insect neighbors are numerous snakes and biting and stinging bugs in the region. In fact, more snakes are indigenous to Texas than any other state. The Brazos Water Snake and Louisiana Pine Snake make their home all over Texas and the endangered Timber Rattlesnake calls The Lonestar State its home. Visit the link below to learn more about the snakes that make Texas their home.

Several different species of insects are also found in Texas, including dozens of different species of beetles including the Tooth Cave Beetle and the Coffin Cave Mold Beetle. Visit the link below to see a list and description of many of the insects found in Texas.

Plants indigenous to the north Texas region include a lot of cacti and wildflowers. Species of plants not found a lot of places in the country including the Star Cactus and Davis' Green Pitaya. Texas owes much of its beauty to the many wildflowers that dot its landscape including the exotic, but rare, Texas Prairie Dawn, Texas Poppy-mallow and Pecos Sunflower.

Here are some resources on the Web to help you enjoy the area's plants and animals:

- **Bird watching in Texas**, *www.birdingpal.org/tx.htm*
- **American Fish & Game Club**, *www.gtbc.com.*
- **Insects in Texas**, *www.tpwd.state.tx.us/huntwild/wild/species/endang/animals/invertebrates/#insects*
- **Reptiles and Amphibians in Texas**, *www.tpwd.state.tx.us/huntwild/wild/species/endang/animals/reptiles_amphibians*, for information on snakes and other reptiles a list of local species.
- **Mammals: Texas Parks & Wildlife**, *www.tpwd.state.tx.us/huntwild/wild/species/endang/animals/mammals*, offers a list of mammals native to the state.
- **Plant Life in Texas**, *www.tpwd.state.tx.us/huntwild/wild/species/endang/plants/index.phtml*

Gardening in Northern Texas

The North Central Chapter of the Native Plant Society of Texas is one of the largest gardening organizations in north Texas. Meeting every month in Fort Worth, the group offers several guidelines for growing a healthy garden in Texas, including tips on cultivating healthy soil, when the best time to plant is and what species of plants will thrive best in a multitude of different conditions. Visit the group's website at *www.txnativeplants.org* to learn almost everything there is to learn about gardening in the north Texas region.

CHAPTER 42

TRANSPORTATION IN PLANO

Plano benefits from a network of interstates and major state roads that make getting from Plano to the Dallas/Fort Worth area to the airport and other points of interest a fast trip. Of course, this the area has grown rapidly, which in turn has helped crowd those roads with traffic. A continuing regimen of highway improvements is in place to accommodate the influx of drivers, though at a pace that can seem slow when you're trying to get to work in the Dallas area. To put some numbers behind that feeling, the Dallas region ranked 7th of 90 major metropolitan areas in 2007 in hours of traffic delays, according to a national study by the Texas Transportation Institute.

For going longer distances, planes -- and increasingly trains -- are convenient options. Within Plano and the surrounding area, Dallas Area Rapid Transit (DART) provides many modes of travel for commuters with options like the light rail, bus service and high occupancy vehicle (HOV) lanes. Old-fashioned ways to get around – walking and biking – are also gaining fans. On the coast, ferries are a popular way to get to and from the beaches and smaller islands.

For more information on getting around, try the Texas Department of Transportation, 800-558-9368, *www.dot.state.tx.us.* DOT works in concert with all branches of government to oversee transportation infrastructure in the state. The North Central Texas Council of Governments, *www.nctog.org,* created a Bicycle and Pedestrian program in 1992 to help encourage walking and bicycling as alternative forms of transportation.

ON THE ROAD

Despite a growing number of public transportation options, driving is still an easy way to get from place to place in Plano, and dealing with traffic is a way of life. A few major highways form the region's major corridors. The Sam Rayburn Tollway (State Highway 121) and the George Bush Turnpike (State Highway 190) provide the city's simplest East-West travel and are the boundaries for the northern and southern ends of Plano. These roads also give travelers access to Interstates 35 and 635, and facilitate travel to the Dallas/Fort Worth International airport.

The Dallas North Tollway (DNT) and the Central Expressway (Highway 75) allow for North-South travel. DNT connects the Granite, Legacy, and International business parks with downtown Dallas and other shopping malls. Highway 75 also takes drivers to Oklahoma.

To learn more about roads in the state, try these resources:

- The Texas Office of the Governor, Economic Development and Tourism offers a free travel packet which includes the Texas State Travel Guide, Texas Accommodations Guide, and an official travel map. You can order the packet by calling 800-888-8839 or visiting *www.traveltex.com/downloads/travel-guide/order-travel-guide.* Or you can download specific parts of the state travel map at *www.traveltex.com/downloads/download-texas-maps.*
- DOT offers information about regional construction projects by choosing Collin County from the drop-down menu at *apps.dot.state.tx.us/apps/project_tracker/projectquery.htm.*

- American Automobile Association (AAA), 214-526-7911, *www.texas.aaa.com,* has an office in Plano that offers extensive travel information to members.

WHAT IS TRAFFIC LIKE IN PLANO?

Commuting is a concern for Plano residents. But let's put this in perspective. We are not talking New York City traffic, nor are we talking Washington, D.C. or Atlanta traffic. A Texas Transportation Institute comparison found that in 2007, the average time commuters in the Dallas area spent stuck in traffic was 53 hours per year. Even during rush hour, traffic generally keeps flowing, albeit at a slower rate than usual. The real enemy of the daily commuter is traffic accidents, which can snarl traffic for hours or even bring it to a dead halt. Highway construction – a fact of life in this growing area – is another culprit.

Dallas Area Rapid Transit has worked to add new developments to help commuters with their travels. Remember, however, that improvement projects don't always show their benefits right away. Especially during construction, the can actually get worse. But once the work is finished, the results can be noteworthy. Research has shown that commuters who spend less time on the road are more productive in the workplace, according to Forbes.com.

The best way to avoid traffic is to try to travel at non-peak times if at all possible. To save hassles and gas, consider carpooling or using public transportation. Many employers allow employees to set flexible schedules that let them avoid traffic. And working from home, at least part of the time, is becoming more and more common. Another time saver is to invest in a "Toll Tag" from the North Texas Tollway Authority *www.ntta.org* which will allow you to access the areas numerous tollways to save time in getting around time. In my experience the tollways maintain good flow most times of the day and still allow movement versus much longer delays on the free roadways.

Try these ways to keep tabs on real-time traffic and construction:

- Department of Transportation: Call (800) 452-9292 or search for specific regions and roads at *www.dot.state.tx.us/travel/road_conditions.htm* or *dfwtraffic.dot.state.tx.us*
- TV station CBS11's traffic center, *cbs11tv.com/traffic*

IS PLANO FRIENDLY TO PEDESTRIAN AND BIKE TRAFFIC?

The answer to the question is, yes. Collin County residents like their exercise. Plano touts itself as easy to travel, but as with any community, there likely are always improvements that can be made when it when it comes to making roads safer for those who share them with automobiles.

Walking

Walkers along the roads in Plano will find ample sidewalks, except on some roads that were not designed for walking due to safety concerns. In addition, rural roads in the outer parts of the city and beyond will have less traffic, but likely very few sidewalks and shoulders to seek refuge from cars.

Downtown Plano and Legacy Town Center are some of the most walkable parts of the city, and many residential areas have walking and biking trails that connect with parks. In recent years, as the trend toward walkable communities has taken root, a number of newer subdivisions further out have also been built with amenities such as shopping and schools within walking or biking distance from homes. In fact, a 2007 American Podiatric Association survey of the 100 most populous, most walkable cities in the United States placed Plano 11th on the list; Dallas came in at 58th.

Bicycling

Avid bicyclists will find that using two wheels for transportation is feasible in many places, but isn't the best bet on some of Plano's bustling roads. However, this and pedestrian transportation are supported in

Texas by organizations like the North Central Texas Council of Governments (NCTCOG). For information on meeting up with other cyclists and finding places to bike, visit the "Sports and Recreation" and "Outdoor Fun" chapters.

In 2007, urban planners in the Dallas/Fort Worth area made a push to encourage cyclists to use their bikes more often for short distance commutes or as a means of getting to mass transit systems. As roads grew more crowded in North Texas and pollution became more of a concern, bicycle use became a hot topic. Officials were excited at the possibility of encouraging "average" commuters to apply alternative modes of transportation as a means of getting to work.

In addition, the DART supports a combination of bicycle and public transportation-oriented commuting. Many DART buses are equipped with bike racks to help bicyclists easily load their bicycles for motorized transportation. Check DART's website for more particulars on using the loading racks properly and following the additional rules that apply to cyclists *www.dart.org/riding/bike.asp*.

For more information on bicycle routes throughout the state, check the Texas Bicycle Coalition website *www.biketexas.org*. The NCTCOG BikeWeb page provides an interactive map of already existing and future bike and pedestrian trails in the Dallas Metroplex area *www.nctcog.org/trans/sustdev/bikeped/bikeweb*. Additionally, the Texas Department of Transportation offers a safety guide on sharing the road with cars and other information for cyclists at *www.dot.state.tx.us/safety/ tips/bicycles.htm*.

WHAT ABOUT TAXIS?

Taxis are widely available throughout Collin County, though they are a more logical option if you are traveling relatively short distances due to their higher rates. Most charge $2.25 just to get in and $1.80 per mile.

Fees for extra passengers or bags may apply. Here is how to contact a few of the area's main taxi companies:

- **Alamo Cab Company**, 214-688-1999
- **Checker Cab**, 972-222-2000
- **Diamond Taxi**, 214-349-3333
- **Star Cab**, 214-252-0055
- **Texas Cab Company**, 214-599-9483
- **United Cab Services**, 817-819-7787
- **Yellow Cab Company**, 214-426-6262

AREN'T THERE SOME FUN WAYS TO RIDE AROUND DALLAS OR PLANO?

There are a few options if you want to see downtown from outside your car without relying on your two feet:

- Horse-drawn carriages are available for special events in Dallas and Plano, such as weddings, parties, or Christmas tours.
- The McKinney Avenue Transit Authority (MATA) *www.mata.org* runs year-round through Uptown and Downtown Dallas for free (except for charters). Hours vary from 7 a.m. to 10 p.m. Monday through Thursday, 7 a.m. to Midnight on Friday, and 10 a.m. to 10 p.m. on Sundays and holidays. Call 214-855-0006, EXT 1 for more information.

TRAVELING BY AIR

How do most people fly in and out of North Dallas?

Just 30 minutes separate Plano and the Dallas/Fort Worth International Airport, 972-973-8888, *www.dfwairport.com*, on East Airfield Drive, and is widely known by its Federal Aviation Administration call letters, "DFW." DFW provides travel to 136 domestic and 37 international locations. The airport is the only facility in the world capable of landing for airplanes at once, and boasts five terminals.

Airlines

Some of DFW's terminals serve different airlines, so it is vital to note which airline you are traveling on. Here's where each airline is and how to contact them:

Terminal A

- **American Airlines**, 800-433-7300, *www.aa.com*

Terminal B

- **American Eagle**, 800-433-7300, *www.aa.com*

Terminal C

- **American Airlines**, 800-433-7300, *www.aa.com*

Terminal D

- **Air Canada**, 888-247-2262, *www.aircanada.com*
- **American Airlines and American Eagle**, 800-433-7300, *www.aa.com*
- **British Airways**, 800-247-9297, *www.britishairways.com*
- **KLM**, 866-434-0320, *www.klm.com*
- **Korean Air**, 800-438-5000, *www.koreanair.com*
- **Lufthansa**, 800-399-5838, *www.lufthansa.com*
- **Mexicana**, 877-801-2010, *www.mexicana.com*
- **Sun Country Airlines**, 800-359-6786, *www.suncountry.com*
- **TACA**, 800-400-8222, *www.taca.com*

Terminal E

- **AirTran Airways**, 800-247-8726, *www.airtran.com*

- **Alaska Airlines**, 800-252-7522, *www.alaskaair.com*
- **Continental Airlines**, 800-523-3273 (for travel to U.S. cities and Mexico) or 800-231-0856 (for international travel), *www.continental.com*
- **Delta Air Lines**, 800-221-1212, *www.delta.com*
- **Frontier Airlines**, 800-432-1359, *www.frontierairlines.com*
- **Midwest Airlines**, 800-452-2022, *www.midwestairlines.com*
- **United Airlines**, 800-864-8331, *www.united.com*
- **US Airways**, 800-428-4322 (for travel to U.S. and Canada) or 800-622-1015 (for other international travel) *www.usairways.com*

Security rules used nationally are in place at DFW, though most travelers will find that security lines tend to move pretty quickly. Passengers will be allowed to the gates, and they will have to take off their shoes and jackets and pass through scanners before getting there. Liquids and gels are not allowed on planes, except for toiletry items of three ounces or less, which must be enclosed in a quart-size zip-lock bag. Laptop computers must be taken out of carry-on bags as you go through security.

Parking

DFW has ample parking available with different rates for different periods of time. For $21 a day, the DFW Airport Valet leaves all cars parked in covered garages and your vehicle will be at the appropriate terminal when you return. Terminal parking, which is close to passengers' gates, costs $17 a day. Parking in Express North/South lots costs between $10 and $12 a day, depending on whether you choose covered parking. For Terminal and Express North/South parking, automated payment options are available. Further out, several economy parking lots charge $8 a day. Bus shuttles pick up passengers from these lots throughout the day.

Getting to and from the airport

Most taxi services in the area will take you from the airport. Taxis *www.dfwairport.com/transport/taxis.php*, 972-574-5878 (use this number between midnight and 8:00 a.m.), may not always be the cheapest, but they are reliable and have consistent rates that add up to about $60 for a trip to Plano City Hall, or $40 to $43 for trips to the Dallas Central Business District or the Fort Worth Central Business District. Taxis are available on the lower level of Terminal D, or the upper level of Terminals A, B, C and E.

The airport is also home to 10 rental car agencies: Alamo, Avis, Advantage, Budget, Dollar, Enterprise, E-Z Rent-A-Car, Hertz, National and Thrifty. A shuttle bus will take you from either terminal to the rental car center.

See the DFW Ground Transportation page, *www.dfwairport.com/transport/index.php*, for more options on getting to and from the airport. They include the Trinity Railway Express, which will take you to the airport from Dallas and Fort Worth for $2.50 or $3.75. Courtesy cars *www.dfwairport.com/transport/courtesy.php* are available from many hotels as well. Greyhound, 800-231-2222, *www.greyhound.com*, will also go to Fort Worth, and Richardson by bus. Amtrak, 800-872-7245, *www.amtrak.com*, offers train service to Fort Worth. Shared rides *www.dfwairport.com/transport/pdf/shared.pdf* are another option, and three services providers are authorized at the airport: City Shuttle, L.L.C. (214-760-1998), Go Yellow Checker Shuttle (214-841-1900) and SuperShuttle DFW, Inc. (972-456-3128).

What about general aviation at DFW?
Are there other airports nearby?

For regional travelers, Love Field, 214-670-6073, *www.dallas-lovefield.com*, the inner city airport of Dallas, may be a more appropriate fit. As a hub for Southwest Airlines, it also allows corporate jets. The airport, known by the letters "DAL," offers more than 100 flights daily to 19 destinations.

Several airlines use the DAL airport. They include:

- **ExpressJet**, 877-958-2677, *www.expressjet.com*
- **Delta**, 800-221-1212, *www.delta.com*
- **Southwest Airlines**, 800-435-9792, *www.southwest.com*
- **Continental Airlines**, 800-523-3273, *www.continental.com*
- **American Airlines, American Eagle**, 800-433-7300, *www.aa.com*

General aviation businesses include:

- **Landmark Aviation**, 214-351-1872, *www.landmarkaviation.com*
- **Business Jet Center**, 214-654-1600, *www.businessjetcenter.com*

Businesses and corporate jets also frequently use Addison, 972-392-4850, *www.addisonairport.net*, and Collin County Regional Airport, 972-562-4214, *www3.mckinneytexas.org/www/airportdefault.aspx*.

CAN I TAKE A TRAIN INSTEAD?

With concerns about traffic delays and the environmental damage done by cars and trucks, rail travel has become an ever more popular option. Railways are also seeing a bump in funding in recent years, which is helping Texas and other states to update aging infrastructure that for decades was used nearly exclusively for freight, not people.

Rail tickets are generally cheaper than airlines, and sometimes comparable to driving, especially since you can use your time aboard for work or pleasure. Unfortunately, train travel remains slow, and improvements are slow in coming thanks to the steep cost of railway upgrades.

DOT's Rail Division, *www.dot.state.tx.us/about_us/administration/ divisions/rail.htm*, oversees the state's railroad system and connects with resources to improve the system. To contact the Rail Division, see the Contact page *www.dot.state.tx.us/contact_us/rail.htm* on its website.

Amtrak, 800-USA-RAIL, *www.amtrak.com*, and its Texas Eagle line provide direct service to 41 cities between Chicago and Los Angeles, including a stop in Dallas. The Dallas station, 214-653-1101, is located at 400 South Houston St. Find schedule information at *www.texaseagle.com/schedules.htm* or *www.bytrain.org/passenger/groupinfo/trips.html*.

What is DART?

DART, *dart.org*, stands for Dallas Area Rapid Transit and is the area's chief means of public transportation resources. A combination of buses, trains and other amenities, the system transports more than 220,000 passengers a day across a 700-square-mile area. Many commuters also use the system's HOV lanes on weekdays. For fare information, see *dart.org/about/aboutdart.asp*.

DART's railway transportation includes the Trinity Railway Express and the Dart Rail Red, Green and Blue Lines.

- Trinity Railway Express, *www.trinityrailwayexpress.org*, is provided by the Fort Worth Transportation Authority ("The T") and DART. It connects downtown Fort Worth, downtown Dallas and the DFW Airport. Services are available Monday through Saturday. For information about fares, see *www.trinityrailwayexpress.org/tre-ridebuy.html*. Trip planning assistance is available through DART at 214-979-1111, or The T at 877-657-0146.
- The DART Rail Red line extends along the North Central Expressway from Parker Road in Plano to downtown Dallas and on to Westmoreland in West Oak Cliff. DART Rail Blue Line runs south from Downtown Garland to downtown Dallas and on to Ledbetter in South Oak Cliff. Meanwhile, the DART Rail

Green Line extends from Victory Station to the MLK, JR. Station. A DART Rail system map can be viewed at *dart.org/maps/printrailmap.asp*.

DART is in the process of expanding its rail service, but the growth has not come without some difficulty over the years. While DART has often been touted for taking cars off the road, ridership has declined recently and when officials assess the financial consequences of lost revenue, they may need to make some decisions about projects not already contracted.

The expansion project as presently planned will double the system's light rail mileage (currently more than 45 miles), by 2013. Plans to extend the Green Line northwest to North Carrollton/Frankford and southeast to Buckner are expected to be completed in December 2010.

A 14-mile Orange Line will head through downtown Dallas to Bachman Station in Northwest Dallas, and eventually to the Las Colinas Urban Center and DFW International Airport. As of the writing of this book, a need to move utility lines has slowed progress of this line, and DART reported that the Bachman Station to Las Colinas portion, which had originally been scheduled for completion in 2011, won't be finished until 2012.

An expansion of nearly five miles on the Blue Line to Rowlett is set to open in December 2012. DART has reported that work on the link between Rowlett and Garland is already underway.

WHAT ABOUT BUSES?

For local or regional travel, your best bet will be the bus lines below. To go longer distances, try Greyhound, *www.greyhound.com*, which has a station at 205 S. Lamar St. in Dallas, 214-849-6831. Prices generally beat trains and planes, but service will be considerably slower, too.

PUBLIC TRANSPORTATION

Want to leave your car in the garage and let someone else drive for a change? You have several options in Plano and the surrounding areas, though it may take a few steps to get exactly where you want to go.

How do the buses work in Plano?

DART has two bus transit centers in Plano. The center on the west side of town is on 15th Street and Coit Road, and near employers such as Dallas Morning News, Medical Center of Plano and Alcatel-Lucent. The east center is near government and county offices and some shopping districts, close to U.S. 75 and Archerwood Street. Passengers have their choice of local buses (route numbers 1 through 185), express buses (route numbers 202 through 283 and the DCTA Commuter Express), Suburban Buses (route numbers 301-385), Crosstown Buses (route numbers 400-488) and buses to rail stations (route numbers 502 through 583). Additionally, shuttle and FLEX routes are also available.

Options for the disabled:
- DART busses are accessible, and guide dogs and service animals are permitted on board. For seniors or mentally disabled residents who need special assistance learning how to use the DART system, call 214-828-8576 for more on the Travel Training program that is available, or visit *dart.org/riding/paratransittraveltraining.asp*. Additionally, riders may qualify for reduced transport fares.
- DART provides curb-to-curb transportation as well for residents who are unable to use DART buses and trains; riders may need to schedule their trips in advance.

DOES TEXAS HAVE A PUBLIC FERRY SYSTEM?

Ferry service has a long history in Texas, and more than 8 million people a year use the Texas DOT's ferry system. Usage generally peaks around the summer months. Port Aransas is known as a place for families to visit for fun activities. The ferry runs on an as-needed basis 24 hours a day all year long. Galveston-Port Bolivar *www.galveston.com/galvestonferry* runs 24 hours a day. To view the schedules at Port Aransas and Galveston-Port Bolivar, see the Ferry Schedule page of the DOT's website *www.dot.state.tx.us/travel/ferry_schedules.htm.*

CHAPTER 43

SPORTS AND RECREATION

If you just moved to Plano then you might have noticed all the sports talk that revolves around America's team—the Dallas Cowboys. Or you heard plenty of chatter about the Dallas Mavericks of the NBA. Don't let that enthusiasm throw you. There's plenty of sporting around to satisfy every flavor of competition. Plano offers everything from hockey, to football, to America's pastime, baseball.

PROFESSIONAL SPORTS

Football

As mentioned before, the Dallas Cowboys are integral to local football lore and, according to Forbes, the most valuable sports franchise of the NFL. The Cowboys play at the brand new Cowboys Stadium, 900 E Randol Mill Rd. Arlington, TX 76011. The stadium is brand new, only beginning to be used during the 2009 season. The stadium holds over 80,000 visitors so you won't be alone if you go to a game. It is the largest domed stadium in the world with the largest high-definition viewing screen. The screen spans from 20 yard line to 20 yard line. It's huge. There are only12,000 parking spaces for the 80,000 ticketholders, so plan accordingly. The Cowboys hold the record for longest streak of sold out games so don't hesitate to get your tickets. You can visit *www.dallascowboys.com* or call 817.892.4400 to get your tickets for the 2010 season.

Superbowl Season

The Dallas Cowboys' Stadium is so spanking new and so one of a kind that the NFL has decided to have the 2011 Superbowl in Dallas. So, as you might expect, it is going to be a full house and you better get your tickets early. More information can be found through the NFL website (*www.nfl.com*) or by visiting *www.northtexassuperbowl.com*. The Superbowl is always an extremely exciting event and to live so closely to a planned location is wonderful.

Basketball

Basketball is a big deal down in Texas. The Dallas Mavericks have been making Texas proud since the inaugural 1980-81 season. The Mavericks play at the American Airlines Center, 2500 Victory Avenue, Dallas, Texas 75201, and can be reached through their website *www.mavs.com* or by calling 214.747.MAVS. The Mavs play a great game and will be perfect for any basketball fans. Some of their superstar players include Jason Kidd and Greg Buckner. The Mavs' current record is 31-18 but every game is a great experience.

Baseball

For those who enjoy America's pastime, baseball, Texas is home to the Texas Rangers, a great baseball team and a great way to spend a Sunday afternoon. The Rangers have been representing Texas since 1972. They play their home games at the Rangers Ballpark in Arlington, Texas. More information concerning the Rangers and tickets can be found at *www.texasrangers.com.* True baseball fans already know the famous Nolan Ryan played for the Rangers until 1993 and his retired jersey can be seen at the field. The stadium holds almost 50,000 fans so if you visit, plan ahead for parking.

NASCAR

For those willing to drive a bit, the Ft. Worth Motor Speedway offers plenty of NASCAR action. Tickets for races can be obtained through the website *www.texasmotorspeedway.com* or by calling them directly at (817) 215-8500. NASCAR races are always full of excitement, fun and the occasional crash into the wall.

PARTICIPANT SPORTS AND ACTIVITIES

Parks and Recreation Departments

Whether you're looking for a place to play tennis or a youth soccer league, a good place to start your search is your nearest park and recreation departments. Most offer youth and adult leagues in tennis, basketball and other sports as well as facilities for those who just need a place to play. Many also offer fitness classes, activities for kids and more:

- **Plano**, (972) 941-7250, *www.plano.gov/Departments/ parksandrecreation/Pages/default.aspx*
- **City of Plano Parks and Recreation: Vines Recreation Center**, (972) 769-4234, *www.planotx.org*
- **Central Park Seven**, (972) 881-1276

Flag Football

- **Plano Sports Authority**, *football@psaplano.org, www.psafootball.org/index.html*

- **Adult Sports Program Office**, Plano *www.plano.gov/ Departments/parksandrecreation/Sports/Pages/adult.aspx*, (972) 941-7278
- **Heritage Yards at Plano**, Plano *www.plano.gov/Departments/ parksandrecreation/Sports/Pages/adult.aspx*, (972) 712-3930
- Big D Fun, Dallas, *leagues@bigdfun.com, /www.bigdfun.com*

Indoor Facilities

If you want to head inside during those super-hot summer months, or in chilly January, these commercial groups offer youth sports at indoor facilities. Some have outdoor places to play, too.

- **CrossFit Plano**, Plano, (469) 757-9227
- **Life Time Fitness**, Plano, (972) 202.8100, *www.lifetimefitness.com*
- **Training Techniques**, Plano, (972) 599.9303, *www.trainingtechniques.com*
- **Ringside Boxing Club**, Plano, (972) 312.8269, *www.ringsideboxingclub.com*

Baseball

In addition to lessons and leagues at most parks and recreation departments, these independent leagues offer baseball for children and adults alike:

- **Plano Baseball Association**, Plano, (972) 517-5800, *www.planobaseball.org*
- **Extra Innings**, Plano, (469) 241-1432, *www.extrainnings-plano.com*
- **Centerfield Baseball Academy**, Plano, (972) 424-0723, *www.centerfieldacademy.com*
- **Premier Baseball Academy**, Plano, (972) 398-3676, *www.premierbaseballacademy.com*
- **Frisco Roughriders Baseball Club**, Frisco, (972) 731-7200

Basketball

- **Fieldhouse USA**, Frisco, (972) 668.6207 *www.fieldhouseusa.com*
- **Rowlett Youth Basketball League**, Rowlett, (972) 412.6170. *www.rowlett.com*
- **Sportsplex at Valleyview**, Dallas, (972) 385.4619, *www.sportsplexw.com*

Golf

There are plenty of places for golfers to play at whatever level they choose. Here are some places to get started:

- **Chase Oak Golf Club**, Plano, (214) 509-4653, *www.chaseoaks.com*
- **Pecan Hollow Golf Course**, Plano, (972) 941-7600 *www.pecanhollowgc.com*
- **Los Rios Country Club**, Plano, (972) 422-8068 *www.irigolfgroup.com*
- **Ridgeview Ranch Golf Club**, Plano, (972) 390-1039, *www.ridgeviewgc.com*
- **Gleneagles Country Club**, Plano, (972) 867-8888 *www.gleneaglesclub.com*
- **The Bridges**, Garland, (972) 205-2795, *www.golffirewheel.com*
- **Waterview Golf Club**, Rowlett, (972) 463-8900, *www.waterview.americangolf.com*
- **The Practice Tee Golf Center**, Richardson, (972) 235-6540, *www.thepracticetee.com*
- **Preston Trail Golf Club**, Dallas, (972) 380-0669
- **Mesquite Municipal Golf Course**, Mesquite, (972) 270-7457, *www.mesquite.com*

Frisbee

Ultimate Frisbee, or Frisbee golf, has a loyal following that enjoys a host of local places to play both competitively and just for fun. Shawnee Park offers a complete disc golf course and plenty of local players to network and play games with. *www.parks.planotx.org/econnect/Facilities/FacilitiesDetail.asp?FacilityId=499*

Gymnastics

The area of North Dallas has been an especially popular area for gymnastics. Plano offers some world class facilities when it comes to gymnastics and they are especially popular with the young ones both boys and girls alike! Here are some of the world class facilities in the Plano area:

- **University of Gymnastics**, 1400 Summit Ave, Plano
  www.universityofgymnastics.com
- **ASI Gymnastics**, 2165 W Park Blvd, Plano
  www.asigymnastics.com
- **Infinite Bounds Gymnastics**, 6300 Independence Plano
  www.infinitebounds.com
- **World of Gymnastics**, *www.woga.net*, home of Olympic champions Carly Patterson, Nastia Liukin, Valerie Luikin and many more

Hockey/Ice Skating

Most of these "ice houses" offer paid skating hours, as well as lessons and leagues for children in hockey and figure skating.

- **Dr Pepper Star Center Plano**, Plano, (972) 758-7528,
  www.drpepperstarcenter.com
- **Ice Training Center**, Richardson, (972) 680-7825,
  www.icetrainingcenter.com

Inline/Roller-skating/Skateboarding

For those that enjoy rolling on wheels instead of ice skates then Plano has several locations available for those looking to have a good time.

- **Thunderbird Roller Rink**, Plano, (972) 422-4447, *www.thunderbirdskatecenter.com*
- **Westlake Skate Center**, Garland, (972) 272-0921, *www.garlandwestlake.com*
- **White Rock Skate Center**, Dallas, (214) 341-6660, *www.whiterockskate.com*
- **Eisenbergs Skatepark**, Plano, (972) 509-7725, *www.eisenbergs.com*
- **Rowlett: Skate Park Skate Zone**, Rowlett, (972) 412-6287, *www.eteamz.com*

Lacrosse

Lacrosse is taking over Texas and in 1991 enough interest was garnered to start the Plano Lacrosse Association (PLA). It is one of the most successful high school lacrosse programs in Texas. More information can be found about schedules and schools at the Plano Lacrosse website *www.planolacrosse.com.* It's fun and exciting.

Martial Arts

Adult or child, amateur or pro, you can find a place to learn and practice judo, karate and other martial arts in Plano, Texas. These groups can also help you find local schools:

- **Martial Arts Center of Plano**, Plano, (972) 612-8919, *www.martialartscenterofplano.com*
- **Plano Martial Arts**, Plano, (972) 867-5665, *www.planomartialarts.com*
- **Janjira Muay Thai Martial Arts**, Plano, (972) 769-8663, *www.saekson.com*

- **Impact**, Plano, (972) 633-5425, *www.impactmaonline.com*
- **Vision Martial Arts Center**, Plano, (972) 758-8622, *www.vmacplanoonline.com*
- **USA Martial Arts and Fitness**, Plano, (972) 985-7738, *www.usamafit.com*
- **Shaolin-Wu Institute**, Plano, (214) 473-6882, *www.swyi.com*
- **Academy of Classical Karate**, Plano, (972) 424-8870 *www.planodojo.com*

Rugby

The local rugby club draws players from around the area and from different schools. You can reach them at 214 726-9190 or visit the website at *www.planorugby.tripod.com/index.htm*

Running

While driving through beautiful Texas on a fall Saturday morning, you're likely to see runners participating in one of the many local marathons put on for sport or for charity. These events are indicator of how big running is in this area of the country.

There are plenty of trails to run in the local parks already mentioned but social runners can join up with fellow minded runners in the Plano Pacers Running Club. Learn more at *www.planopacers.org.*

Soccer

A number of youth and adult soccer leagues are sprinkled throughout the area, in addition to privately run soccer facilities.

- **Plano Youth Soccer Association (PYSA)**, Plano, (972) 422-7972, *www.pysa.com*
- **Andromeda Soccer Club Incorporated**, Plano, (972) 423-3449
- **Dallas Texan Soccer Club**, Plano, (972) 612-5589, *www.dallastexans.com*

- For our Spanish speaking friends there is the **Plano Hispanic Soccer Association** (972) 881-8384
- **Garland Soccer Association**, Garland, (972) 530-2636, *www.garlandsoccer.com*

Swimming

There are several public pools in Plano as well as private health clubs offering professional-grade swimming facilities, swimming instructors and more. Some of the pools are even open year round.

- **Oak Point Recreation Center**, Plano, (972) 941-7540, *www.planotx.org*
- **Jack Carter Outdoor Pool**, Plano, (972) 208-8081, *www.planotx.org*
- **Texas Pool**, Plano, (972) 881-8392
- **Plano Aquatic Center**, (972) 964-4232, *www.planotx.org*
- **Colony the Aquatic Park**, The Colony, (972) 624-2225, *www.the-colony.tx.us*

Tennis

Tennis is popular around Plano and there are plenty of clubs available for those who are ready to burn up the courts in their tennis whites. Check out these clubs for play times and lessons.

- **High Point Tennis Center Plano**, Plano, (972) 941-7170, *www.highpointtennis.com*
- **Tennis-Tykes**, Plano, (214) 708-8335, *www.tennis-tykes.com*
- **Eubanks Financial Group**, Plano, (972) 392-3443, *www.eubankhutson.com*
- **Lakes Tennis Academy**, Plano, (972) 668-5253, *www.lakestennis.com*

Volleyball

Although volleyball isn't as popular as several other sports in the area, several places in Plano still host competitive leagues:

- **Volleyball Institute of Plano**, Plano, (469) 229-0700, *www.volleyballplano.com*
- **Allstate Volleyball Inc.**, Plano, (972) 712-2009, *www.allstatevolleyball.com*
- **Garland Volleyball Association**, Garland, (972) 496-0002, *www.garlandvolleyball.net*
- **Fieldhouse USA, Frisco**, (972) 668-6207, *www.fieldhouseusa.com*

Yoga

Check your local recreation department for yoga classes, as well as the listing of gyms and fitness centers below.

Health Clubs and Gyms

- **Pranaa Ayurveda Spa and Yoga**, Plano, (972) 608-0402, *www.pranaa.com*
- **Sunstone Yoga Preston Towne Crossing**, Plano, (214) 764-2119 x103, *www.sunstoneyoga.com*
- **Natural Trends**, Plano, (972) 398-9727, *www.naturaltrends.biz*
- **Plano Stretches Yoga With**, Plano, (972) 758-0974
- **Move Studio**, Dallas, (972) 732-0206, *www.movestudio.com*
- **The Studio Yoga Plano**, Plano, (469) 438-3463

Plano YMCA

There are several YMCAs in the area for families and individuals to visit, socialize and workout. Most locations have pools and programs such as summer camps for children, as well as daycare.

- **YMCA**, Plano, (972) 378-9622, *www.ymcadallas.org*
- **YMCA**, Plano, (972) 335-2331, *www.ymca.net*

County Town and State Parks

Northern Texas is populated with beautiful parks that highlight the area's history in addition to offering places to hike and bike. The websites for these parks can be found by going to *www.texasoutside.com/parks.htm* and clicking on the park of your choice. Most county parks are free and open to the public from 9 a.m. to dusk year-round, though staffed centers will have more limited hours. Contact each facility for more information on tours.

- **Haggard Park**, Plano, (972) 941-2117
- **Willow Creek Park**, Plano. Willow Creek is a community park with picnic tables, grills, and sports fields for everything from softball to kickball. It features a playground, swings, hiking and bike trails, and plenty of big trees to climb.
- **Lake Lavon Parks**, Visitors both young and young at heart enjoy a variety of outdoor recreational opportunities. Camping, fishing, boating, biking, and picnicking are all favorite pastimes. The campground offers 50 sites with water and electric hookups and 12 tent only sites. Additional amenities include hot showers, a dump station, a boat launch, a group shelter and public telephones. The shelter is available year round.
- For the RV riders visit *www.texascampgrounds.com* and find the nearest (or not so near) campground to meet new people and enjoy the scenery of Texas.

State Parks

There are many State Parks in Texas and accordingly there are a quite a few new Plano. A complete listing of the state parks can be found by visiting *www.tpwd.state.tx.us/* and honing in on where you would like to visit.

- **White Rock Lake Park**, just twelve miles from Plano, is a unique 1,015 acre lake which offers a variety of activities. It has almost ten miles of hiking and biking, bird watching, fishing piers for catfish, sunfish, and bass fishing. White Rock is a popular place for picnics, so popular that you can make reservations. Call (214) 670-8740 to get that great spot for a nice Sunday afternoon.

We enjoyed writing this book for you, and we hope it was a big help! If you would like to talk to us about buying or selling a home, we would be honored to help you.

We work with local buyers and sellers every day. The initial consultation is always free, and there is no obligation.

Just send an email to

james@planorealestatebook.com
or visit
www.planorealestatebook.com

We're never too busy to help
you and your friends!